The School Librarian's Technology Playbook

The School Librarian's Technology Playbook

Innovative Strategies to Inspire Teachers and Learners

Stacy Brown

LIBRARIES
UNLIMITED®

An Imprint of ABC-CLIO, LLC

Santa Barbara, California • Denver, Colorado

Library of Congress Cataloging-in-Publication Data

Names: Brown, Stacy (Librarian), author.
Title: The school librarian's technology playbook : innovative strategies
    to inspire teachers and learners / Stacy Brown.
Description: Santa Barbara, California : Libraries Unlimited, 2020. |
    Includes bibliographical references and index.
Identifiers: LCCN 2019043676 (print) | LCCN 2019043677 (ebook) |
    ISBN 9781440870392 (paperback) | ISBN 9781440870408 (ebook)
Subjects: LCSH: School libraries—Information technology. | School librarians—
    Effect of technological innovations on. | School librarian participation in
    curriculum planning. | Libraries and teachers.
Classification: LCC Z675.S3 S764 2020 (print) | LCC Z675.S3 (ebook) |
    DDC 027.8—dc23
LC record available at https://lccn.loc.gov/2019043676
LC ebook record available at https://lccn.loc.gov/2019043677

ISBN: 978-1-4408-7039-2 (paperback)
      978-1-4408-7040-8 (ebook)

24   23   22   21   20   1   2   3   4   5

This book is also available as an eBook.

Libraries Unlimited
An Imprint of ABC-CLIO, LLC

ABC-CLIO, LLC
147 Castilian Drive
Santa Barbara, California 93117
www.abc-clio.com

This book is printed on acid-free paper ∞

Manufactured in the United States of America

Contents

Acknowledgments

I consider this book a love note to librarians and the passion they embody every day to be successful in their increasingly challenging roles. If you are a school librarian lucky enough to work in a school as open to entrusting creative endeavors to its faculty as The Davis Academy is, then you are fortunate. Regardless of the level of support you receive in your school environment, though, the goal for this book is to provide a series of strategies to inspire your own sense of bravery to explore uncharted waters and achieve collaborative partnerships. A special thank-you goes to the administration and faculty of The Davis Academy for always inspiring me to stretch my knowledge in order to work among incredibly talented educators and for being willing partners to brave the unknown.

I also am grateful to my support squad. If you ever want to know who your people are, put 80,000 words to paper and consider who you feel inclined to tell first after typing that final punctuation mark. Thank you to my parents for instilling discipline in me that serves as an invisible hand driving me forward to finish the big tasks. A big thank-you goes to my family for allowing me to create the space to write and for supporting me every step of the way. It's not always easy to raise little readers and writers, and I am grateful to my husband for maintaining my momentum on writing days. Together, we have written a beautiful life.

Introduction

"Librarians are tour guides for all of knowledge."
—Patrick Ness, author of *A Monster Calls*

Not long ago, I was at a conference in which a pair of librarians referred to themselves as the "triage center" within their school. No request was too trivial or beyond their job description. A student is missing a shoe? They craft one out of duct tape. A student couldn't pack a lunch? They scrounge together something nutritious. A child needs to escape her current reality? They introduce her to a different time and place through compelling stories. For me, this is precisely how I view school librarians: as advocates for meeting students' needs.

Imagine if the school librarian could tag-team with the classroom teacher so that together, they could alter the school's culture positively using creativity, innovation, and technology, resulting in a Future Ready School that meets every student's needs. Imagine if the school library were the launchpad for innovation, and teachers saw the school librarian as their coach, providing them with expert plays to help them drive the ball across the finish line. Imagine if even the most reluctant of teachers, who made it clear that they were not willing to "get in the game," came to rely upon the school librarian as a valuable resource, critical to their success in the classroom. You don't have to imagine it, though, because this is the reality.

When I was asked to create a playbook for school librarians to work with teachers to integrate technology and influence innovation in the classroom, I quickly realized that writing a playbook of any kind needs to come from a place of passion. While I am not necessarily a sports enthusiast (unless we are talking about the Texas Longhorns), and thus am not that familiar with playbooks, I have a strong passion for the dedication and flexibility exhibited by school librarians. Having presented at numerous library and educational technology conferences throughout the country, I am always reminded that anyone would be hard-pressed to find another group of professionals more dedicated to promoting access to high-quality resources, advocating for their patrons, or devoting themselves to lifelong learning. I consider all of us school librarians as being "on the same team." We are all working to encourage our students to be the best they can be, and we have powerful resources at our disposal to lead them on a positive path to fulfillment.

School librarians are analogous to the coach and the center in football. They evaluate the options, suggest the plays, and kick off the game. They give the locker-room pep talks, spurring others to take action toward an unknown outcome. School librarians lead cheers of encouragement for teachers to keep their head in the game when things don't go as planned on the field. With school librarians crafting the plays, the teachers represent the quarterbacks. Teachers receive the ball from the center, and they carry the play forward to their students. It's a team effort and with a little preplanning, a willingness to accept the unknown, and a drive to press forward, a successful play moves the rest of the team across the field to score a touchdown. Over time, these plays accumulate into a strategic playbook that can be revisited often.

If there were a "one size fits all" formula to working with teachers to reach positive learning outcomes, a playbook would not be necessary. However, I have worked with just about every type of teacher: newbies, master teachers pulled out of retirement to share their magic but very much stuck in their ways, angry teachers, always cheerful teachers, negative teachers, almost perfect teachers (yes, there are some of these), "I want to be your friend and not your teacher" teachers, idealistic teachers, passionate teachers, and so many others. After all, human beings by nature are complex. Throw a classroom of children into the daily mix and, well, things get even more complicated. It's not easy being a teacher, and it's certainly not easy being a school librarian. After all, you are working with all of these teacher types, as well as a diverse student body. However, as the school librarian, you have a few unique superpowers that you can leverage to cultivate strong teammates: an instinct for curation, technological prowess, and connections to all stakeholders, to name just a few. There are ways to tap into your superpowers to create a school library that serves as the incubation hub for positively influencing school culture. Before you launch any strategic play, however, the known factors have to be evaluated and considered.

As the coach, the school librarian has to recognize that for the nonlibrarian who is not trained to curate, infobesity is a real hurdle. Otherwise referred to as *information overload* or *information explosion, infobesity* is one of the significant obstacles to finding focus. The number of technological advancements and resources to spur innovation can feel daunting. Do not worry. As someone who has been there and dealt with that reality, I urge you to keep reading. You will discover how to join forces with classroom teachers and inspire them to be brave and develop the trust to make powerful plays that move students and other colleagues down the field.

This book will serve as a strategic manual for school librarians to support teachers in implementing innovative technological advances within their classrooms. It is divided into fourteen chapters. Chapter 1 focuses on vision so that first, you can get your head in the game and become the change you wish to see. Chapters 2 through 12 outline specific innovative learning strategies and technology tools, defining what they are and how they can be launched within the school library and integrated throughout the school. We have all probably heard the mantra, "It's not about the tools." And that's right; in this case, it's about what the tools can do for us in our quest to support teaching and learning. Therefore, sometimes it is about how we learn to use the tools. These chapters tackle three-dimensional (3D) printing, virtual and augmented reality, podcasting, coding, gamification, engineering, YouTube, makerspaces, social media, QR codes, and video chats. Examples of lessons and activities are provided to support core curricula, specials curricula, and extracurricular programs. Chapter 13 features practical approaches to shaping student leaders into ambassadors for literacy, technology, and innovation, as well as positively influencing the school culture. The conclusion provides strategies for reflection, revising, and redoing to fail forward, or to leverage mistakes both as teachers and learners, and cultivate an introspective community of learners. This is where transformative growth occurs.

In recent years, I have heard my students invent new words and phrases to describe innovative learning opportunities in the classroom. "Hard fun" and "try-fail" are two of my favorites. As champions of change and access to information, school librarians are the warriors who can support teachers so they can be brave and implement innovation and technology in the classroom so that students can experience hard fun and learn to try-fail. Welcome to *The School Librarian's Technology Playbook*!

CHAPTER ONE

Be the Change You Wish to See

"When you give a ripple power and direction, it becomes a river."
—Jennifer Kahnweiler, in Mariam Pera, "Championing Introverts"

We are ideally situated to emulate the change we wish to see and spread that change throughout our school community. The Future Ready Schools initiative continues to influence school leadership so that school leaders are focused on implementing digital learning strategies to positively affect student engagement and retention. However, school administrators cannot create Future Ready Schools alone. This is where school librarians are essential. School librarians work with all stakeholders within the community: students, parents, faculty, and office staff. Few others, outside of administrators, can make this claim. School librarians should leverage these connections to establish themselves as the driving innovators within their school.

If you close your eyes and picture your professional role model, whom do you see? What superstar school librarians do you admire? Who has been a pioneer within their school community that you wish to emulate? When you measure your path to innovation against whomever you envision, there is no doubt that your journey will look different from theirs. However, the result of creating an incubation hub within the library for exploration and experimentation is within reach. Where do you start? To answer that question, I will share with you where I started. While your journey will undoubtedly look different from mine, I hope that my story will spark some ideas in you to ignite innovation in your learning community.

Consider a Game Plan

The Billboard Strategy

A likely path to success is to expose your decision-makers to those change-makers that you wish to emulate. This can be done in a variety of ways. One approach is what I call the *Billboard Strategy,* or putting your decision-makers in front of whomever you consider to be a "poster child" for innovative approaches that you wish to see within your school. Sometimes it can be as simple as pointing to a teacher at your school who is already teaching outside the box, with your support. Ask your administration if this teacher can take the first five minutes of the next faculty meeting to showcase an innovative strategy that they have used in their classroom. Encourage the teacher to share what worked and what they learned to do differently next time. This will help build trust. Not all of us succeed in every aspect on the first try. Raise an army of teachers who are willing to pilot new technology tools and tap them to take the stage during faculty meetings, a bagel breakfast for teachers in the library, or a teacher in-service day.

Attend a conference with your decision-makers and ensure that they attend a session that is facilitated by a superstar school librarian or innovator who is representative of the change you wish to see. In 2013, my principal and I attended an educational conference in Boston known as "Building Learning Communities," hosted by Alan November, founder of November Learning (https://novemberlearning.com). At breakfast each morning, my principal and I would map out our schedules together so that we could ensure that each of us was attending the "right" sessions, and we also wanted to attend some sessions together so that we could discuss any changes that we may wish to implement within our school.

That particular year, Shannon Miller, school librarian extraordinaire and author of the Van Meter Library Blog (http://vanmeterlibraryvoice .blogspot.com), was making presentations on several topics related to innovation and digital tools in the school library. One session that my principal asked me to attend with him happened to be Miller, talking about change in the library. I had already been to one of her previous sessions and was pleasantly surprised when he inquired about attending one. In hindsight, I should have been the one to make this suggestion. As it happened, because I had already seen a related presentation of Miller's, I had planned to attend a different session at that time, but I encouraged him to go without me and we would compare notes later. While he was sitting in that session, however, I was receiving numerous texts from him asking me about the tools, resources and learning strategies that she was sharing. Specifically, he was curious as to where we measured in integrating these types of programs and tools in our library. At the same time, he was realizing that we were already doing some incredible things in our school library. Through Miller, he was hearing some of the same language that I have used and was being exposed to some of the same tools that I had advocated for in the past. I was thrilled. Not only was he growing his library knowledge base, but he was learning that we were what would now be considered a "Future Ready Library."

The biggest takeaway from his attending that session is that it opened his eyes to new possibilities of how we can drive our school forward when supporting the librarian as a change agent. There is serious power in creating the school library as a place from which innovation originates and spreads throughout the school when the library is highlighted, supported, and marketed. Prior to attending this session, my principal had always been supportive. This session, however, allowed him to hear from another convincing source about the value of having access to a strong e-book collection, various digital applications that support the learning, and strong media programming, to name some examples.

I attribute that day to being a game-changer for our library. We had always had strong support, but now we had an influential advocate who truly understood the value of partnering with us to transform the learning culture within our school. I share this story with the hope that school librarians will think about how they can get their decision-makers in front of persuasive, passionate librarians and educators who are vocal advocates, sharing the value of a robust school library program and how it can revolutionize the learning environment.

The "Red Bull" Strategy

Another strategy for emulating the change you wish to see is to quite simply add some creative energy to your school culture, with *energy* being the keyword. I refer to this as the "Red Bull" strategy. When you appear energized and are having a good time in the school library, students notice, and so do their teachers. To get our school community's attention and influence their willingness to be brave and try new tools and resources in their classroom, we dress up in themes that support our goals. For example, I have been an Internet Boss, who imparts the value of using databases. I have been an Information Ninja, who shares the tricks of the trade to avoid violating copyright. I have been a Media Maven, who shares my resourcefulness to accessing high-quality information. It is natural that when you see someone dressed unusually, you ask what the occasion is and inquire about their costume. These little conversations sprinkled throughout the day are powerful learning opportunities to expose students and faculty to the library resources that can be used in the classroom and the value that can be gained in learning how to use those resources.

The "Tumbleweed" Strategy

One of my favorite strategies to cultivate change reminds me of a tumbleweed as it gains momentum and gradually grows in size. I pick a digital tool that I believe can add value to the learning, and I use it with the faculty. One such example was introducing the faculty to Breakout EDU, which is an immersive learning game platform. During preplanning one year, I used the Breakout EDU concept to create a team-building opportunity for our faculty to learn some history about our school. We were kicking off a year in which we would be celebrating our "Next Stage" capital campaign and our school's 25th birthday. In recognition of this milestone, I created a digital Breakout EDU, in which our faculty were divided into approximately eight groups. Each group was assigned to a classroom, and with the use of some computers, was tasked with being the first to "break out" of their room by solving the school-related clues. Of course, the group that was lucky enough to include our head of school was the first to break out, but every group learned some fun facts about our school's history, strengthened their relationships with one another, and had fun in the process. This active approach to gamifying the learning had successfully engaged them.

After having their own experience with Breakout EDU, some of our faculty felt comfortable enough to launch this tool within their own classrooms. For example, one fifth grade language arts teacher created a digital Breakout EDU about the novel *Maniac Magee* as a way to evaluate the students' reading comprehension. After hearing about how much the students enjoyed this activity, a fifth grade math teacher was inspired to create a Breakout EDU using the physical Breakout EDU kit, in which students had to solve division problems to discover the clues that would unlock a box. The momentum quickly spread, and we were seeing this innovative tool being used across grade levels on both our lower- and middle-school campuses. Additionally, I created a smaller version of our school-themed Breakout EDU for our parents to solve at a parent-teacher organization (PTO) meeting. It was a huge hit, as the parents were able to experience firsthand the innovative ways that their children are learning. ~~In turn, when we model for the parents the learning that their children experience, they are more likely to provide the financial support we needed to help grow our resources.~~

Once the use of Breakout EDU, both in digital and nondigital form, had spread widely throughout our school, we decided to use it as a powerful tool to learn about another faith. Our school is the largest reform Jewish day school in the country, and to expose our students to religions different from their own, we participate in several interfaith days of learning with other faith-based schools.

During one such visit from Mount Vernon Presbyterian School, we created a digital Breakout EDU with questions that focused on both Christianity and Judaism. Setting the scene for the students, pipe organ music was playing as they filed into the room. Projected onto the whiteboard was the following scenario: "The church and the synagogue share a place of worship. Unfortunately, the key to the building has gone missing. Help the rabbi and the minister on their quest to retrace their footsteps to locate the missing key. To prove their reentry into the building without the key, they need to demonstrate their religious knowledge to the building manager. Time is running out! Religious services start soon!" We combined students from both schools into small groups to work collaboratively to tap into their knowledge and, using the clues provided, unlock the mystery. It was a powerful day of learning, connecting, and making new friends. And to think it all started with a faculty meeting during preplanning. ~~Starting small and building the momentum can ultimately lead to establishing the school library as the hub of innovation, creativity, exploration, and as the heart of the school.~~

The "Rewind and Evaluate the Footage" Strategy

Initiating change that drives your school forward can also come from an evaluative place. As mentioned previously, the school librarian is unique, in that this position allows interactions with all stakeholders within the school community. Within these interactions, school librarians have a unique vantage point—they can gauge the school's strengths and weaknesses in various areas that affect the curriculum, sometimes at a level of evaluation that is closed off to school administrators. ~~Making the case to partner with teachers to strengthen areas of weaknesses not only demonstrates that you are on their team, but also reinforces the value of the school librarian as being a synthesizer of informat~~ion who can positively affect the learning culture. In many schools, some grade levels are stronger in some areas than others. Different factors can influence this, such as the age of the children and the comfort level of the teachers. Some teachers feel intimidated by technology. This may be more about mindset than experience, but some teachers take considerable convincing and hand-holding before they feel brave enough to implement technology tools in the classroom.

One such example to positively influence change with the power of technology and coming from an evaluative place is regarding the home-to-school connection. In the younger grades in elementary schools, parents tend to have plenty of opportunities to volunteer in the classroom. As their children get older, however, these opportunities dwindle. Our third grade team was looking for an innovative tool to continue the home-to-school connection, allowing parents to feel that they were a part of a classroom community, even if they were not physically in the building as often as they might like. As discussions between myself and the teachers ensued, we experimented with Padlet, a digital board that allows users to share documents, images, files, texts, and videos so that anyone with the link can contribute to and view the board. Padlet requires an Internet connection and the web address to the specific Padlet board to which you wish to contribute.

After brainstorming, the third grade team came up with the idea to use this technology tool as a "dinner discussion" activity. Each week, students were sent home with a link to the Padlet board, and it included a weekly topic that each family could reflect on and talk about on the board. One of my favorite examples was during the Olympics, in which the teachers posted on their class Padlet walls asking students and their families to discuss at dinner what values they think Olympic athletes should demonstrate. Each family member contributed with a response to this question on the Padlet board. During the class morning meeting time, the teacher would review all the responses projected onto the Smartboard with the students.

An unintended outcome of this activity was that students learned a lot about one another's family structures. Some students on some weeks had only one parent post, as the other parent traveled for a living, or parents could post from another location outside the home, but they still could participate. Some weeks, siblings would post too, and the students and teacher had the opportunity to learn more about the personalities of the classmates' family members. Librarians and teachers can join forces and use technology like this to build community.

Cultivate Team Players

Consider what approach will work best for you. Regardless of the strategy you choose, be sure to work at making professional friends along the way. It will help grow your army of innovators and help you build trust when you ask teachers to be brave for their students and implement new technology in their classrooms. In addition to taking the time to make personal connections with our students, it is equally as important to make personal connections with our colleagues. Chances are that there is only one, or very few, librarians in your school. Consider how you can create a stage for yourself to showcase all the ways that you can amplify a teacher's classroom.

As George Couros (2018) writes, "While we focus on being 'champions' for our kids, remember that 'championing' the adults in education IS serving the students. The impact on one educator can influence thousands (if not more) of students over a lifetime." Sharing personal connections with our colleagues will allow them to increase their trust in us, with the goal of establishing partnerships in teaching. Transforming our relationships with teachers and administrators brings us closer to transforming the education of our students.

CHAPTER TWO

It's Not About the Tools, but . . . 3D Printing Has a Lot to Offer

"I enjoy the excitement of 3D models coming together. It takes time but it's so much fun."

—Sara, age 9

Be Your Best Cheerleader

If there ever were a contraption that caused quite the controversy at our school, it would be the three-dimensional (3D) printer. For about three years, there was a running joke between myself, the vice principal, and our principal and associate head of school. It went something like this:

Me: "I want a 3D printer for our library. We could do so much with it."

Administration: "I'd like to have a clear understanding of how it would be valuable to the curriculum before purchasing a 3D printer."

Me: "There are so many opportunities to amplify the curriculum with a 3D printer. We can enhance the second grade unit on rocks and minerals and simple machines, for example."

Administration: "Oh, look. It's 3:05 and Stacy's mentioning the 3D printer again. What has it been, like five minutes since her previous request for this? Look, it's not about the cost. It's about whether or not it will add value to the learning."

And so it went for three long years of touring schools, seeing their 3D printers (and my principal was correct—in some cases, they were just sitting in a corner unused), interviewing 3D printing vendors in preparation for that day when we were ready to make the purchase, and continuously exploring how a 3D printer could add value to our school's library and our school's curriculum. After I spent all this time significantly advocating and doing my homework on the added value of a 3D printer, the timing was finally right. In conjunction with our school building expansion, known as "The Next Stage," which also included the addition of some alternative learning spaces, we got a 3D printer.

We chose to purchase the Zortrax M200, developed in Poland. I learned about this particular printer at our local Regional Technology Fair. I stopped by a 3D printing vendor table where the vendor was showcasing the Zortrax products. I started asking questions and discovered that among many excellent features of this particular printer, a significant benefit was that if there was a problem, it was easy for a layperson such as myself to take apart and repair. In my research, I also discovered that this printer is also sold at a reasonable price point compared to other 3D printers on the market.

It has been almost two years since we purchased the Zortrax M200, and we have not had a single regret. I have learned quite a bit from handling that machine, and we have since added another Zortax M200 to the school library on our middle school campus. Having gone through the process of working to acquire a 3D printer and implementing it into our curriculum, I will share what I have discovered to be the most effective, least painful, and in fact, enjoyable way to maintain and operate a 3D printer so that it enhances the school's learning culture, all while forging partnerships between the school librarian and the teachers.

There are several ways to acquire a 3D printer. Many school libraries purchase them with funds raised through DonorsChoose.org, while others budget for them in advance. Sometimes a generous parent will offer to donate the funds to purchase a 3D printer or will donate the actual machine. In our case, we raised money as part of a larger capital campaign to innovate our learning environment. Before acquiring any 3D printer, I recommend taking the time to thoughtfully consider how it can best serve your student population. Ensuring that it will be put to good use and not fall victim to being a gimmicky acquisition is critical to garnering support for future requests. In other words, have a plan. Survey your teachers and ask how they would like to use a 3D printer in their classrooms. Ask them to share how they see a 3D printer improving their teaching and learning. Solidify that they stand behind you in printing with a purpose in order to add value to the curriculum. It is worth noting that we have embraced the hashtag #PrintWithPurpose when sharing our 3D printer creations on Twitter.

Get Your Players Fired Up

A 3D printer is typically very exciting for students. At first, they will be drawn to it for its novelty, and then when they realize that just about anything can be replicated using a 3D printer, it opens up a world of possibilities in their minds. It becomes fuel for the imagination, and it is one of the few "toys" that does not have to be powered on to be interesting. Even our students who are lucky enough to have their own 3D printers or have a relative with a 3D printer become animated when they see the printer in the school, especially when it is in action. Leverage this enthusiasm and use it strategically. Break out that 3D printer and use it to teach some of the more mundane subjects. Flip the excitement level so that those topics that had been boring in the past suddenly become the hottest topics in the school. In this same spirit, Hope and Wade King (2018), authors of *The Wild Card: 7 Steps to an Educator's Creative Breakthrough,* say, "Go for application instead of memorization" in order to instill academic rigor and student engagement (88). Learning through the use of our hands is more engaging than memorizing data.

Innovation, which *Merriam-Webster* defines as "a new method, idea, or device," can look many different ways in the classroom. 3D printing encourages novelty, in which iterations of various objects can be reproduced, which therefore supports innovation in education. There are several approaches to incorporating 3D printing in the classroom through partnerships with teachers:

- Ask the teachers for their "big" themes throughout the year and pick two to integrate 3D printing into (I will share examples later in this chapter).
- Interview students in various grade levels and find out which units they tend to struggle with and lack the motivation to study. Approach the teacher with some ideas to incorporate 3D printing into those particular units.
- Do your own analysis of areas where you think 3D printing can enhance the curriculums and pose suggestions to the classroom teachers on how to do so.
- Propose the integration of 3D printing to the teachers in a way that ensures that you are leading the charge, so as not to discourage them from wanting to try something new out of fear that they will have to do all the work. Let them know that you will shoulder the responsibility of implementation, with their support. You will pilot the change.

- Explain to the teachers ahead of time that you are comfortable with failure, as it is part of the learning process that ultimately leads to success, and that you hope that they will feel the same way. Learning how to persevere in the midst of failure leads to cultivating the grit necessary to continue pursuing goals. You are experimenting together, and the students will follow our lead.

- After the activities conclude, thank the teachers for taking a chance on you and let them know you appreciate their support. This is how you segue into a solid partnership for future activities together.

Make Strong Plays

Early Elementary Students

If you intend to integrate 3D printing into your schoolwide curriculum, introducing your students to 3D printing as early as the pre-K level helps cultivate an understanding of two-dimensional (2D) versus 3D objects at an early age. Sharing the difference between reading about different shapes within the pages of a book and holding those shapes in one's hands helps students conceptualize how a model can go from being on a computer screen to then being printed in 3D to become an actual object within our world. For example, explain to students that before adding new rooms to a preexisting house, an architect has to draw up blueprints to show what those spaces will look like before construction starts. Point out to students that seeing ideas in a 2D format on paper, transferring these ideas to a 3D model on a computer screen, and finally creating tangible objects from those models using a 3D printer help young children understand not only the relationship between 2D and 3D objects, but also the 3D printing process itself. While most students at this age still believe in the tooth fairy, it is not uncommon for them to believe that a 3D printer creates objects by magic. It is our role to start helping them translate how everyday inventions come to life. Therefore, walking students through the various parts of the 3D printer, showing them how to load the printer with the filament, and describing how the filament is melted and expelled from the extruder give them an overview of the technology behind the machine. As a result, when these same students start to create 3D models throughout the curriculum, they have a basic understanding of the technology behind it. If your school subscribes to BrainPop (https://www.brainpop.com/), a collection of animated educational movies on a variety of topics, there is a fantastic BrainPop movie that explains 3D printing from start to finish in laymen's terms.

There are a variety of practical applications for 3D printing in the kindergarten classroom. In our school, kindergarten teachers teach students about geometry—specifically, how to identify, name, and create cubes, spheres, cones, and cylinders, as well as to identify the faces, vertices, and edges of each of these shapes. Their instruction encourages the following questions: How can you identify and describe 3D shapes? How can combining shapes make new shapes? Active learning may include going on a "shape hunt" throughout the school, using Play-Doh to combine 3D shapes to make a new shape, and playing 3D shape bingo. This is where the school librarian comes in and plays a vital role in helping students and teachers with innovative learning using 3D printing. The first step is to create a free account within a 3D modeling software. We like to use Tinkercad, which has a free, child-friendly website (https://www.tinkercad.com) designed to create 3D models.

Invite the kindergartners and their teacher into your library or the computer lab, or else roll a set of laptops into their classroom. Before the students and the teacher arrive, sign into Tinkercad and create a "classroom" so that students can be logged into the Tinkercad class with a special code. Once students are sitting in pairs in front of the computers, have them designate their project with their first names so that you will be able to identify the ownership of each design. Then, ask the students to create objects in Tinkercad made of 3D shapes. For example, students can create ice cream cones made of a sphere and a cone, a house made of a cube and a triangle, and a car made of a rectangle and four spheres.

Allow the students to choose their object, and advise them that they will be assessed on their ability to work together as a team and for their creative ideas. Then, invite a few faculty members into the class and allow the students to share their designs and explain the shapes they used to create their objects. Have those faculty members evaluate their projects based on how well the students work together to describe their process, as well as the originality of the design. Be strategic about which faculty you invite to evaluate the designs. Who are your decision-makers for acquiring resources? Is it your principal, your head of school, your school's chief financial officer (CFO), or your curriculum specialist? Consider using this as an opportunity to showcase the thoughtful ways in which the school librarian and the teachers are joining forces to integrate technology into the curriculums.

Advise the visiting faculty members to ask the students the following reflective question: How many faces, edges, and vertices do the shapes have that were used to create their object? Connect their questions back to the learning. The adults can share their feedback using the "I like, I wish,

I wonder . . ." format, which originates from Stanford's d.school program (Doorley 2018). Then those faculty members can select one team's design to be 3D-printed so that students can see the finished product.

Because we have the Zortrax M200 3D printer, we save the Tinkercad creation as a stereolithography (STL) file and transfer it into the Z-Suite software so that it can be 3D-printed on our machine. If the designs are small enough (and you can always scale them down in size), it can take anywhere from approximately forty minutes to two hours to print one design. If you have enough printers in your school, you can 3D-print all the students' designs. In our school, however, by allowing faculty members to come in as a *Shark Tank*–style panel to evaluate the work based on specific criteria and to select one design, students can experience the creation of 3D shapes and see them come to life with the use of just one printer. Be sure to invite the students in to watch the 3D printer as it prints their designs, even if it is just for a few minutes. This activity can be paired with the book *The Greedy Triangle,* by Marilyn Burns and Gordon Silveria, and/or with the BrainPOP video entitled *3D Printing* to reinforce the concepts of 3D shapes and the technology behind 3D printing. More than likely, this is the students' first experience with creating a 3D object from concept to finished product. Starting in the early grades will help build a strong foundation for learning with 3D printing throughout subsequent grade levels.

In many school curriculums, students learn about water scarcity. In our school, this is a central theme throughout the first grade, focusing on the water cycle, conservation, and social action, and 3D printing plays a vital role in bringing this unit to life. Doing a basic Google search will demonstrate that many organizations around the world are devoted to water conservation. Connecting with one of these organizations as it shares its firsthand accounts of other children in different parts of the world who are similar in age to first graders who have to miss school in order to travel to obtain safe water sources is a powerful learning opportunity. Often, these organizations are highly motivated to educate others about their mission to expand clean water to countries threatened by severe water shortages, and they often embrace the notion that inventors can be of any age. Typically, they have received direct feedback from those children for which they are trying to serve when developing water filtration systems, or even just raising money for others to develop water filtration systems.

Make this connection among your students and challenge them to become young inventors. Inspire them to create a water filtration system with other children who need access to safe drinking water in mind. This type of innovative activity builds empathy, encourages creativity, develops social consciousness, cultivates problem-solving skills, and fosters collaboration. Encourage students to work in small groups of three to five people. Challenge them to put their ideas on paper, have them create 3D models of those ideas in Tinkercad, and 3D-print each group's water filtration model. Share them with an organization that you previously connected with to educate your students. Pairing this activity with the book *The Water Princess,* by Susan Verde, reinforces the critical need for access to clean water in various parts of the world, some of which may not be very far from where we live. Demonstrate that you are invested in working with teachers to develop socially responsible global citizens and future leaders.

The integration of 3D printing in school can become more sophisticated at each grade level. When evaluating points of entry for 3D printing in the curriculum, do not lose sight of the possibility of incorporating this technology where interests may not be naturally sparked. Some second graders love learning about simple machines—others, well, not so much, unless, of course, you integrate some LEGOs and the 3D printer. Again, simple machines is a standard topic for a unit in most schools, but the grade level in which it is taught is different for different schools. Teachers responsible for leading this unit usually have their own approach to introducing students to the various simple machines.

Partnering with the homeroom teacher, as the school librarian, and asking them to visit the library to first build 3D models of simple machines out of LEGOs, is a fun, hands-on approach to grasping how simple machines make up many of our most useful everyday objects. Build upon this activity and challenge students to create their own simple machines in Tinkercad. Similar to the approach outlined for kindergarten students, encourage the second graders to work in pairs to create 3D models of everyday objects and to identify the simple machine within that object. Some favorites that we have seen created within our school include hoverboards, playground slides, and seesaws.

As mentioned previously, we only print with purpose within our school. Again, invite faculty into your space to evaluate the designs and require that the students articulate the simple machines within their objects and explain how they work. Faculty should again provide feedback using the "I wonder, I wish, I like . . ." model. This creates a valuable opportunity for students to feel empowered by the work they are creating, while being given a stage on which to share what they know. Having the *Shark Tank*–style

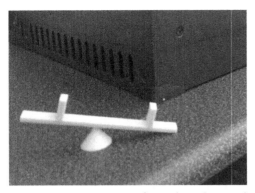

Figure 2.1   A 3D print of a student-designed simple machine.

panel select one design for print, which can then be sent back to the classroom to integrate into the unit as it continues, is exciting for both the students and the teachers. Due to time constraints, it is often unrealistic to 3D-print a model for each student involved in the design process to take home. We explain to students that we would like to exhibit their models at school and showcase them to visitors, while also using them as learning tools for future second graders, as they too will explore simple machines. Over the last couple of years, our second grade team has created a small collection of 3D-printed simple machines to help them introduce the unit, such as the example in Figure 2.1.

Third grade is often cited as the year in which there is a migration from learning to read to reading to learn. Literacy can come in many formats. With this in mind, invention literacy is making its way into many school curriculums. There is a renewed interest in entrepreneurship as a stand-alone unit, including social entrepreneurship, as well as an emphasis on project-based learning. In our school, we focus on invention literacy by starting with a problem and challenging students to solve it. We allow the students to choose the degree of seriousness of the problem. For example, students may decide to focus on a broader social issue that affects a community, such as developing a "pooper scooper" that allows elderly people to clean up after their dogs while walking them without having to bend down or exert themselves physically. Otherwise, they may decide to focus on an invention that solves a very personal problem, such as continuously misplacing eyeglasses, resulting in being late to appointments, meetings, work, or school.

Invention literacy can also be tied into a lesson in economics that integrates math, financial prowess, social studies, and technology. There are many opportunities for cross-curricular connections. As Colleen Graves writes in her *Create Collaborate Innovate* blog (2016), "I'm tired of seeing apathetic kids that look like digital zombies. I want to see kids that are curious and that want to know how stuff works because they want to make the world a better place." With this in mind, cultivating students as content creators can create a rich learning experience infused with proud teacher moments.

Conceptualizing prototypes of inventions in 3D is a natural transition into 3D printing. Introducing invention literacy in third grade in conjunction with the homeroom teacher's social studies unit has worked well at our school to cultivate a partnership between the librarian and the teacher. Through this partnership, we have been able to launch this topic into other areas of interest throughout the learning, as mentioned previously.

Here is what this partnership looks like for us, and what it can also look like within your learning environment: We use a variety of tools to build upon this lesson. With a primary goal of developing students as content creators, there are different technology tools used at different stages of the invention literacy process. First, in homeroom, teachers facilitate students working together as a class to crowdsource common problems that they face or that they see in the world around them. Then, students work together to synthesize these issues and decide which ones they believe, as a community, are the most important.

After narrowing the issues down to three, students work in small groups of three to five to create a public service announcement outlining the problem they have selected and the way in which they intend to solve it. The public service announcement is filmed in front of a green screen using an iPad. Then, students use the Green Screen app by DoInk to drop in a relevant background for their public service announcement. At this point, the school librarian must instruct students to ensure that they are selecting appropriate backdrops from Creative Commons Search to avoid violating copyright. The public service announcements are then hosted on a class Padlet board, which is an online bulletin board that invites collaboration so that they can be shared beyond the classroom walls.

Now that the issues have been settled upon and solutions have been considered, students can choose to work alone or in a group to create prototypes for their inventions that will resolve one of the three issues. These prototypes can be built with littleBits, small magnetic circuits that snap together, first as a way for students to think through a model with their hands. Then, they can be re-created using Tinkercad. Often, building first with littleBits has resulted in more sophisticated prototypes being created in Tinkercad. This second stage of prototyping helps students create a well-thought-out design. The homeroom teacher and the school librarian then work together to determine which prototype for each of the three issues that were presented will be 3D-printed and put on display.

Exhibiting student work is beneficial to inspire younger students, to gain parental support, and to demonstrate the value behind the school librarian innovatively collaborating with the teacher. Be sure to recognize that sharing student work is a vital component for reinforcing continued partnerships in teaching and learning among the school library, the teachers, and the students.

One of the strategies for inspiring teachers to try new and innovative learning strategies in collaboration with the school librarian is by reassuring them that the students have previous exposure to innovative learning strategies. While a specific type of technology may be new to the teacher, it may not be new to the student. It is the school librarian's responsibility to help a teacher who teaches within the confines of one grade level to gain an understanding of the knowledge that their students have brought to that teacher's class. Otherwise, for example, a teacher may shy away from using 3D printing in her or his core curriculum because it may feel intimidating.

Often, knowing that their students have previous experience working with specific technology tools is the influential motivator that allows teachers to be open to the usage of these tools. Upper elementary students are at a perfect age to build upon their previous exposure to innovative tools and take creative risks. The trust has already been established between students and their teachers, which fosters the ability to use 3D printing to enhance learning. At this stage, it is time to reexamine the idea of leveraging 3D printing to achieve learning goals. It is in upper elementary school that, more than likely, girls have been identified as not being as skilled in math and science as boys. It is also in the upper elementary grades that students can start to understand the value in studying specific subjects to achieve career goals. For instance, they can understand through programs like Hour of Code and Girls Who Code that there is a dramatic shortage of individuals who are qualified to fill many positions in computer science. Furthermore, upper elementary students can grasp that there is also a shortage of women and minorities in this field.

As reported by Code.org, a nonprofit devoted to supporting schools to provide access to computer science education, there were 500,000 computer science–related jobs available in 2016 and only 40,000 qualified individuals to fill those jobs. Additionally, females make up only 25 percent of the students studying computer science in the classroom, and those statistics do not improve in technology-related workplaces (Code .org 2018). School librarians can improve this situation by establishing a path to encouragement for girls to pursue science, technology, engineering, and math (STEM).

Upper Elementary Students

Because of the limitless possibilities for creating with 3D printers, fourth and fifth graders tend to be at an age that is a sweet spot for cultivating an interest in pursuing STEM-infused learning activities. Consider your audience, especially when thinking about ways to encourage an enthusiasm for 3D printing among all genders and ethnicities. For example, a group of students who love to read and that consider themselves to be "bookish" might enjoy designing props for the stories that they read and 3D-printing them to be cataloged and checked out with the books as they circulate. However, students can also design and 3D-print their own props to serve as extensions to the books that they read outside of the school library. Knowing they are playing a role in bringing part of a story to life for future readers can be motivating. Does your school host a Tech Fair, a Science Fair, or a Math Fair? If so, allow students to design pieces of their project in Tinkercad or Microsoft's free 3D Builder and 3D-print them as a component of their project. Is there an opportunity for students to learn drag-and-drop programming beyond the Hour of Code? If not, schedule a series of library visits with these grade levels and upon arrival, encourage them to build their own robots out of cardboard. What parts of their robots can be designed in 3D modeling software and printed to add a unique characteristic to their robots?

This age group also loves to compete. Host a competition in which students are challenged to design a 3D model that promotes social action. The winning model will be 3D-printed and on display in the school lobby, highlighting the student designer's work. Allow 3D printing to generate technology leaders among your students. Those who take a real interest in understanding the mechanics should be present when you perform routine maintenance on the machine. Allow them to see how the parts are disassembled and reassembled. Ensure that the students go through the safety measures of wearing protective goggles, as it is important for them to learn how to take appropriate precautions. Give these students an opportunity to teach younger students about the process of 3D printing. Let them serve as mentors and "libratory" assistants, and grow student leaders through technology usage.

Note that 3D modeling does not have to start with software and end with printing. Investing in 3D pens, such as the 3Doodler, can be useful in encouraging upper elementary students to be enthusiastic about STEM-related fields. The price of the base model of the 3Doodler 3D pen typically starts at $50. The pens are handheld and plug into an electrical outlet. Once the plastic filament (in stick form) is inserted into the heated pen, the plastic melts so it extrudes a flexible substance that hardens into the design that is drawn. After reading the book *Loot,* by Jude Watson, in our upper elementary book club, students created their own loot (jewelry) with the 3Doodler. They were able to choose their own colors for rings, earrings, and bracelets. Add a bauble bar to your school library, where students can come in and create their own jewels with 3D pens.

Middle School Students

Middle school provides endless opportunities for sophisticated learning with 3D printing. In my collaboration with a middle school math teacher, the eighth grade advanced math class was challenged to design tools for the teacher. In order for the tools to be approved, they had to have a beneficial purpose, be scaled to a usable size, and have an original design. Working in pairs, students invented a graph-paper liner, a desktop organization system, and a pencil holder shaped like the school that honored the current graduating class with personalized text. There were significant try-fails, or unsuccessful attempts, throughout this process, as students were challenged to take measurements and revise their 3D models in Tinkercad according to their data.

After doing this project last year, this same math teacher and I are currently working together to have the advanced math class design, prototype, and build a free little library for our school campus this year. After collaborating once on a smaller project, we are now feeling brave enough to try a more significant project. Additionally, this project will allow us to work with the art class for the finishing touches.

At our school, students are taught to give charitably at a very young age, often donating their time to causes they believe in strongly. One such example is a student in seventh grade who loves to rock climb. It dawned on her that people who don't have all of their limbs may not have the opportunity to experience the same joy that she gets from rock climbing. As a result, she was inspired to create a 3D model of a prosthetic foot that has ball bearings in the right places, so that individuals who are missing a foot can experience rock climbing with a prosthetic limb. Not only printing with purpose but printing with personal connections can inspire powerful learning opportunities in STEM.

Does your school's middle school science curriculum include a rocket launch? In working with a middle school science teacher, students at my school were able to design their rocket's nose cone or fin in Tinkercad software and then upload their Tinkercad design into the 3D printer's Z-Suite software. This allowed them to alter the rocket piece's density, which would improve its flight trajectory. Students designed their rockets in pairs and could choose whether they wanted to 3D-print a component of their rocket.

To make the 3D printing demands manageable, the teacher and I agreed upon a timeline for 3D designs to be completed so that a schedule could be implemented that allowed each team's part to be 3D-printed in enough time to complete the assignment before rocket launch day. Allowing students to personalize their rocket design with 3D technology added an element of engineering to the project that is lost when designing the rocket solely with recyclable materials. Students can also design and 3D-print medals for school-related events. Writing contests, athletic events, costume contests, summer reading challenges are all examples of opportunities for middle students interested in 3D printing to design and create recognition rewards.

There's More to 3D Technology Than the Print

Learn Beyond the Library

Consider exploring whether your area has a 3D printing facility. If so, take a group of students on a field trip. The local vendor that introduced us to the Zortrax M200 also has a 3D printing facility, where customers can outsource prints and get their machines repaired. He allowed us to visit, gave a presentation about 3D printing technology, and took us on a tour of his studio, where the students saw a wide variety of 3D printers in use. It was an incredible learning experience. If no such facility exists nearby, investigate local businesses that rely on 3D printers and schedule a visit to see how they use these printers to fulfill their professional responsibilities. Exposing students to 3D printing in professional settings allows students to grasp the value of the technology in real-world applications.

Mining Minecraft to Your Advantage

When it comes to 3D printing, even if you do not have access to an actual printer, there is much to be gained by solely focusing on integrating 3D modeling software into the curriculum. The love of Minecraft is serious business—use it to make learning an amazing experience for the students. For example, our third graders learn about Native Americans every year. With MinecraftEdu, however, we have added an element of collaborative learning to this unit. In one exercise, students create a Native

American village in a multiplayer world. Tapping into the knowledge that they have acquired about the resources that were available influences the materials that they elect to use within Minecraft to build their homes. They also consider the landscape, climate, common foods, and the tools that were accessible to the Native Americans historically. Using that information, they build a village, working together as a virtual community to achieve a common goal. The students who play Minecraft regularly at home teach the novices about the function keys in Minecraft. Sometimes these are the same students that have a more difficult time connecting with their peers. All of a sudden, they are the experts in the room. It. Is. Awesome.

I have seen this be a "gamechanger" (pun intended) for some of these students. They become the teachers, the experts, the pacesetters, the pioneers. Minecraft is not the only option for a simulated collaborative activity in 3D design building; 3D Builder and Google SketchUp are both strong alternatives. Once other teachers learn of a partnership between the school librarian and another teacher to integrate 3D modeling software into a lesson and the students are buzzing about the experience, you improve your credibility. For those teachers who do not know this success story, be sure to set a stage where the teacher that you partnered with can share his or her positive experience. The stage can be a variety of platforms, such as sharing during the first five minutes of a faculty meeting, a tweet that is directed to other teachers, or a faculty email from the principal. Highlighting the rewards of such a partnership is a critical component to the integration formula. These sharing opportunities encourage teachers to have an open mind and discover that the possibilities are endless with 3D modeling software integration. For example, our Judaics teacher was inspired to work with me so that her students could build a digital sukkah in Minecraft in observance of the Jewish holiday Sukkot. Additionally, one of our school's eighth grade middle school language arts teachers differentiated her instruction with the novel *Speak,* by Laurie Halse Anderson, using Minecraft. She allowed some of her students to use the 3D Modeling program to represent themes in the novel. For example, one student created a tree that the other students could collaborate to build, just as Melinda, in the novel, decides to fulfill her art teacher's class assignment by creating a tree that represents herself as a way to signify her own personal growth. Minecraft is a powerful tool to allow students to build invention prototypes, even if they are not ultimately 3D-printed. Prior to owning a 3D printer, our middle school students participated in a course that focused on the role of technology in entrepreneurship. While they could not 3D-print their inventions, they could create a 3D model of their invention. Some students chose to use cardboard to build their prototypes, while others preferred Minecraft for prototyping. Incorporating choice to differentiate the learning and assessing is often preferable to accommodate different learners. Another fabulous way to introduce 3D modeling software is to create an opportunity for other teachers and their students to rely upon it for information. One of my favorite examples of this was discovered on Pinterest, in which a librarian in Mattituck, New York, created a digital representation of her library in Minecraft and used it to orient her patrons and show them where resources were located (Barack 2013). It became an interactive library orientation.

The Initial Play: Start with Questions

To get started with 3D printing, start with the following questions: Where can the curriculum be enhanced? How can 3D printing reinvigorate the learning process? What are my learning goals, and how can 3D printing help me achieve those goals? What are ways that I can partner with teachers to incorporate 3D printing to build their confidence and positively affect students' learning? How can I make teachers comfortable enough to sustain the learning with 3D printing? What type of positive encouragement can I offer teachers when trying new technology tools? Considering these questions will launch school librarians into a successful partnership with teachers and the use of innovative technology.

CHAPTER THREE

Alter Reality to Elevate Learning

"Virtual reality is fun to create because you can put what you want in the environment with different people."

—Anna, age 8

Be Brave: Put Yourself Out on the Field

I introduced our faculty to augmented reality by embarrassing myself. Truly. I asked my principal if I could borrow the faculty meeting time (or hijack the time, depending on how you choose to look at it) to share an innovative technology tool with the teachers. The key to success in this request was giving advance notice. A year early was not too soon to ask my administration if I could be allotted faculty meeting time.

As the school librarian, you know that you will have beneficial tools to share. You may not know what they are yet, as they may not have been invented yet. However, you know that these tools ultimately will be available. These same tools will be all the rage, in that they will appeal to the students and improve classroom engagement.

The day that I chose to embarrass myself was a day like any other. It was after a long day of teaching on a Tuesday afternoon, and the teachers were filing into the library for a 4 p.m. faculty meeting. Our school days tend to run longer than at many schools because we have a foreign language requirement of Hebrew and a Judaic Studies curriculum, in addition to all of the other core and special subjects. As a result, our faculty meetings always come after what has already been a very long day. To combat any feelings of drudgery, I decided to sacrifice myself for the sake of gaining my audience's attention. As faculty filed into the library, I had posted on the large drop-down screen (approximately 9 feet × 7 feet in size) instructions to grab an iOS device with a camera (iPad 2+ or an iPhone), download the Aurasma app (which would become HP Reveal, from Hewlett-Packard) from the App Store, and to download the i-nigma QR Reader.

After the staff scanned the QR code with Aurasma, I advised them to click Skip at the top-right corner of the app, as they could go back and sign up for a free account later. Then, I instructed them to open the Aurasma app on their phone to scan a large picture of my face. Here's where things get embarrassing. I am an introvert, tried and true. I had already put my face on the huge screen in the library for all to see. This took courage— serious courage—on my part. Once they scanned my face, though, something even more embarrassing happened. Once they scanned the image, it looked as though my hair were on fire, while the song *Girl on Fire,* by Alicia Keys, blared from their devices. After thoroughly humiliating myself, I said that *augment* means to add on and *reality* signifies the world that actually exists, so *augmented reality* means to digitally enhance what already exists.

We have a slew of master teachers at our school who have been teaching successfully for many years. Many of them are not necessarily looking to make changes. In the interest of not scaring them off, I found it helpful to break down the concept of augmented reality after first demonstrating its possibilities and then simplifying the meaning. Once they were introduced to augmented reality, it was time to expand their augmented reality vocabulary. To do this, I showed another slide stating that the term *overlay* is the addition to reality. In the example of my hair on fire, the overlay would be video that played showing my hair on fire. The *trigger image* is the image that triggers the overlay. This was the static image of Stacy *not* on fire. Think QR Code. Finally, *aura* represents the total package of the trigger image and the overlay.

Again, if using this technology today, be sure to replace the word *Aurasma* in this narrative with the words *HP Reveal,* as that is now the name of the app. But I find it is important to present my experience to you in its original state so that you can have an accurate picture of the events as they happened. I made it a point to break down the concepts into simplistic terms so that the faculty could understand the relationship that these new words have with one another. Then, I asked this critical question: "How can you use augmented reality in your classroom?"

This is a great time to "Turn and Talk." If you follow our model, you can ask each faculty member to turn to a neighbor and brainstorm the various ways that augmented reality can alter the learning experience for the students in their classes with the subjects that they teach. As they shared, I walked around the room, jumped into the conversations, and noticed the enthusiasm level. If it feels right, you can select faculty members to share what they came up with as they turned and talked. If you feel hesitant to call on individuals to share, you can also share other known examples of when augmented reality has been used in the classroom.

This is, in fact, what I did in my presentation. I shared an example of how Northwest High School in Justin, Texas, created an entire set of interactive bulletin boards with Aurasma that highlighted student work throughout the school (Cooper 2013). Another example that I shared was a YouTube video of a science teacher who created augmented images of her lab equipment so that students would move around the room, scan each image, and learn about how to use each piece of equipment safely (Smith-Science 2013). My third and final example included a YouTube video of students in music class scanning images of famous composers to learn their biographical information (Herring 2013).

The last step in this process was to allow the teachers to use the last ten minutes of the sixty-minute faculty meeting to create their own augmented reality with the following instructions:

1. Partner up!
2. Open the Aurasma app on your device.
3. At the bottom, press the A button above the Home button.
4. Press the plus sign at the bottom of the screen.
5. Create an overlay by clicking on Device (at the bottom) and clicking the plus sign (in the upper-right corner).
6. Select Camera.
7. Take a video and select Use Video.
8. Give the overlay a name and press Finish.
9. Touch your video and press Select.
10. Find a static image (such as a book cover or sign) and capture it by pressing the purple camera icon, making it a trigger image.
11. Press the right arrow icon and type in a name for your augmented reality creation.
12. Select Private and Finish.
13. Hover over your trigger image and view the augmented reality that you created with Aurasma!

As the final order of business, I asked them to scan a QR code linking to my Pinterest board of resources on augmented reality in education. This board can be found at https://www.pinterest.com/21ststacy/augmented

-reality, and the link to my complete faculty presentation can be found here: https://tinyurl.com/ybwmm5zt. Please feel free to make a copy and change it to work within your own learning environment. Remember to ask your administration if you can "take over" a faculty meeting next year, or even a portion of a couple of meetings. Approaching your administration when the meeting dates are being set and before the agendas are created is a solid strategy for setting the stage for you to inspire your teachers.

Recruit Teachers into the Game

To bring teachers into the game, consider exposing them to augmented reality in a manner that is not intimidating so that they can all learn together in concise steps. In my experience, after I broke down the plays for the entire faculty, some of the teachers took it upon themselves to stay an hour after the faculty meeting to create their own augmented reality opportunities in their classrooms. Some of those teachers integrated augmented reality the very next day. Once teachers have been exposed to the technology tool, the game-changing play for the school librarian is to keep an eye on the curriculum calendar. Create your own playbook that notes when specific topics will be taught so you can strategically connect with teachers at the right times. This will help in your efforts to forge partnerships for innovation. There are a few ways to discover this information about what and when:

- Seek out your school's curriculum map or "year at a glance" for each grade level.
- Email teachers to inquire about their upcoming units and discover ways that you can support them.
- Attend grade-level planning meetings.
- Request a check-in meeting with teaching teams to plan a lesson partnership.
- Snag teachers in the teacher workroom while they are making photocopies and ask questions about upcoming lessons.
- Invite teachers to a planning breakfast in your library before school starts.
- Host a partnership powwow, in which teachers can sign up for a one-on-one strategy session with you via a Google document.

Once you have identified when teachers will focus on specific topics, go for the play. What follows are some examples of innovative plays across the grade levels, in which altering reality and making curricular connections can bring learning to life.

Augmented Reality in Action

App-Smashing with HP Reveal

At some point in their elementary years, most students are taught about animals and their habitats. By partnering with the school librarian, our kindergarten team integrated augmented reality into their animal unit. In homeroom, students selected an animal to research. Then they came to the library, as a class, to browse for books on their chosen animal and learn about note-taking. Using nonfiction books, the students jotted down notes and drew illustrations representing what they learned about their animal. After the students' notes were compiled, students created their own nonfiction books and drew illustrations of their animal. The kindergarten teachers felt that producing their stories on paper was an important part of the process for students to synthesize their information in a tangible format and to gain additional handwriting experience. Then, using the PixNTell app and the iPads, students took pictures of their writing and their illustrations and turned them into a digital presentation. PixNTell has a voice record feature so that the writers can read their books aloud. With the help of Creative Commons Search, to avoid copyright violations, or using students' animal illustrations, teachers hang a picture of each student's chosen animal, along with the student's name underneath, in the hallway outside the classroom. Using HP Reveal, when the images of each student's animal are scanned, the students can be heard reading their books, while their writing and images are shared visually via PixNTell. By partnering, we were able to create interactive displays of the students' animal research books, as seen in Figure 3.1.

Figure 3.1 An interactive display of students' animal research books.

Figure 3.2   An interactive display of students' poem collages.

The third grade teachers used augmented reality to spice up their poetry unit. Each student created a poem about a color, with a collage to accompany it. They created a stop-motion film of their collages being made using the iStopMotion iOS app. Once their video was complete, they hung their collages on the wall, along with their poems, and when the collages were scanned, visitors could see their collages being made in the stop-motion effect, as seen in Figure 3.2.

One of the fifth grade language arts teachers set up a bulletin board outside her classroom so that parents could scan their child's face while waiting for their turn to go into parent-teacher conferences. Upon scanning their child's face, they were directed to a video of the student showcasing some of the schoolwork that she or he was most proud of producing. In another example, a middle school math teacher decided to have his students augment their final exams. To do so, students made posters consisting of math problems. When each problem was scanned, a video of the student solving the problem and demonstrating knowledge of the concept popped up. The problem served as the trigger image. Their interactive exams were then hung on the wall for all to learn from and enjoy. And a middle school Judaics teacher had students create social action–oriented projects using a lesson in *tzedakah*, which means to give charitably in the Jewish faith. Students had to invent a charitable business and create advertisements for it using posters that were augmented to include more information about the business's goal. As people walked the halls, they could learn about these charities through these interactive displays and decide where they would make their charitable donations.

Pai Technology

First graders at the Davis Academy in Atlanta, as part of their yearlong theme of learning about water, explore ocean habitats. They take a trip to the Georgia Aquarium as one of their field trips. In preparation for their visit, they journey underwater via augmented reality using Pai Technology's free Ocean Pets app and a purchased box of materials entitled Ocean Pets that can be found on Amazon.com. Ocean Pets (costing $29.99 at the time of this publication) contains a mess-free putty that students can mold into different fish with the guidance of the Ocean Pets app. Once students have molded their unique fish, they scan them within the Ocean Pets app, and they come to life in an underwater background. Students journey through the ocean along with their fish as they learn about caring for the ocean and facts about marine life. There are eight types of fish that students can create, scan, and animate into the ocean.

QuiverVision

QuiverVision has developed an augmented reality app for young learners. Apps like these, which can be used on both Android and iOS devices (and many of which are free), allow young learners to experience augmented reality in conjunction with their elementary school units. One of the Next Generation Science Standards for kindergarten through second grade specifies that students "Develop and use a model of the Earth-sun-moon system to describe the cyclic patterns of lunar phases, eclipses of the sun and moon, and seasons" (2013). Using the Quiver 3D Coloring App, students can develop two-dimensional (2D) models of the phases of the moon and turn them into three-dimensional (3D) models by scanning them.

Here's an example of how it works: Go to http://www.quivervision.com and select a worksheet that ties into the curricular focus. When I facilitated the use of the Quiver 3D Coloring App, I partnered with a second grade teacher who was teaching her students about the solar system and the phases of the moon. I printed out a QuiverVision worksheet entitled "Moon Phases" for each student. Students colored the worksheets, scanned them using the QuiverVision app, and watched as their phases of the moon were brought to life off the page. The worksheets contain additional interactive activities once they are scanned.

The students love putting their personal touches on the subjects that they are learning about before the subjects are augmented. QuiverVision has a variety of worksheets that support content beyond the standards requirements. The website includes content that is important to school librarians, sparking creativity beyond core curricular subjects in ways that can be integrated into library programming. For example, QuiverVision now has an augmented reality worksheet to coincide with Peter Reynolds's book *The Dot*. The activity is well suited for participating in International Dot Day, the author's designated day to celebrate creativity, courage, and collaboration. Sharing augmented Dot Day creations via social media platforms with other learners using the #DotDay hashtag provides participants with a global audience. Exposing students to augmented reality apps for informal learning opportunities creates student leaders who are then well suited to serve as mentors for younger students using the same technology in their classrooms. Teachers benefit from this too, as they can rely upon more senior students to help navigate the technology used with the younger students in their classrooms.

Virtual Reality

Virtual reality differs from augmented reality in that it is an immersive learning experience. With augmented reality, objects jump off the screen into another dimension. In virtual reality, there is no separation of space between the audience, other players, and the experience. Without separations in space, virtual reality can create an intimate bond between the participants and the virtual environment.

Google Expeditions

Google Expeditions is a free education app that allows students and teachers to explore virtual worlds through both augmented and virtual reality field trips. With virtual reality immersive experiences, students who are learning about a particular geographic location can travel to that location using a variety of tools. A virtual reality viewer, also known as an oculus rift, is required. While pricey versions are undoubtedly available, a commonly used version is Google Cardboard, which costs approximately $15. However, there are some versions available online for as low as $8, and sometimes businesses will give them away for free as promotional items. Also, students can build their own oculus rift using cardboard, lenses, magnets, Velcro, a rubber band, glue, scissors, a ruler, and an Exacto knife. There are several sources online that will describe how to put an oculus rift together, including Instructables.com. In addition to the virtual reality viewer, students will need access to a mobile device such as an iPhone, which must fit into the oculus rift. In order to serve as the virtual reality guide, the teacher will require a tablet. Finally, a router is necessary so that Google Expeditions can run on its own local Wi-Fi network. The free Google Expeditions app will need to be installed on the mobile devices and on the guide's tablet.

Throughout the school year, Google Expedition offers site visits to schools free of charge, typically on a first come, first served basis. The facilitators will bring all of the required technology for the students and the guide to use. This is a prime opportunity for the school librarian to partner with teachers to ensure a meaningful virtual reality experience. There are hundreds of potential Google Expedition experiences. Communicating with the teachers so that their students participate in expeditions that are relevant to their curriculum is critical. The school librarian can suggest that the teacher and the librarian copilot the expedition together. The biggest obstacle is convincing teachers that this experience will be worth taking a break from their regularly scheduled program. Here are several selling points that the school librarian can share with the teacher:

- Together, the librarian and the teacher can select an expedition that is relevant to the teaching.
- Students will not just learn about the teacher's topic; they will be immersed in a simulated learning experience in which they discover the topic with their senses.
- The teacher will benefit from learning innovative technology along with the students.
- The teacher will not be alone—the school librarian will be right there too.
- Students will find a different way of learning to be interesting and engaging.

To sign up for a potential visit, visit the Expeditions AR Pioneer Program (https://goo.gl/esYsBg).

When we worked with a Google Expedition team at our middle school, we also invited parents to come explore right along with their children. We set up a daylong schedule of classes that would come to the library. We created a spreadsheet specifying the class name and subject, the time that it would come, and the virtual reality field trip destination. Parents could attend during their child's Google Expedition time slot, or they could come at a time that was more convenient and explore a topic that personally interested them. It was a great opportunity for parents to experience the innovative practices implemented within our school, while also inviting them to come into the school, which does not happen as often once students reach the middle school level.

YouTube

YouTube offers its own virtual reality channel, broken into subtopics, such as concert experiences, immersive storytelling, exploring the world, gaming, thrill-seeking tours, musical experiences, and others. Using headphones in conjunction with a YouTube virtual reality exploration can enhance the experience. With YouTube's virtual reality channel, all that are required is the oculus rift and a mobile device that can fit within the oculus rift, as previously specified. For instance, architecture students can take a tour of New York City skyscrapers, archaeology students can explore Mayan temples, and science students can visit the InSight Mission Test Lab at the National Aeronautics and Space Administration (NASA). Instead of reading about the significance of Mexico's Day of the Dead, experience Day of the Dead and journey to Mexico virtually. Again, when paired with relevant curriculums, virtual reality can transform the learning experience.

Unity

Interested in having students create their own virtual reality explorations? Check out Unity (https://unity3d.com). A free version of Unity's software is available to download for beginners and offers free licenses for education. Educators can fill out an online application on behalf of their educational institution. Virtual reality creation tutorials help users build their own unique immersive worlds via Unity's software. A free educator toolkit is available to assist in using Unity in the curriculum.

Considered the most widely used virtual reality development platform, Unity makes virtual reality creation accessible to students ages ten and up and provides a wealth of online resources to support learning and creativity. While so many destinations already exist through virtual reality, not everything can be found. Connect the creation of virtual reality worlds to your school's own curriculums, such as studying novels. Do your students read *Hatchet,* by Gary Paulsen, in their classes? If so, have the readers recreate the Canadian wilderness scenes as Brian describes them in the novel. What an innovative approach to reading comprehension.

CoSpaces Edu

CoSpaces Edu is a website with a free companion app that individuals can use to create and explore virtual reality in the classroom. An educator resource guide available on their website provides a step-by-step guide for usage in the classroom. There are a variety of lesson plans, free for implementation, that focus on science, technology, engineering, and math (STEM) and coding, social sciences, language arts, and maker spaces. There is also a free online teacher training course available. Students can create within the app and explore using both the app and the website. The app allows a wide range of complexity to accommodate users ranging from early elementary students all the way to adults. Teachers can create and manage classrooms through the website as well.

One of my favorite recent partnerships was with a kindergarten teacher. She was new to her grade level, but I had earned her trust through partnerships that we did together when she taught third grade. So she agreed to be brave and implement CoSpaces Edu into her literacy unit focusing on nursery rhymes. Ahead of her class's visit, I created a CoSpaces Edu account for myself, created a class that I labeled with the teacher's last name, and input all of her students' names into it. Then, I created a space and an assignment to recreate a nursery rhyme using virtual objects. Upon their arrival, in order for the students to grasp the concept of virtual reality, I shared some common examples of virtual reality experiences, like the Roller Coaster VR app. I contrasted the concept of virtual reality with that of going to the movies. At the movies, you are an audience member watching a story unfold, but you are not necessarily a part of the story. In virtual reality, the students have the opportunity to become a part of their newly created environment, and as a result, their role in the story is one of active participation. They immerse themselves in a new experience.

Before they started creating their own virtual worlds, students were able to experience the story of the Three Little Pigs using Google Cardboard, an iPod, and access to 1st Playable Production's YouTube creation of "The Three Little Pigs" tale in virtual reality. Once students experienced virtual reality in a world that was created by someone else, they were motivated and inspired to create their own worlds. Each student used a specific iPad that was signed into their student account through the CoSpaces Edu app. Our iPads are numbered so I could keep track of which student was assigned to which iPad number. Then they selected a nursery rhyme and dragged objects and scenery into their scene to re-create their chosen nursery rhyme.

Their creations were unique and symbolic. Using the mirroring feature on the iPad and Air Server on the computer that is connected to the projector, the students' creations were projected onto the Promethean board in Play mode. They became the "tour guide" of their version of the story for a wider audience. The teachers and the students loved hearing what went into each child's creative process. Discovering the "story behind the story" was fascinating. The students shared how they decided to include specific structures, characters, and the inspirations behind their environmental choices, such as weather and scenery. Need an escape from your reality? Take students on a trip to their own Neverland with CoSpaces Edu. It is a journey that they won't soon forget.

Cheering for Your Team

As I started to see more and more of our teachers being brave and integrating augmented and virtual reality experiences into their classrooms, I felt that it was important to highlight their bravery. At the end of the school year, at our closing faculty meeting, I made a point of spending five minutes highlighting our "Techtastic Teachers" and some of the projects they implemented in their classrooms. Here is an example of my bragging efforts that were showcased on our large screen in the library at the end-of-year faculty meeting, as seen in Figure 3.3.

The example in Figure 3.3 highlights our school's science teacher, Meredith Hegarty, who enhanced her rocket launch lesson with Aurasma.

BLAST OFF WITH AURASMA

Bring science to life with virtual reality. Students create badges that when scanned with Aurasma, demonstrate the launch of their bottle rockets. Creativity, design build skills, technology tools, math, and science are all rolled into one. Genius.

Figure 3.3 Students turned their mission badges into scannable images that take viewers to their rocket's launch.

I also made a point of sharing Mrs. Hegarty's wall of pizza boxes, in which each student decorated a pizza box to represent a different element of the periodic table and when scanned, viewers were taken to a video in which the student educates the audience about that particular element. Mrs. Hegarty used the same innovative technology, with her students completing two very different projects, which grew not only her own comfort level, but that of her students.

The school librarian is an innovation coach. As such, it is important to circle back with the brave teachers who agree to try something new, risk failure, lean into the novelty of innovative teaching strategies, and take a chance on an unknown outcome. Be sure to congratulate them, recognize them, and perhaps even ask them to work with you to present your experiences in front of a larger audience, whether it be within your school community (parents, board members, or other faculty members) or at a local or national conference. Allow other stakeholders to learn from your bravery, as you and a cocaptain may inspire someone else to attempt a similar play.

CHAPTER FOUR

The Power of Podcasting

"Podcasting is fun to do, and it is fun to pick your own instruments to make the podcast have sound in the background."

—Amy, age 6

There is such power in podcasting, for both listeners and creators. Anyone can become a podcasting superstar. The term *podcast* has been around since 2004, when Adam Curry (the former MTV VJ now known as "the Podfather") and Dave Winer (another "Podfather" and the former entrepreneur and *Wired* magazine writer) worked together to generate on-demand content to listen to on an iPod, modeled after the technology that the Boston-based journalist and radio host Christopher Lydon used to generate Really Simple Syndication (RSS) feeds to curate blogs. In simple terms, a podcast as defined by *Merriam-Webster*, is an audio file that can be downloaded via the internet and listened to at one's convenience through a computer or mobile device. The *pod* in *podcasting* comes from the iPod, Apple's portable MP3 player, which at the time was the primary portable music player, reminiscent of the Sony Walkman.

Podcasts, however, are not limited to iPod use—any mobile device or computer will work. We can also think of *pod* as a (lowercase) acronym for the phrase "personal on demand" or "portable on demand." By subscribing to podcasts, listeners can access their favorite hosts or listen to audio on just about any topic that may interest them. People listen to podcasts for a variety of reasons. Podcasts can help their listeners achieve learning goals, such as how to speak a foreign language. They can also be for entertainment, like the antics of a favorite comedian, or for personal growth, such as discovering tactics to practice mindfulness.

Podcasts inspire the imagination of their audience. While some podcasts do have a visual component, many are listened to while on the go, making audio the primary mode of engagement. Podcasts can feel personal. They make famous and celebrated individuals feel accessible to the listener—they are invited into one's own living room, sharing casual conversation. Audiences can curate podcasts based not only on the people who are the subjects of the podcasts, but also by the topics of their choosing. Melissa Plaskoff, president and cofounder of ON-AIR MEDIA, LLC, a successful Dallas-based boutique podcast network and studio, notes that "people are inspired to create podcasts as a forum to connect with others, to process and navigate life-changing events, and to benefit those that are seeking reaffirmation or exposure to experiences not unlike their own" (2019). For learners who are discovering their voice, podcasting helps connect content creators with an interested audience that is drawn to their stories. The ability to customize exposure to content is a primary benefit to podcasting. There is power in this level of personalization.

Podcasting does not require significant technology, nor does a podcaster have to rely on an outside authority for publication. There is power, too, in this level of independence. Storytelling is a key component to successful podcasts. Everyone has a story to tell, and podcasts create a stage that allows just about anyone to share their story.

Interestingly, there is healing power in podcasts too, for both the creator and the listener. There is emotional value for the podcast creator to share their thoughts, interests, and knowledge with others. This process allows podcast creators to know themselves better and validate what they view to be their contribution to society. As for listeners, podcasts can connect them to like-minded individuals, or else expose them to unfamiliar people and places and change the way they view the world. Podcasting represents accessibility. They can be enjoyed at any time, at any place, and by anyone. There is power in this level of accessibility, too.

The Voice Inside Your Head

With the rise in podcasting, it is evident that we have something to say, and a desire to listen exists out there. As stated by Calvin Reid (2018), "podcast listening continues to grow, with an estimated 73 million people listening to podcasts of all kinds each month." In other words, podcasts are all the rage. In education, podcasts can help students find their voice. Just as students spend years in school learning the mechanics of writing, verbal expression can be fine-tuned not just through the natural progression of growth, but also with purposeful coaching.

School librarians are well situated to serve as the purposeful coach in podcasting. They can guide learners and teachers through the technical components, while also helping them discover and share their inner voice. Meanwhile, teachers can serve as the assistant coach throughout the podcasting process. In doing so, they are ultimately training to become the head coach. This chapter shares what podcasting can look like for learners of all ages and ways in which you, the head coach, can make podcasting a painless yet, powerful play in education. It also will share strategies for integrating podcasting into your school library to encourage content creators throughout the school. Discover how to move off of the sidelines and into the bleachers to celebrate teacher and learner success, allowing you to move on to scoring new goals with other players.

We all have different technology tools available to us in our school communities. However, one of the benefits of podcast creation is that it can be done with a variety of technology tools, including older devices. There may be some aspects of the podcasting process outlined in this chapter that the coach may decide to eliminate. There are multiple approaches to podcasting, each of which is influenced by time constraints, the ages of the podcasters, the type and amount of technology available, and the goal of the podcast. Any recording device and a little creativity can result in a world-class podcast.

The Warm-up

To begin finding one's inner voice, it is always helpful to start with a warm-up exercise. Give everyone a word, such as *learning,* and invite the students and teacher to write down three words that come to mind when hearing their word. Walk them through this exercise at least three times with different words. Now, compare the words that were written down. More than likely, there will be variations in what words came to mind. For example, one student may have written down "serious," "focus," and "hard" in response to *learning,* while another student may have written "fun," "interesting," and "curious." As you compare the different reactions that the students and the teacher had for the prompts, explain that each of us has our own diverse experiences, which shapes our thoughts and creates a unique voice within our heads. We all have our own personalities and experiences that influence our inner voice. In podcasting, we want to allow our inner voice to shine through and influence how we share our content. This is one of the factors that makes podcasting interesting. Each podcast host has a unique style.

In order for learners to grasp the concept that will drive their own podcast creation process, they must realize that exposure to the power of podcasting in a variety of contexts helps podcasters discover their own voice. Curating various types of podcasts and encouraging listeners to consider how specific podcasts made them feel, how they shaped their learning experience, and whether a podcast changed the way they think will help them create their own powerful podcasts. There are different approaches to exposing students to podcasts and how they can evaluate their impact. I will share some strategies next, but keep in mind that some of these examples may not suit every age group. However, the examples can be altered to meet the needs of different learning communities. As the coach, consider what will work best for your learners.

Podcasts as a "Pregame Activity"

Podcasts are a powerful introductory tool to an activity related to science, technology, engineering, art, and math (STEAM). For example, students who are working in small groups or in pairs can be challenged to build a weather-resistant structure to withstand natural disasters. As a pregame activity, share a podcast about the housing shortage that can occur after a natural disaster, when supplies are difficult to acquire and the access to areas that are in ruin is limited. National Public Radio (NPR) has a robust collection of short podcasts in which victims of natural disasters and reporters share their firsthand experience with the difficulties people face locating new housing after a natural disaster. One such example can be found at https://n.pr/2X7HKKN.

Once students listen to a podcast related to the housing shortage after a natural disaster, have them work in small groups to complete a STEAM challenge by designing and building a weather-resistant housing shelter using duct tape, cardstock, straws, rubber bands, cardboard, pipe cleaners, and other supplies that may be on hand. After building, be sure to have them share and reflect on their process. Finally, ask them how the podcast influenced their approach to the activity. Did the activity feel more meaningful? Were they able to make a deeper connection to it with a more serious sense of urgency surrounding the housing shortage? Did they have a personal connection to the activity that gave them the ability to put voice to the problem they were working to solve? In this instance, podcasts can be used to create an emotional hook that aims to educate and connect listeners to a social cause.

Podcasts as a Team-Building Activity

Demonstrating that podcasts can connect people to each other is another strategy that shapes how students share their own voices via podcasting. As students are exposed to stories through picture books, novels, and nonfiction books throughout school, pairing these readings with author interviews so that students can learn the "story behind the story" deepens their connection to the content. This helps connect readers to authors. Schools that subscribe to TeachingBooks (https://www .Teachingbooks.net), which is an online collection of resources focusing on children's and young adult books and their authors, have access to short podcasts in which authors share their name pronunciations and biographical information about the history of their name. When students have the opportunity to hear an author's own voice, it connects them to the author, breaking down the boundary between imagining the author as a distant figure as opposed to a regular person sharing her or his work.

All forms of storytelling, whether through works in print or audio recordings via podcast, connect people. After allowing students to hear from the authors themselves, whether through an interview or in learning about their name, reflect on how this changed the students' perspective on the story that they read. Did it alter their perspective on the story? Did they have a better understanding for who the author is, and possibly why he or she shared the story? Did they form a deeper connection to the story?

In our school, we host parent book clubs, and we read both fiction and nonfiction books that are relevant to parenting and education. A recent book that we read was Emily Giffin's *All We Ever Wanted*. As part of our discussion, we listened to a two-minute clip of a podcast produced by Barnes and Noble, in which the author is being interviewed about the inspiration behind this fictional story. After listening to the podcast, we learned that one driving question that inspired the events in the story was this: At what point does privilege morph into an entitlement for children? We were able to make deeper connections with the story through a better understanding of the author's thought process.

Podcasts as a Tiebreaker Activity

While some students may be visual learners, others are auditory—they rely on what they hear to process information. Poll your students and ask which of them consider themselves to be auditory learners and which believe that they are visual learners. Give the students a book to read to themselves and ask them follow-up questions to assess their reading comprehension. Next, share an audiobook with the students and ask follow-up reading comprehension questions. Poll the students to determine which set of questions was easier for them to recall: those with audio, or without? Do the responses make sense, demonstrating that those who believe themselves to be auditory learners were able to better comprehend the story that was read aloud to them? Ask the students to reflect on this and assess their preactivity responses with that of their actual experiences. Use this exercise to demonstrate that often, podcasts can make learning stick for specific students.

Once the podcasters have warmed up to their purpose and tackled their topic, they are ready to press forward. There is a variety of approaches to podcasting, depending on the type and the amount of technology that is available. As a result, next I will share how to create podcasts in a variety of formats, including analog podcasts, which mimic the process but in which access to technology is limited; mobile device podcasts created using a tablet or smartphone; and finally, computer-generated podcasts that can be created using a desktop or a laptop computer. The number of devices available will also influence whether each student creates her or his own podcast or if students will work in small, collaborative groups, each owning a part of the process. When students are working in small groups, it is helpful to either assign them specific roles or to allow them to select their roles within the production process. I will share an example of creating a group podcast later in the chapter.

What's My Story?

Consider the goal of the podcast. Is it to accompany a written project that your students created to explain their process? Is it simply to teach them technology tools that can be used to create a podcast in order to add digital tools to their toolbox? Or is it to share what they learned about a particular topic? Honing in on the goal of the podcast will influence how you frame the podcast project going forward. If the podcast is centered around any topic of interest to the students, it will be helpful for them to complete a storyboard beforehand, which will outline the podcasting process. Podcast storyboards can be divided into sections or, as in the example in Table 4.1, shared in menu format as a four-course meal.

When podcasting with emerging readers, visual storyboards can be used as an alternative to written storyboards, which I will discuss later in this chapter.

Table 4.1   Podcast Storyboard Shared in a Menu Format

Course of the Meal	Content	Notes
Appetizer *Introductory music:* What type of mood are you wanting to create?		
Salad *Spoken content:* Introduce yourself and your guest (if there is someone besides yourself taking part in the podcast)		
Main Entrée *Spoken content:* This is where the primary purpose of your podcast is delivered. It could be an interview, a poem, opinions on a specific topic, or advice. Don't forget to thank your guest and/or your listening audience.		
Dessert *Concluding music:* Again, consider the closing mood. Often, this can be the same music shared in your introduction.		

What's in a Name?

Just as the voice in our head guides our everyday thoughts and actions, so does the labeling of what we encounter shape our impressions. For this reason, what a student chooses to name the podcast is important. It sets the tone for the audience. Depending upon the technology used to create the podcast, sometimes multiple podcasts are hosted on one channel, which is similar to creating a collection of YouTube videos and inputting them into one playlist. If each student is creating his or her own podcast, you will need to have a podcast channel name, and each student will need to have a name for the episode within the channel. If small groups of children are creating a few podcasts, allow each student to suggest two episode titles, and then ask the group to vote for the one they will choose. When podcasting with emerging readers, it is helpful to preselect three to five podcast titles and then ask the students to vote on their favorite. Deciding on the name for the podcast channel and/or individual podcast episodes should be fun. Some questions to consider when generating a strong podcast channel name and/or individual episode titles are the following: What is the goal of the podcast or podcasts? What type of mood do I wish to establish: serious, fun, silly, joyful, calm? What one word best describes the content? What will be memorable, on point with the subject matter, and easy to remember? When word gets around that your students are podcasting superstars, it will be important to be able to recall podcast titles to suggest to potential listeners. Encourage creativity in the naming process.

Making Podcasts Accessible for Participants of All Ages

My first teacher–school librarian partnership for podcast production was with kindergarteners. While this may sound daring, I strategized a few key plays ahead of time. First, I selected a teacher to work with whom I had already established considerable trust through previous partnerships. Next, I made a point of emphasizing that this class would be "piloting" this activity for the rest of the grade. I asked the teacher and her students to approach podcast production as flexible thinkers and to be sure to put on their "patience hats" before arriving to the "production studio." Before each

Figure 4.1 The Podcasting Teacher Cheat Sheet.

visit to the creation space, I made a point of reminding them to be sure their patience hats were on tight. Most important, I created a "Teacher Cheat Sheet," which I have modified twice as I have noticed areas that require more detail. Scan the QR code in Figure 4.1 with a QR reader and access the latest version of "The Podcasting Teacher Cheat Sheet."

I prioritized getting the teacher's buy-in by reassuring her that I was calling the plays and would ease her onto the field. My first approach in doing this was to assign her three students who were strong listeners to work in a separate area and walk through the steps together. I emphasized the importance of breaking down each step one by one and advised them that there was no time constraint. We would be flexible with our time and not feel as though we needed to complete these podcasts in one learning session. I also reminded the teacher that we were adding digital tools to the students' (and the teacher's) toolbox by exposing them to a series of apps. They would become *app smashers*, which meant they would have the ability to use multiple apps to create one project that demonstrated their learning. Finally, I made a point of emphasizing to the teacher that after these podcasts were complete, she would have high-quality projects to share with her parent community that reflected her students' growth.

Solidifying the Team Mindset

As I was emphasizing to the teacher the importance of being flexible and allowing expectations to be fluid, I also realized that I was reminding myself of this as well. For example, after successfully getting a small group of strong students a third of the way through the production process before the bell rang, the teacher was feeling confident. The following visit, however, she had a more challenging student, with whom she was struggling. The instant that I recognized this, I made a point of having that student work with me, as I could sense that the experience had the potential to dampen the resilience that she had shown this far in the project. As the coach who is training the assistant coach to be the lead, flexibility is critical to building up strength in the process before pulling back. Again, this reinforces that the school librarian is working hard to set both the teacher and the students up for success.

Students were eased into the concept of podcasting through a series of steps as well. The teacher and I agreed that each kindergarten student would create her or his own podcast to share tips for having a successful year in kindergarten, based on what they had learned and experienced so far in their school year. First, I shared an example that I had asked a fifth grade student to create, in which she played the role of a kindergarten student giving advice about how to be successful on the playground, to behave respectfully in the dining hall, and to maintain strong friendships. After playing her podcast example for the students, I walked them through her creation process:

1. She drew a cover for her podcast with her own face in the center.
2. She made a storyboard to serve as a script to trigger her memory of what she wanted to share while recording.

3. She opened up the Book Creator app on an iPad and created a colorful cover with the title of her podcast in the center.

4. She opened the Garageband app on the same device and created a musical piece to accompany the introduction and the conclusion of her recording.

5. She saved her musical score and input it into the book cover within Book Creator.

6. She took a photo of her drawing with the camera app and saved it in the camera roll of her photos.

7. She advanced to the next page in the Book Creator project and inserted her drawing that included her face.

8. Using a storyboard, she recorded what she wished to say onto this page.

9. She advanced to another page and created another image with the name of her podcast and inserted her Garageband musical score again on the final page.

10. With my help, she uploaded it to YouTube and marked it as unlisted in the privacy settings so that anyone with the link could view and listen to her podcast.

Walking the students through the overall process beforehand was not only interesting, but also exciting to see all the various applications that they would be entrusted to use for this project.

Podcast creation does not have to be an independent activity. Powerful podcasts can be created collaboratively, in small groups. With this approach, students are well served to have specific roles during the podcast creation process. These roles can be chosen by drawing out of a hat or through voting. When establishing the roles, it is important to consider the technology that is available, as well as the ages of the students. For example, younger students who are working in small groups may have more abstract job assignments. Examples of roles for younger students include the following:

- Musician: Responsible for producing the musical scores to accompany the podcast.
- Researcher: Draws information from external sources to expand the information that will be shared.
- Artist: Creates the visuals, including the podcast logo, if any.
- Production manager: Ensures that the group is staying on task and assists with overcoming obstacles.

The audio can be recorded by each group member so that it becomes a shared task. With older students (ages ten and above), the jobs may become more sophisticated. Examples of podcast positions for upper elementary students and beyond include the following:

- Composer: Creates an original music score to accompany the introduction and conclusion of the podcast.
- Interviewer: Speaks with outside sources to gather data.
- Researcher: Peruses credible sources to increase the group's knowledge of the topic.
- Editor: Manages the storyboarding process and the revising of the content.
- Copyright expert: Works to ensure that there are no copyright infringement violations or instances of plagiarism.
- Production assistant: Oversees that each role comes together harmoniously to create an effective, efficient project.

Unless the group votes otherwise, allowing each student in the group to have a voice in the recording process will reinforce the team mentality and help ensure group ownership of the finished product.

The Storyboard

The storyboard is the backbone of a podcast project. It is the tool that will allow the students to feel confident prior to their big play—the recording of the podcast. Keep it simple and consider your audience. When working with older students, perhaps a more fun approach to storyboarding, as suggested in the four-course menu example given in Table 4.1, will help ease some of the pressure that comes with creating the content. For younger students, consider that it may be necessary to rely on visuals displayed next to topics written in text and/or give the students the choice to write or draw pictures as their content.

Some students choose to draw, some choose to write, and some choose to do a combination of both. Storyboarding also allows the students to form their own pictures in their mind, visualizing what they intend to say in their recording.

App Smashing

The technology that is available for recording will influence which applications are used to create podcasts. Luckily, there are a variety of podcasting tools that are suitable for different types of devices. If working with desktop computers or laptops, it will be important to ensure that the microphone is enabled or that a stand-alone microphone is available.

Stand alone microphones can often connect through the universal serial bus (USB) port and are sold online via Amazon.

There are a number of online platforms that allow users to create podcasts with a computer. Vocaroo (http://vocaroo.com) is one such tool. Simply hit Record, and a link is generated to share the voice recording. The recording can be downloaded onto the computer as an audio file, such as an MP3 or WAV file. Vocaroo also allows the link to the audio recording to be generated into a QR code with one click. Our students use the app to create podcasts in Hebrew so that the teacher can evaluate their conversational skills. They can either email the teacher the link to their recording or post it onto the class's Padlet wall.

Spreaker is another audio recording tool, and it allows for a few more advanced options. Tracks can be layered on top of one another to generate additional sound effects, such as audience applause. An important factor in considering Spreaker is the age requirement; users (who must be registered) must be thirteen years or older. Therefore, usage within this application for students below the age of thirteen requires that students create their podcasts under the teacher or school librarian's Spreaker account.

One of my favorite web-based podcast creation tools is Anchor. Anchor makes it easy to create professional-sounding podcasts via your computer by following a series of simple steps. There are built-in musical scores to add to each episode to designate a pause in the recording or simply add flavor to the episode. Once the podcast is complete, Anchor hosts it and generates a unique link for sharing. The site also has a library of cover art, or you can create your own cover art to upload to your episode. Anchor has a thorough, yet easy-to-understand, section on their website that provides tips for successful podcasting.

Audacity is another web-based podcasting tool that can be downloaded for free on a Mac or a PC. Audacity allows significant alteration of the recording. The user can adjust the pitch, the bass and treble, and the background noise by expanding the audio file and editing it in detail. While it is easy to create a simple recording via Audacity, it is also well suited for those that wish to make more complex technical edits. Audacity users are recommended to wait three to five seconds after pressing Record before speaking so that the microphone can normalize itself.

Another strategy is to record directly from the computer using its microphone. The audio file can be saved as an MP3 and uploaded to a free podcast-hosting site, such as Podbean (http://Podbean.com) or Soundcloud (http://Soundcloud.com). Both are excellent choices for creating a podcasting channel that hosts multiple episodes and generates a unique link to the podcast channel.

If you are using a mobile device, such as an iPhone, iPad, or Android, there are a variety of free podcast creation apps that can be used too. One of the most well-known podcasting apps is Garageband, as previously discussed, which can be used on an Apple device, such as an iPad, iPod Touch, or iPhone. Garageband is particularly useful for not only recording vocals, but also for creating musical scores that can be used to add flavor to the podcast as part of the introduction and/or conclusion to the voice recording. To use Garageband, simply select the plus sign at the upper-right corner within the audio recorder section. Tap the red Record button. Make sure that the pitch is turned off by ensuring that the triangular icon to the right of the Record button is gray. If it is blue, tap it one time to turn it gray. When you are finished, tap the white square to stop the recording. To save the recording, click the white arrow at the upper-right corner, select the drop-down menu that appears, and select My Songs, and it will save onto the Garageband dashboard. By holding down the podcast icon in the dashboard, a menu pops up that provides a Share option. By selecting Share, you can save the podcast as a song and upload it to a cloud-based tool, such as Dropbox, Soundcloud, or Google Drive. In addition, the sound file can be shared via text or directly imported into iMovie for additional editing. If you do not wish to include music or fine-tune the pitch, then the Voice Memos app on an iPhone or iPod Touch will allow you to record and publish directly to iMovie, Google Drive, or Dropbox, or send it elsewhere via text.

VoiceThread (http://VoiceThread.com), which is both a website and an app, is another valuable podcasting tool in education. In addition to being device agnostic, VoiceThread allows educators to sign up with their school email addresses to receive 50 free student accounts for every educator account. This version is considered the classroom account. Teachers can create a prompt via an audio recording and ask students to respond to it. Students can also create cover art and include video with their recordings. VoiceThread allows versatility in podcast creation, in that students can follow the educator's lead by responding to a topic in detail, or they can generate their own unique audio recording within their own framework.

Other podcast creation apps that will work on either Apple or Android devices include Audioboom, Spreaker Studio, Anchor, and the Voice Recorder app. The level of complexity of editing will help determine which apps you want to use to create podcasts. Some are simple audio recorders, while others have sophisticated editing tools built into them. No matter the level of sophistication, however, allowing students the experience of creating their own content and sharing their voices is a powerful lesson in media creation. These efforts support the Shared Foundations and explanatory Key Commitments of the American Association of School Librarians (AASL) to inquire, explore, and engage (AASL 2018).

Curricular Connections

With podcasting, students are empowered to use technology tools to amplify their voices. Connecting podcasting to the students' curriculums not only engages learners but allows the content to stick as well. As Chip and Dan Heath share in their book, *Made to Stick,* "Concrete, sensory experiences etch ideas into our brain—think of how much easier it is to remember a song than a credit card number, even though a song contains much more data!" (2008, 272). There are a variety of ways to leverage podcasting to influence how a curriculum is made to stick.

For a Love of Literature

The school at which I work is the proud host of an author podcast series. Every time we have a visiting author, whether in person or via Skype, we have a team of student experts who create a podcast in which they interview the author. Students in upper elementary levels can apply to become part of the author podcast team. Teams are typically comprised of two students. One serves as the researcher, to discover meaningful questions to ask the author about her or his life and work, as well as being the interviewer. The other serves as the technical partner, recording the interview with an iPad and producing the podcast, including mixing the music into the introduction and conclusion. All questions are approved by the school librarian after the research is complete. This activity is also a great opportunity to start a conversation about etiquette. Reviewing the do's and don'ts of interview techniques is a powerful learning opportunity for all students, regardless of whether they are active participants or audience members, as reflected in Figure 4.2. Once the podcast has been completed, we host it on a Soundcloud channel. The link can be found at https://tiny url.com/davissound. Creating podcasts surrounding author visits generates excitement, encourages exploration of the author's work to ensure a meaningful discussion, and exposes students to published authors.

Podcasts are excellent formats for student book reviews. Whether the work being reviewed is for a book club, a book report, or a book fair, providing the opportunity for students to create podcasts that not only summarize the book but that make other students want to read it is a powerful way to encourage literacy. Our students have recorded podcasts by speaking into a microphone plugged into the computer via the USB port, and we have hosted them on Podbean.com. Once the podcasts have been saved as audio files, we have linked the book reviews into Follett Destiny, our library catalog, so that when other students are searching for

Figure 4.2 The student technologist, with the iPad, is purposefully placed at an elevated level to capture better sound quality, while the student interviewer sits at eye level to her guest, photojournalist Kate Parker, as Kate shares her story.

books, they can receive recommendations and synopses of the books from their peers. Over the years, quite a collection of book recommendation podcasts can be acquired. We have some book reviews within our library catalog that date back to 2008.

Our school also hosts a program entitled Young Authors Night every spring. Students have spent months writing books on different topics or themes, depending upon their grade level. For instance, our youngest learners create a book that is within the theme of "all about me," and our fourth graders create a biography of someone in their family tree. Creating podcasts to coincide with this project adds a multimedia component, in which students learn note-taking skills, research skills, "netiquette," and technical skills. Our fourth graders record an interview with their subject, which also introduces them to the idea of using primary sources, or they interview someone who knew their subject.

Again, formulating interview questions, producing the technical aspects of a podcast, and showcasing the interview as a QR code within their "Young Authors Night" piece, highlight an interesting part of the writing process. It also allows the students to go back and listen to the interviews to aid them in their writing.

Ask an Expert

~~As referenced previously, one strategy for making content stick is to be the creator of that content. The process of researching and sifting through information to learn about a particular topic to meet an end goal is a powerful learning experience.~~ Podcast production can encourage students to research an aspect of their curriculums to be able to interact with an expert on a particular topic, all while increasing the depth of their knowledge on the topic. Here are some examples:

- Ms. Frizzle Podcasts: Remember Ms. Frizzle, the kooky science teacher who took her students on science-rich journeys of discovery through *The Magic School Bus* series? Why not bring Ms. Frizzle to life with podcasts that connect students with scientists to help them uncover the mysteries of the universe? Joanna Cole, the author of *The Magic School Bus* books and a former school librarian, notes that she started each book with a science-related question that she was trying to answer by creating a fictional story. Modeled after this approach, students can agree on a scientific question, research information to help them generate additional questions to uncover the truth, and interview an expert to help them address the question. For example, the Next Generation Science Standards denote that climate change is taught as part of the Middle School Science curriculum (2013). Students can formulate a question related to climate change, such as what the rate of global warming is and what conditions influence this rate. Researching and generating interview questions for a climate scientist and setting up a podcast interview with this person allow students to become more knowledgeable about global warming and the conditions that influence it.

- Are You Smarter Than a Fifth Grader Podcast: Despite the name (which comes from a television game show), this can actually be done at any grade level. Ask students to formulate trivia questions that cover their particular curriculum, just as the game show does. Select an expert, such as a teacher at that grade level, to respond to those questions via a podcast. This is a playful way to flip the learning process, empowering students to formulate trivia questions that relate to their curriculum and quiz the experts—their teachers.

- Students Are Experts Too: Often, teachers make the bulk of the decisions on issues that affect student learning. However, podcasting offers an opportunity to encourage students to develop their own expertise and share their knowledge. For example, many schools use Seesaw, a digital portfolio learning tool that is a mobile app and a website (https://web.seesaw.me/), to create content and showcase their work. Teachers determine whether their classrooms will use this tool. Ask students to give the tool a try and create a podcast reviewing it. They can share their personal experiences of how this tool has affected their learning, demonstrating the value of students sharing their voices and recognizing student-centered learning.

Review and Reflect

Some clever parents hide vegetables inside a more kid-friendly food like macaroni and cheese, or even cookies. Using podcasts as a rubric replacement can have a similar effect on assessing a student's learning. I've noticed that sometimes when we use the word *rubric* with our students, it can take some of the joy out of completing a project. Students may feel that their creativity is being staunched when asked to follow a checklist of standards. Disguising the rubric as a podcast can generate the same self-evaluation effect of asking students to measure their work against a set of standards. As an alternative to a rubric, ask the students to generate a storyboard that denotes specific areas to be covered. Then, upon completion of the project, have students use the storyboard to create a podcast that addresses the areas from the storyboard as a review and reflection of their work. For example, our students were asked to create a landform project in second grade that required research and an oral presentation. The original version of the rubric is given in Table 4.2.

The storyboard for the podcast, used in place of the rubric, is reflected in Table 4.3.

Instead of including point values, as is done with a rubric, consider adding a reflection column that encourages the podcaster to reflect on the level of importance of each piece of the project. Students can note how important it was for them to be able to share three facts about their project, for example, and how that influenced their overall presentation.

Low Tech/High Impact: The Analog Version

For some, the idea of creating a podcast can be intimidating. The act of recording audio is such a simple concept that it is difficult for a potential podcast creator to believe that there is not more to the process. However, if we focus on the writing and the talking, the technology behind podcast creation can be perceived as less daunting. The art of creating content for a podcast is what drives the learning within the process. Although the technical skills in the production process are valuable, they can be thought of as secondary. It's the next component after scoring a goal, similar to kicking the extra point after a touchdown. It's worth another point, but the touchdown, the main event, has already been scored. It is possible to produce an analog version of a podcast. With a little creativity and a shift in expectations regarding how the audience will receive the information, an analog podcast can be a powerful play in learning!

As shared earlier in the chapter, identifying the content, researching the knowledge gaps, tapping into experts, generating an outline to ensure that

Table 4.2   Original Landform Project Rubric

Name: _____

Landform/ Bodies of Water Project: Rubric

Project Due Date: January 23, 24, or 25

Specific name of landform or body of water:_____

Please use this rubric as a guideline to know what is expected for this project. The students are graded on their oral presentation, so please make sure your child has plenty of practice presenting to the family! You do not need to return this sheet. Your child will be graded on these requirements.

Project Requirements	
My name is on this project. (1 point)	YES or NO
I was creative in designing my project. (1 point)	YES or NO
Oral Presentation	
I explained why I chose this landform/body of water. (1 point)	YES or NO
I explained how I made my project (materials, how it is constructed, etc.). (1 point)	YES or NO
I shared the resource(s) that I used to find my facts. (1 point)	YES or NO
I was able to share three facts about my landform or body of water. (3 points)	YES or NO
I shared my project with my family, and I spoke loudly and clearly. (1 point)	YES or NO
I practiced explaining my project to my family. I used my notecards. I made eye contact. (1 point)	YES or NO
I practiced three or more times in front of my family. (Recommended)	YES or NO

content is shared in an organized manner, delivering the content, and reflecting on the process are what drive the learning of the curriculum. These actions also reinforce the value of tackling a project within a specific framework to ensure it is well organized. Following a game plan, such as the one shown in Figure 4.3, which includes organizational tactics, reinforces the value of building strong executive skills that will positively affect academic success.

This brings us to the analog piece of the podcast. Rather than using a mobile device, a computer, or a technological device of any kind to record and share their experience, have students deliver their "podcasts" before a live audience. Set the stage so that a fan group is available to hear the

Table 4.3   Storyboard, or Rubric in Disguise

Landform Podcast Storyboard	
The Scene	**My Script**
Introductory music (optional): *Yes or No?*	
Introducing the host of the show: *How do we know this landform project belongs to you?*	
Creativity: *How were you creative in this project? What made your landform unique?*	
Explanation of your project: *How would you explain why you chose the landform/body of water that you did?*	
Explanation of materials: *How did you make your project? What materials did you use? How did you construct your landform/body of water? Be specific.*	
My source(s): *Where did I find the information that I shared in my oral presentation?*	
The content: *Was I able to share three facts about my landform/body of water?*	
The practice process: *When I shared my oral presentation with my family, was I able to speak loudly and clearly? Was I able to make eye contact? Did I use my notecards?*	
Repetition: *Did I practice three or more times in front of my family?*	

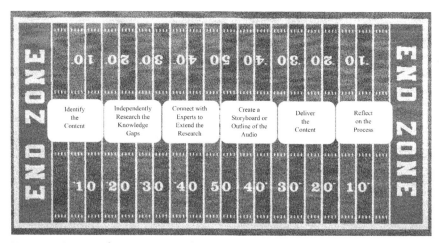

Figure 4.3   A podcasting game plan to score a touchdown.

audio production in person. The benefit of podcasting in such a low-tech way is that the audience can become a part of the reflection process as the creator crosses the goal line. Similar to a live taping of a show, in which the audience can participate, a comparable environment is established in an analog podcast creation. Live podcasters have the benefit of bringing their audience into the process with them, receiving real-time feedback and direct interaction from listeners. Once the podcast has concluded, asking audiences to participate in a live question-and-answer session can enhance the reflection process.

Celebrate Success

An aspect of all this that is sometimes overlooked, and yet critical to solidifying the partnership between the school librarian and the teacher, is to celebrate successes. During my first attempt at joining forces with a homeroom teacher to create podcasts, I received a text from the teacher one evening with an image of an empty wine bottle—she was noting that I had driven her to the bottle after an afternoon of podcasting. While meant as a joke, it was a solid reminder that as the head coach, I had to keep encouraging her all the way through the process.

After all, we are asking teachers to go beyond their comfort zones and try the unknown, with a group of students depending on them. Remind those brave teachers whom we have convinced to innovate with us that it truly is about the journey of learning. Be sure to tell them that we will encounter highs and lows along the way, as even strong teams do. For me, the success comes from the joy of sharing. The power of podcasting lies in the ability to personalize the content, control the publication process, and make the podcasts accessible to listeners, whether it is in front of a live audience or through a digital platform.

CHAPTER FIVE

Curricular Connections to Coding

Coding done through the library."

What about tech classes?

> "I like coding because I like being on computers and making projects work."
>
> —Suzie, age 9

Coding has created incredible opportunities for our school as a whole, and for our students as individuals. It has been a vessel for students' personal growth and for our school's ability to gain recognition, and therefore acquire additional resources to support learning. It has proved to be a skill set that connects us to our local community and expands our exposure to opportunities beyond our school. There are a variety of ways that school librarians can approach creating a culture of coding. Regardless of which approach you take, it is imperative to take one.

Anyone can code. Truly. I was an English major with a negative self-image of my math abilities. My mother claims that she put my math tutor's children through college. Yet I would grow up to inspire a culture of coding in my school community. Coding, as defined by *Merriam-Webster*, the act of putting "into the form or symbols of a code." Reminiscent of translating the meaning of the Dewey decimal system to determine the proper location of a book, coding is using another language or system as an intermediary between humans and machines. Coding creates a bridge that allows people to communicate and connect. The Future Ready Librarians framework outlines the role of the school librarian as one that cultivates community partnerships, leads beyond the library through collaborative leadership, empowers students as creators, and facilitates professional learning (Future Ready Librarians 2018). Coding is a gateway to fulfilling these responsibilities. In this chapter, I will share strategies for building your own culture of coding, starting in the school library and merging into the curriculum through teacher partnerships.

The Super Bowl of Learning Experiences

Coding is a game changer in every way. It is a skill set that takes the players by surprise, changing their perspective on what learning can look like. As school librarians, we love to nurture the library as a safe haven. The library is a place for learners of all ages, interests, habits, and aptitudes to find knowledge with which they can connect. For some students, coding in school is the first opportunity for students to feel empowered and have a sense of belonging. As I write this, I have countless examples of students running through my head that illustrate this point. The moment these students discovered coding in school, they felt like the expert in the room, with a strong interest in growing their knowledge of coding and sharing their creations. This is one reason that it is important to introduce students to coding early in their school career. Another reason is that the more exposure they have to code, the more sophisticated they can become in computer science.

Learners build upon a foundation starting at an early age and are more likely to consider computer science an important component to their learning. It becomes another language in which students strive to become literate. It is no longer an "extra," but rather a critical piece of their academic development. Cultivating a culture in which both students and teachers recognize coding as a fundamental literacy can be tricky. In this instance, I find it valuable to start with the students. Nurture their coding interests to gain teacher support and showcase the results within the parent community to solidify the value placed on coding in the curriculum. In a short time, coding can become an expectation, as opposed to a special treat.

Practice Drills, Then Join the Team

The beauty of creating a culture of coding is that you don't have to wait for teacher buy-in before you can successfully implement. Students will support your efforts, even if the teachers are not yet ready to embrace the value of coding. I suggest introducing kids to coding during their library visits. If you haven't participated in Hour of Code before, this is the year to start. Hour of Code started as a grassroots effort to introduce kids to computer science and demonstrate that coding is an accessible skill set that can be learned. In just five years, there are over 200,000 registered Hour of Code events in over 180 countries (Code.org n.d.). Hadi Partovi, the founder of Hour of Code, could not have made it easier for school librarians, or anyone interested, to sponsor an Hour of Code event. Each year, Hour of Code takes place the first week of December. The Code.org website hosts a variety of coding activities that support drag-and-drop programming, text-based programming languages, and app development.

Having just completed our fourth year participating in Hour of Code, I have bought into it now more than ever. Here's why: Hour of Code started as a fun, manageable way to introduce our students' ages four to fourteen to coding. It was an accessible way for me to dabble in coding, too. From the start, I made a point of asking teachers not to drop off their classes for their library visit and leave, but rather to stay and code with us. One of my favorite and most memorable moments was when, in our first year of Hour of Code, one of our fourth grade teachers, who definitely does not consider herself a technology expert, was mentioned in a tweet with a picture of her coding with her class. As it turned out, Shakira, the famous pop music star, is a huge supporter of Hour of Code and was monitoring the #HourofCode hashtag. In response to seeing our school's tweet, Shakira tweeted back that she loved that this teacher was coding with her students. It was a memorable moment, in that in no other scenario would this teacher have expected to connect with a famous music icon such as Shakira. I started to realize just how much a program like Hour of Code can affect a school, connect unlikely individuals to each other, and transform the learning environment. Next, I will share in more detail how Hour of Code has transformed our coding culture through creative programming, leaving a lasting impact. Hadi Partovi was on to something.

Beyond Hour of Code week, designating student visits to the library as a time to expose students to coding is a strong way to start, too. Coding in the library certainly does not need to be limited to the Hour of Code week. If you see students on a fixed schedule, consider reserving some time during these visits to code. These coding opportunities can also be connected to their core curriculum, which I will share in detail next. As you explore the activities that are hosted on Code.org, many of which are available all year long, you are likely to find coding activities that encourage problem-solving and independence, such as animating a name in Scratch or completing a maze in Minecraft with Blockly. Create a menu of choices for students to toggle back and forth between different activities, or create coding challenges within Code.org so that learners attempt to experience one programming language before they advance to another.

For example, I chose three Code.org activities (one that involved Scratch, one that used Blockly, and one that used JavaScript) and had each activity's link saved in the favorites of our web browser. Once students finished an activity in Scratch, they could choose to advance to the Blockly activity, and then progress to the JavaScript activity. Once they were exposed to a variety of coding scenarios through the menu options, they could settle on their favorite for the remainder of their class period.

~~When students are able to spend a library visit coding, I make a point of ensuring that we have books about coding available should they~~ wish ~~to channel their interest beyond the classroom.~~ Often, I will receive parent feedback that their child loved the coding experience. I make a point of encouraging parents to nurture their children's interest outside of school by exploring coding camps, participating in after-school coding programs, or entering a technology competition that will motivate them to challenge themselves. ~~School librarians do not need to be coding experts. They only need to have the will to facilitate the time in which students can learn to code.~~ For those activities that require technical instruction, Code.org has created video tutorials for the student to watch in short snippets before practicing a new coding skill. The students will naturally start talking about how much fun their library time is and how much they enjoy coding. Teachers will hear them. Parents will notice. And so the momentum of creating a coding culture will begin.

Once students have had the opportunity to practice coding with Code .org during a library visit, they quickly discover how to navigate the website and select activities independently. As a result, consider soliciting time for substitutes to do coding with students when either a teacher or you require a substitute. Coding through Code.org is a great activity for a substitute teacher to facilitate. Because Code.org has a video component for teaching the more challenging concepts, students can learn at their own pace and be fairly self-sufficient. The next time that it is known that a substitute will be required, consider suggesting a lesson in coding rather than checking out a video.

No One Has to Sit on the Bench

You may have noticed that I haven't mentioned specific devices yet. Amazingly, Hour of Code (and going beyond Hour of Code) can take place with a variety of technology devices, or even no devices at all. There are many times that I prefer to explore coding unplugged, even when the technology is available. This is another valuable component of the Code.org resource. On the website, you will notice that activities are broken down based on the technology that is available. If working on desktops or laptops, mobile devices, or without enough technology for the students, there are a variety of ways that coding concepts can be taught. There are meaningful stand-alone activities that can be connected to the core curriculum as well, regardless of whether learners are discovering coding through technology usage or as an unplugged exercise. I will share my favorite unplugged coding activities in the next section.

As further evidence of Code.org's mission to spread the gospel of the value of learning computer science, the site offers a teacher training program in which a Code.org representative will come out to your school, free of charge, and do professional development training with the faculty. This training shows teachers how to integrate coding concepts into their curricula. All of the lesson plans are made available online too, free of charge. The Code.org website makes coding fun, stress free, and accessible to all. Once students are exposed to coding through the library, word will get out that it's the place to be.

The Heisman Trophy of Computer Science Education: Hour of Code

Many school libraries recognize the value of participating in coding all year long, as opposed to just during the week of Hour of Code. Even so, there is considerable value in marketing Hour of Code as though it is the event of the year, even within an already established coding culture. Hour of Code week is the perfect excuse to display your coding efforts. You are backed by millions of other Hour of Coders who are reaching out on social media to share their Hour of Code efforts. You have an army of invisible supporters. Use it to your advantage. Make it known that this is a global movement and that "everyone's doing it." Whether you are an early adapter or a newcomer to coding, take advantage of the flyers, posters, statistics, activities, and ideas that flood social media to create the vibe within your school that if all of you are not participating wholeheartedly in Hour of Code, well, you are doing a disservice to your students and damaging your school's reputation. This is the time to be dramatic. Work it. Leverage it. Run with it.

Make Your Best Plays through Programming

The programming opportunities with Hour of Code are endless. If you can dream it up, you can implement it. The reason for this is that, as I mentioned before, Hour of Code provides all the resources. Your role is to facilitate with creative marketing schemes, provide the space, and bring on the coders. Here is a list of alternative program ideas to link with Hour of Code:

- "Program in Your PJs"—Invite kids to come in their pajamas and code comfy-style.

- "Grandparent/Parent Hour of Code"—Host a separate Hour of Code event for parents and/or grandparents, but be sure to have student technologists on hand to help answer coding questions.

- "Faculty Hour of Code"—Ask your school administration if you can reserve a faculty meeting time slot to host Hour of Code for teachers.

- "Coffee and Coding"—Serve flavored coffees, give a mini-introduction about the value of coding as the participants sip, and then have them discard their drinks and begin to code.

- "Code with Compassion"—Encourage participants to create animated greeting cards in Scratch, the free visual drag-and-drop programming language.

- "Code a Critter"—Using Scratch, ask coders to draw a unique critter called a "sprite," create a habitat or background for it, and code the critter to act as it would in its natural environment.

- "Digitally Dine with Us"—Think about your favorite foods and code them within Khan Academy's free "What's for Dinner?" online tutorial using JavaScript.

- "Accessorize with Coding"—No technology? No problem. Create binary bracelets with colored beads to represent 0s and 1s and personalize them by encouraging participants to code their initials into the bracelets. Check out the activity here: https://code.org/curriculum/course2/14/Teacher.

- "Cuckoo for Coding"—Make this what it sounds like: cuckoo. Ask coders to come dressed wacky, tacky, and ready to code. After all, many coders get so lost in their coding missions that they neglect to match their attire.

- "Code Like a Dance Mom"—Showcase the "Dance Party" coding activity on the Code.org website and get participants coding to their favorite tunes. They will have the pleasure of watching their avatars on screen dance to the music of their choosing. Don't forget the headphones!

- "Code a Comic"—Make like Marvel and use Scratch to code superheroes, villains, and wild scenarios to tell a digital story with a protagonist and an antagonist.

- "Codes Against Humanity"—Tap into students' love of popular card games and turn them into coding activities. Best suited for coders in high school and up, mimic the strategy behind Cards Against Humanity, in which players put unlikely words and/or phrases together to create hilarious sayings (depending on one's preference for humor). Use Pencil Code Gym: Imagine (https://gym.pencilcode.net/imagine/#/imagine/first.html) to code your own Cards Against Humanity phrases and words.

- "Code in a Galaxy Far Far Away"—Zone in on *Star Wars* and take advantage of the *Star Wars*–themed coding activities hosted on Code.org. Make it out of this world and encourage coders to come as their favorite *Star Wars* character, like Princess Leia, Han Solo, Rey, Finn, C-3PO, or maybe even Darth Vader.

Tap into pop culture, communal interests, or favorite themes and host an event that makes your community curious enough to come and see how you will pull it off. When in doubt, poll the students and find out what would attract them to coding events. Create a coding committee that helps you plan and market the events through grassroots efforts.

Advertise with Coding Commercials

Super Bowl spectators love to watch the commercials, some as much as or even more than the actual football game. Audiences anticipate the level of creativity that will go into the annual event's commercials. A prestigious media award is designated specifically for Super Bowl commercials. With over 100 million Super Bowl viewers, that is serious marketing power. When it comes to promoting Hour of Code, think big. Think like a Super Bowl commercial. Tap into resources within your community, both locally and through social media, to grow your Hour of Code community. Suggestions for local resources include the following:

- Coding boot camps: If you live in an urban area, near a college or university, or both, chances are that there is at least one coding boot camp nearby, to which you can reach out and ask them to partner with your school library to support your Hour of Code event. One of the ways that coding boot camps can add value is by bringing in a coding expert, or even a coding student, who is proficient in a coding language that you plan to emphasize during Hour of Code. They can not only assist with questions, but also share the value in learning to code as a literacy. Additionally, coding boot camps can help spread the word about your Hour of Code event, especially if you are planning to open it up to a larger community. They may also donate swag to give away as door prizes and offer to be the future destination for a student field trip. We have done this type of field trip on two occasions, and during both visits, students were drawn to the unique work environment, nap rooms, and all. Cultivating these community partnerships has served us well in related events. In addition, it has helped us gain Technology Fair judges and *Shark Tank*–style panelists for various in-school technology-related projects and competitions.

- Local start-ups: Consider if there are any entrepreneurs in your parent population who work in the technology industry. If so, there is a great chance that they know programming or know someone who knows how to program. Invite them in for your Hour of Code event. They will love that your school is supporting computer science. Sometimes it just takes the first step in communicating to grow our resources. I have acquired some fabulous unexpected resources through some of these efforts. One parent had ten Spheros sitting in unopened boxes, which he had received as a promotional item; he donated them to our school when he learned of our interest in coding. Several parents offered to come in and speak to our students about their programming jobs and teach them some new tricks in coding. Another parent offered to have us tour his high-tech work environment, which is an incubation hub for start-ups. Another gave us insight into free field trips hosted by Apple and Microsoft, which we took advantage of by visiting with our students and learning about three-dimensional (3D) modeling, coding, and animation. Employ these speakers, resources, and field trips as teasers leading up to Hour of Code, or as a prize for having participated in Hour of Code. It's not just about the one hour spent coding during the week of Hour of Code; rather, it is about the opportunities that arise from the connections that Hour of Code encourages us to make.

- Institutions of higher education: They need us just as much as we need them. We can help each other out in many ways. Graduate students in computer science may be seeking volunteer hours and may help facilitate an Hour of Code or Beyond Hour of Code event. Computer science professors may be conducting research for publication and are interested in piloting programs or ideas in a coding classroom. Universities often have sophisticated workspaces with advanced technology. They may enjoy the outreach opportunity of hosting younger students, who are also potential future students. These are the ways in which mentorships form. Through partnerships with Georgia Tech, we have gained student interns that come twice monthly to work with our kindergarten students. Georgia Tech graduate students facilitate technology workshops and summer camps at our school. We have been able to tour the digital technology studios at the Atlanta campus of the Savannah College of Art and Design (SCAD). We learned how one SCAD student created an algorithm from Instagram photos that people posted of enjoyable vacations to design a dream hotel. If there is a university nearby, reach out to it. This can be the beginning of a powerful partnership to nurture coding-related opportunities and strengthen communities.

While there may be organizations within driving distance, plenty of organizations advertise through social media that they are interested in supporting Hour of Code events, including the following:

- American Library Association (ALA): ALA offers a robust number of grants to support a variety of creative programming ideas. It is worth reaching out and asking if they can support your Hour of Code event. They may have funds set aside through their Libraries Ready to Code initiative. They may also help connect your school library with public, academic, or other libraries that are launching coding programs and are willing to partner in events and/or share resources. This year, we earned a microgrant sponsored by Google through ALA's Ready to Code initiative. It was a simple application, and over 250 libraries received these grants. Next year, make it your library.

- International Society for Technology in Education (ISTE): ISTE offers awards that highlight educators doing powerful, positive work with technology. Consider applying for one of these awards to achieve school recognition, which often results in being able to grow the resources. ISTE also publishes resources to encourage educators to take novel approaches to integrate coding in the curriculum. Curious about a new technology tool for Hour of Code? Check out ISTE's EdTech Advisor to see educator reviews of these products.

- Code.org's Regional Partner Program: Code.org has a section on their website in which U.S.-based organizations have agreed to serve as partners in their community to host professional learning in coding. Code.org funds these endeavors, and a map of community partners can be found on their website at https://code.org/educate/regional-partner. There may be one in your area. Check it out.

- Local library association chapters: Most state-level library associations offer awards and/or grants for library programming. If you don't apply, you can't receive. Check out your local library association and see what resources they offer for financial support to kick off an eventful Hour of Code program.

Media blasts through email, Twitter, Instagram, Snapchat, and Facebook are also useful channels to spread the word about Hour of Code. You never know whose attention you will grab. Use the right hashtags and bingo—you may have just put your school library on the map. The benefits to this include connecting with coding experts to enrich Hour of Code offerings, potentially gaining more resources, and growing your professional network to inspire new ideas. Not only is it important to put your Hour of Code events out there, but also search the following hashtags to see what others are doing around the globe: #HourofCode, #ReadyToCode, #CSEdWeek, and #GoogleforEdu.

The Future Ready Librarians group on Facebook presents a wealth of information for connecting with a diverse group of forward-thinking librarians interested in sharing innovative ideas, soliciting feedback, and seeking advice. Don't overlook this powerful group for Hour of Code inspiration.

Other resourceful Facebook groups include the School Librarian's Workshop, ISTE Librarians Network, Librarians as Tech Leaders, Makerspaces and the Participatory Library, and the Librarian Co-Op, which is where librarian's share lesson plans. Some Hour of Code gems can be found within these Facebook groups.

A benefit of searching Instagram is that rather than combing through text, you can curate ideas easily through imagery and videos. If an image or video catches your eye, you can click on it to read more or listen to discover the ideas. Instagram, too, can be searched with hashtags such as #HourofCode, #Coding, #CSEdweek, and #ReadytoCode. Following Code.org on Instagram will generate videos of celebrities sharing their support for Hour of Code, as well as spotlighting interesting Hour of Code programs around the globe. Meanwhile, Snapchat is great for marketing to school library patrons who are ages thirteen and up. Post a photo highlighting an upcoming Hour of Code event to stimulate interest among the teens.

Marketing professionals suggest that businesses have a presence everywhere, through a multitude of social media applications, in order to reach the largest possible audience. However, as a school librarian wishing to encourage patrons to support Hour of Code events, to solicit resources (directly or indirectly), and to share programming ideas, I suggest focusing on those platforms in which you feel most comfortable. If Snapchat isn't your thing, don't force it. Ultimately, you will be most successful reaching audiences through the social media platforms where you feel most at home. You will be more likely to routinely visit these platforms, and therefore gain supporters and cultivate a digital network. If there is one social media app that you already feel most comfortable with, stick with that one at first and slowly venture onto new platforms one by one. I started with Facebook, became a Twitter fan, and eventually got on board with Instagram, which I have grown to appreciate for its emphasis on visuals. I have not yet embraced Snapchat—perhaps I never will, and, that's okay too. When it comes to leveraging Hour of Code programs through social media, you do you. Just remember to do something.

Beyond Hour of Code: Take It and Run with It

Speaking of leveraging, perhaps you realize by now that Hour of Code is about so much more than an hour of coding. It's about what you do with coding all the days before and after the week designated as Computer Science Education Week. Coding is a vessel by which student leaders can be developed. By launching an Hour of Code event, you suddenly have a platform for students to serve as leaders, mentoring other students with their coding skills, providing outreach beyond the library to encourage other coders, and striving to grow their own skills so they can represent the school library as a coding communications specialist. We have a group of student technology leaders about which I will divulge more about later in the book; however, for now, suffice to say that these students have made it their mission to advocate for the benefits of coding to other students and their families.

Partner upper-elementary students with kindergarten students and allow them to use Hour of Code as the launchpad for a lasting mentorship in the area of technology skills. Use an Hour of Code program to cultivate those relationships. Once Hour of Code concludes, don't stop creating opportunities for older students to work with younger students in the areas of technology, media, and literacy. Employ Hour of Code as a launchpad for future opportunities to do coding together. All parties will benefit significantly by building interpersonal relationships, while growing their skill sets as both leaders and learners.

Be on the lookout during Hour of Code week for those students who suddenly come to life in ways that you had not yet seen at school. Grow relationships with your students using their enthusiasm for coding. Encourage these students to participate in a Technology Fair hosted by your school. Ask them if they want to code a robot and present it during a board meeting, a parent-teacher organization (PTO) meeting, or during a faculty meeting. Recruit them to copresent with you at an educational technology or library conference. Give them a stage that inspires them to further explore their interest in coding. As librarians, we love to put books in children's hands as a refuge and as a way to see the world. What if we approached coding in this same manner? Empower students by using Hour of Code as a gateway to bigger experiences.

In addition to real-time experiences, Hour of Code can be used to create positive virtual experiences for learners. As content creators, students benefit from showcasing their work. It allows them to reflect on their process, consider their presentation skills, and grow their own network. Using digital platforms to share students' coding projects is rewarding for all these reasons. There are a number of platforms that can be used for this purpose. Some suggestions include the following, which are both mobile apps and websites: Padlet, Seesaw, Google Drive, and YouTube. Seesaw lends itself to educating students about being strong digital citizens, and the site has a comments section that can be monitored. Students can learn the do's and don'ts of commenting on one another's coding projects. Once a student has built up a solid portfolio, Seesaw makes it easy for educators to share her or his work with parents or other interested parties. Seesaw has a built-in QR code generator that provides direct access to an individual's digital portfolio and a ready-made email message that can quickly be sent to an audience. Don't let Hour of Code just be about an hour of coding. Leverage it to create a coding culture that celebrates positive digital citizenship.

Curricular Connections with Coding

Before you can connect coding to the curriculum, you, the school librarian, must have general knowledge of your school's curriculum. With a supportive administration, this is much easier. Without an administration that sees the value and the superpowers that lie within your role, well, it can be a bit more challenging—but it still can be done. If your administration is supportive, ask if they can mandate that teachers meet with you at least three times a year so that you can be part of their planning process. I meet seasonally: fall, winter, and spring. Starting in the fall, I send out a Google doc with my availability and ask that everyone sign up for a thirty-minute time slot to meet with me. My principal backs me up in his weekly team meetings and reminds everyone that they must sign up.

My first order of business is to demonstrate that I am on their team. Sometimes I will bring candy to these meetings to lighten the mood, especially with those teachers that I feel may not want to particularly be there, if they feel they have a million other things to do that are more important. Then we get down to business. I ask open-ended questions about their upcoming units, where I can help them innovate, and most important, we schedule times on their calendar for their classes to come visit me so that we can collaborate on these upcoming units.

If necessary, I get creative with my scheduling too. Having done this for several years now, I have learned to spread out these meeting times over the course of a month. When I first started doing this, my principal allowed me to get a sub for the week that I had these meetings. I cleared my calendar and got a substitute to demonstrate how important these sessions were to me. As our collaborative culture has grown, however, and the trust is more established, I can schedule these over the course of a month and not feel the need for a substitute. I can be creative in my scheduling and meet before school, after school, during lunch, or during the teacher's planning period. I try to work around them, while being cognizant of balancing my other professional responsibilities.

Without a supportive administration, you will have to earn your own buy-in with the teachers so that they truly want to come and meet with you, and so that they see the value of the sessions on their own. After one visit, this probably will be obvious, but getting them to come the first time is the challenge. Here are some tactics:

Bribe them with nourishment: This can take the form of candy, coffee, cake, protein bars, or whatever tempts to your audience's tastebuds.

Tell them the truth: You are going to elevate their lessons and take them to an innovative place, all while making them a superstar. They would be foolish to pass up this opportunity.

Corner them in the breakroom and guilt them into a session with you by sharing some vulnerability: Start by saying, "As part of the requirements of my role, I am obligated to partner with teachers, but I am getting pushback. Will you be kind enough to help me fulfill my role and partner with me? I promise to make it a positive experience."

Find a friend: There is usually one teacher in the building that adores you instantly because he or she values your role. Perhaps one of their relatives was a librarian. Perhaps the library was a safe haven for this person as a kid. Whatever it is, use this to your advantage. Seek this teacher out first and conjure up something fabulous—and most important, broadcast it to the rest of the school! Make it so that kids are running home to tell their parents what awesome coding activities they did in math today. Before you know it, all the other math teachers will be seeking you out because their students told their parents what the other class got to do with the school librarian, and they want to be able to do that too. It happens. Trust me.

Once you have cultivated a routine time with teachers in which they will plan with you, tap into their curricula through meaningful discussions so that you can elevate the learning experiences. The teachers may not realize it yet, but it will be a learning experience for everyone. Similar to the 3D printing approach, inquire about the units that teachers do not enjoy and would love to spice up a bit. Starting in the doldrums will emphasize that you are on their team, wanting to elevate their teaching and learning experiences both for themselves and for their students. I once found myself combing through the second grade social studies textbook, making connections to coding, pitching my ideas to the second grade teaching team, and solidifying the schedule of when they could come with their classes to implement these ideas with me.

I always send a calendar invite to the teachers once we have settled upon a date and a time. This step is important to make sure that your session ends up on both of your calendars once the lesson and the logistics are confirmed. Now that you are set up to collaborate through coding, what does this look like? Read on to discover lessons that integrate coding into the curriculum in unique and creative ways.

The Rookies

The littlest learners, four- and five-year-olds, are often the most open-minded. Their creativity hasn't been squandered as much, or they haven't been discouraged from asking questions quite so much. They are open to an innovative learning experience. Plus, they will think that everything you do is cool and interesting. In some ways, rookies are the ideal teammates. I am a huge fan of Ann Gadzikowski's book *Robotics for Young Children: STEM Activities and Simple Coding.* This book has become my go-to guide for coding with our four- and five-year-olds. The author approaches coding as a literacy, as opposed to a technical skill, and shares how to reinforce coding concepts without additional screen time. Instead of focusing on how to code, she emphasizes the language of coding and its meaning.

Algorithm. In coding, an *algorithm* is considered a list of steps to accomplish a specific task. While this is a rather large vocabulary word for young learners, they can certainly be taught the concept behind an algorithm. For example, one of our favorite activities is to read *Thunder Cake,* by Patricia Polacco. In the story, a young girl has to follow a series of steps to be able to acquire the ingredients and successfully bake a cake. At the end of the book, there is a recipe for thunder cake. Comparing recipes to algorithms can help little learners grasp the concept of following a series of steps to perform a specific task, which in this example is baking a cake.

Sequencing. In prekindergarten and kindergarten classrooms, a common skill is sequencing, or understanding how objects, events, or times occur in a logical order. To teach this skill, educators may read a story to children and ask them to recite the order of events as they occurred. Or they may be given pictures of their morning routine, such as brushing their teeth, driving to school, listening to their teacher, and asked to put them in sequential order. In coding, sequencing can be explained as the order in which we tell a computer to do something. If we don't program the computer to follow commands in the correct order, it cannot do what we want in the way that we want. This may create a bug or an error in our computer's program.

There are many ways that we can demonstrate the concept of sequencing in coding with young learners, both with and without screen time. There has been a growing educational initiative to develop robotic tools for young learners that teach the concepts of coding, but again do not require screen time. One commonly used tool is the Bee-Bot, which is a robot that looks like a bumblebee. It has directional arrows on its body that the child can press to control in which direction the Bee-Bot runs.

The Bee-Bot can be purchased with large mats on which it can move to reach specific targets by inputting the directional errors in the correct order. Learners and educators can also create their own unique maps for the Bee-Bot.

Students can work with the Bee-Bot in small groups. They can take turns setting goals for the Bee-Bot, such as to move to the blue square, and they can take turns inputting the program for the Bee-Bot to achieve the goal. Once the students appear to be master coders, they can make the challenges more complicated, such as to reach the blue square in three commands or less. Individual Bee-Bots cost around $100, and class bundles can be purchased for around $500, which typically includes four bots, two mats, and command cards.

Cubetto is another favorite coding tool for young programmers that does not require screen time. It is a wooden robot that comes with a separate control panel that children can code by inputting directional arrows onto the panel, pressing a button, and watching the Cubetto move. Like the Bee-Bot, there are colorful maps that children can use to create programming challenges for Cubetto. Cubetto can be purchased for about $225, and it includes a map, the coding blocks, and a guide to help the facilitator tell a story to coincide with Cubetto's goals of reaching a specific destination. For example, if you acquire the "big city" mat, Cubetto's goal may be to reach the bridge. There are several class bundle options that include four, eight, or twelve Cubettos ranging from $1,300 to $3,500.

Cubetto is so much fun to work with in small groups. With four learners, one person can establish the programming goal or destination for Cubetto to reach on the mat, one person can program Cubetto, another person can execute the program, and someone else can watch and give advice. Then, rotating each learner's role allows everyone to take a turn while working collaboratively. We enjoyed hacking Cubetto and turning it into a drawbot. By putting down white butcher's paper, drawing simple shapes onto the paper with a pencil, and attaching a marker to the side of Cubetto, students created a program that would cause the marker to trace over the pencil drawing. In this way, learners can create programming challenges for one another.

There are coding opportunities for every budget. LEGOs is another powerful coding tool for young learners in which storytelling can be integrated. Have students work in pairs, in which one child creates a simple maze out of LEGOs along with a story to accompany it, as shown in Figure 5.1. The other child uses sticky notes to draw arrows to code the direction that the LEGO figure would need to follow to get from point A to point B to complete the maze. Then, the coder can test the program by

| Create an algorithm using arrows to solve the maze | Code the cat to get to the witch |

Figure 5.1   Coding with arrows and LEGO mazes.

following the arrows within the maze using the LEGO figure. If the LEGO figure cannot make it to point B, then the pair can work together to debug the program and start again.

Allow students to choose a mask to wear and to work in pairs to program each other as sprites or characters. Tell the students that in Scratch, which is a block programming language created by students at the Massachusetts Institute of Technology (MIT) for young children to learn to code, characters are known as "sprites." This activity, shown in Figure 5.2, reinforces the importance of sequencing when creating algorithms. Once the coders have successfully created a program that allows their human sprite to reach their intended destination without running into a wall or a piece of furniture, have them switch places.

Loops. In coding, *loops* represent the act of doing something over and over again. One way to demonstrate this aspect of computational thinking is to give each child several manipulatives in various shapes and colors, such as red squares, blue circles, green rectangles, and orange triangles. Explain that in coding, symbols are used to create shortcuts. In this instance, the manipulatives will serve as symbols that have a specific meaning. For example, the red square represents "sit down," the blue circle represents "stand up," the green rectangle represents "jump," and the orange triangle represents "repeat." Tell the students that you are

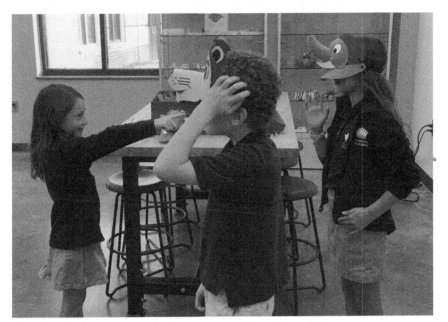

Figure 5.2   Human sprites taking turns coding one another.

going to give them a series of commands, but instead of following these commands, they will put down the manipulatives in the correct order to signify those commands. If I say, "Stand up, sit down, jump," then the coder should put down a blue circle, red square, and a green rectangle, in that order. If I say, "Stand up, sit down, and jump two times," then they should put down a blue circle, a red square, and a green rectangle followed by an orange triangle. Some students will be quick to catch on, while others may take longer to process the meaning behind the symbols. That's okay. This can be an active learning experience too, so that before you quiz them on creating the correct algorithm, have them act out each representation of the manipulative. For example, lay out a blue circle, a green rectangle, and a red square. In response, the learners should stand up, jump, and sit down. These active motions will help them learn what each manipulative represents. Break up the activities so that the learners alternate between active learning and executing programs with objects.

A product called Hands-On Coding has created colorful manipulatives that are modeled after coding blocks and designed for children ages five and up to learn computational thinking skills. An interesting twist to this product is that its resource page, which can be found at https://www

.handsoncoding.org/resource-page, shares math challenges that encourage students to use sequencing skills to create mathematical equations. For example, students can arrange the coding block manipulatives so that a turtle moves onto a three, then the plus sign, then the two, then the equals sign, and then the five. They have just coded a simple math problem and solved for it using coding block manipulatives that mimic online drag-and-drop coding blocks. There are several board games on the market that reinforce computational thinking skills too. Our students have enjoyed Robot Turtles, a board game made by Thinkfun and designed for ages five and up, which can be found on Amazon for less than $17.

When school librarians partner with teachers to demonstrate these basic coding skills, they can be related to students' curricula within their other subjects. Examples include unpacking for the day, in which the series of steps to unpack make up the algorithm. The order in which the unpacking process is done is the sequence of events. Identify that if the students had to unpack each morning all week long, then they are creating a loop with the act of doing it over and over again. These learning experiences are not limited to the library. Coding vocabulary can become the word of the week and be established as a rotational center within the homeroom class, and a coder can be added to the job board as the student responsible for relating the vocabulary to her or his everyday actions.

While learning about coding as a literacy creates a strong foundation for early learners, with plenty of age-appropriate coding apps available, screen time within limits can be a fun way to expose young students to coding. Daisy the Dinosaur, Kodable, and ScratchJr. are all free mobile device apps that reinforce sequencing skills with directional challenges. ScratchJr. also allows children to create digital stories through animated sprites and coding blocks specifically designed for early learners. Ask students to program an alternative ending to a picture book in ScratchJr.

Learners can also benefit from curricular connections with the previously mentioned Sphero, a small robotic ball. As students are learning how to write the alphabet, they can use the Sphero Draw 'N' Drive app to trace the letters. Challenge early readers to use drag-and-drop icons within the SpheroEdu app to move the Sphero in the correct directions to write the letters of the alphabet. Sphero allows teachers to differentiate the learning to accommodate both prereaders and early readers.

This same approach can be used when learning foreign languages as well. Our students start learning the Hebrew alphabet at an early age. Our Hebrew teacher enjoys treating the students to a Hebrew letter-writing lesson with Sphero's Draw 'N' Drive app. They are motivated to learn their letters faster when they know that they will have the opportunity to move Sphero to trace the letters. No mobile devices? No problem. If working with computers, Code.org has online computer games for prereaders that teach computational thinking via fun themes and animated characters. Thoughtfully integrating limited screen time to reinforce a coding concept that coincides with daily activities can help early learners grasp coding as a literacy.

The Elementary Players

Teaching rookies, or the youngest learners, the fundamental concepts of coding allows the school librarian and teachers to tag-team on coding connections in core curricular subjects. The teachers are learning right along with the students, which builds up their confidence level and increases their exposure to coding concepts. Thanks to Hour of Code and many passionate educators, there is a multitude of resources available to teach coding to learners of all ages and skill levels, regardless of the available technology. As I share various coding integration activities in the following section, keep in mind that these can be fluid across the grade levels. It is not imperative that these activities be done within the grade levels emphasized here. One activity, for example, I did with our Kindergarten Prep students and then repeated it with the third graders, adding more sophisticated parameters. Coding within the curriculum can be modified to best suit the grade level with which you are working.

Consider a variety of approaches to making meaningful connections to coding within your curriculum. In our school, first graders are tasked with creating Torah scrolls and putting them together to share at a special Torah service. When students are arranging the Five Books of Moses in the proper order, there is a curricular connection to coding as it relates to order or logic. For example, Genesis, which literally means "in the beginning," must be the first book. Otherwise, the Torah scroll would need to be re-created or debugged to correct the error. Sharing coding vocabulary across the curriculum reinforces its meaning. At this age, our students also start learning map skills. They learn about the compass rose, map keys, and how to orient and create a map of their street. In the past, students were mesmerized by first creating their street map on paper and then accessing Google Earth to compare their handdrawn maps with the view of their street in Google Earth. Seeing their street and home both in the aerial view and in the street view on Google Earth was very exciting. Students can also merge the two concepts and create their own digital version in Scratch on the computer. Using the draw tool within Scratch, they can create their street, the trees, their home, other relevant landmarks, and a compass rose. Students can program a human sprite to walk to their house on their street.

Students can also hand-draw a map and program the Ozbot, which is a tiny robot that can read colors drawn on paper to move in specific directions. Different color patterns mean different actions to Ozbot. For example, if the learner draws one continuous line that has the colors black, blue, red, green, and black (in that order), this tells Ozbot to turn right. Using this color-coded system allows young students to program Ozbot to follow directions on a map without a screen. As an alternative, students can also program the Ozbot to move using drag-and-drop programming via the Ozoblockly app. This makes for an easy way to differentiate the learning based on coding skills and age levels. Ozobots can cost between $42 and $77 per robot, but there are also classroom sets available for educators to purchase in bulk at a lesser cost.

School librarians and teachers can partner to integrate coding into the curriculum using Scratch in a variety of other areas as well. Our early-elementary students learn about the water cycle. Students can re-create animated diagrams of the water cycle, demonstrating the collection of water, evaporation, condensation, and precipitation. Programming with Scratch to mimic the water cycle allows students to build in wait times between each part of the cycle to illustrate the chain of events while sequencing the order for each sprite.

Scratch can be used to illustrate math word problems in a variety of ways. For example, learners can create a background scene that includes a bird's nest with one bird (sprite) sitting on top of it. They can program that bird to fly away, and in its place, four more birds fly to the nest. How many birds total have visited the nest? Five. Using Scratch animation to create mathematical word problem appeals to visual learners, while improving their coding skills. In literacy, students can use Scratch to improve their vocabulary and understand context. For example, if each student is assigned a spelling word to re-create in Scratch, the students have built an animated study guide for their spelling test. If the spelling list is a list of adjectives, such as "flat," "empty," "loud," and "late," one student gets assigned the word "flat" to illustrate the meaning and share the spelling in Scratch. As a class, review each child's animations to help them remember the words and their meanings.

Other ideas include leveraging Scratch to demonstrate reading comprehension. Instead of quizzing students on the chapters that they read, have them code scenes from their books in Scratch. In reading groups, ask students to create alternative endings to their novels as an extension activity.

In science, ask students to demonstrate gravity and the laws of motion through an animated scene.

Once learners are comfortable with Scratch, this programming language can be used to understand how other drag-and-drop programs work or to program small robots beyond a screen. BirdBrain Technologies created two great robotics products to inspire coding skills, the Finch and the Hummingbird Robotics Kit. Finch is a robot that looks like a bird. It can scoot around on the floor when connected via universal serial bus (USB) to a computer and programmed to move in certain ways. A variety of programming languages can be used to control the Finch. These include, but are not limited to Snap (a drag-and-drop program designed for pre-kindergarten through second grade), Scratch (for all ages), CREATE Lab Visual Programmer (one of my favorites, and suitable for all ages), Python (text-based and designed for seventh grade and up), and JavaScript (a text-based program for tenth grade and up). Partner with other teachers for creative curricular connections to coding. School librarians can simulate the *American Ninja Warrior* experience for students in collaboration with the physical education (PE) teacher by using Finch. Students can create prototypes of obstacle courses and program the Finch robots to go through the obstacle courses successfully, as seen in Figure 5.3. Then, these same obstacle courses can be recreated in PE class for the students to attempt in reality.

BirdBrain Technologies offers a program for schools who wish to receive twenty Finch robots on loan for a couple of months. Interested schools can contact them at loanprogram@finchrobot.com to learn when the annual application period is open. Starting early in their education, students are taught to prototype their ideas. With this approach, and by collaborating with the PE teachers, coding is not limited to academics but can also be integrated into a physical activity.

Third graders are sandwiched between early-elementary and upper-elementary students. This can be a great opportunity to elevate their learning experiences with coding. School librarians and teachers can invent engineering challenges to demonstrate core concepts in coding that include a culmination of curricula that they learn in social studies and science while learning the language of coding. For this, we use the book, *Hello Ruby: Adventures in*

Figure 5.3 Prototype of an obstacle course tested with Finch robots.

Coding, by Linda Liukas. This book is part of a great series that helps teach young kids important topics in technology. In this particular book, Ruby goes on a journey to obtain five gems. In each stage of her journey, she encounters scenarios that symbolize the fundamentals of computational thinking. For example, she has to identify patterns, repeat functions, and create an algorithm to achieve her goal of finding all five gems. Along the way, she encounters challenges, which can be related to having a bug in a computer program. One such challenge is that she needs to construct a bridge to get across a river.

Pause throughout the story and have students participate in engineering challenges that are relevant to the story. I give students a finite set of supplies, such as eight toothpicks, six Popsicle sticks, four pipe cleaners, and scissors. Working in groups of three to five, students use these supplies to build a bridge to help Ruby cross the river. Each group shares its bridge creation before we move onto the rest of the story. The teacher helps facilitate the sharing process by interjecting with questions, such as the properties of minerals as they relate to the gems in the story and the states of matter as it relates to using a solid to build over a liquid. The students have to problem-solve for Ruby to be able to continue on her journey. We make sure to point out that problem-solving is a significant component to coding.

To reinforce the concept of sequencing with third graders, they are tasked with working in small groups to build a Rube Goldberg machine. It must be Hanukkah themed to demonstrate their learning in Judaic Studies class. One action causes another. With third grade, we ask that they have two or more actions; however, the requirements can be more sophisticated for older students. Other coursework, beyond faith-based themes, can be built into the Rube Goldberg machine-building process. Examples include demonstrating the laws of physics, incorporating animal habitats, and portraying facts about their state to highlight what they have learned in social studies. Each group is given crafting supplies, such as Play-Doh, straws, paper, pipe cleaners, Popsicle sticks, glue, tape, scissors, feathers, colored pencils, and marble, as well as an idea map for them to sketch out their plans before they start building.

These students also do a unit on sound in their science curriculum. In collaboration with the teacher, we use Scratch and the Makey Makey kit, which is an invention kit that can connect to Scratch and turn everyday conductive objects into touchpads in order to demonstrate that energy can be transferred through sound. Have students work in pairs to select a musical instrument that they can create in Scratch, such as a piano. Students can then draw a picture of a piano keyboard on white paper in pencil and hook up the alligator clips from the Makey Makey to a piano key. By programming the piano in Scratch to play a music note when a specific piano key that is drawn on the paper is pressed, the sound of that note is generated, as shown in Figure 5.4. Through this process, students also learn about conductive and insulating materials.

Figure 5.4 A third grade student playing sounds on her hand-drawn keyboard created with Makey Makey.

Students also learn about light in middle- to upper-elementary curricula. They discover that light can pass through or bounce off of objects. Students can program light-emitting diode (LED) lights to blink on and off using the Humming-bird Robotics Kit. When the LED light is turned on, does it shine through tissue paper? What about cardboard? Why or why not? These hands-on learning activities that integrate coding make powerful learning experiences.

LEGO Robotics creates amazing learning opportunities that tie into science curricula as well. Students can build animals out of LEGOs and program them with the LEGO WeDo software to mimic animal life in their natural habitat. In doing so, it is also relevant to integrate previous knowledge of simple machines. Each of the LEGO robotics animals is able to move through the use of simple machines. For example, an alligator's jaw moves with the transfer of energy and with the help of a pulley and a belt. Learners can program the animals and the background scenes to give off sounds that are natural to their environment.

The best curricular connections in coding come from joint brainstorming sessions between the school librarian and the teachers. The librarian provides the innovation, and the teacher fills in the curriculum goals specific to their content. Working together, they coach one another through abstract ideas to generate tangible and memorable learning experiences.

Upper-Elementary Players Dominate the Field

Fourth and fifth grade students are eager to code! They typically have some experience with gaming, and they know that coding is the gateway to gaming. Curricular connections abound. Take music, for example. Pick a song that everyone knows well, loves, and would be happy to break out into song in the middle of the school day. I chose a song from *The Greatest Showman* movie soundtrack. Ask students to step into your recording studio. (This is where their imagination has to kick in unless your school really does have a recording studio.) First, I define a *function* (a piece of code that you can call over and over again) and share its purpose. For example, a song is like a computer program. Defining the chorus in a song by using a function, which makes it easy to call up the chorus over and over again without having to write it out every time. Not only does this save time, but if a mistake is made, it has to be corrected in only one place. Additionally, the program feels less complicated, with the repeating parts being defined only once, at the beginning. This process is helpful to computer scientists, just as it is helpful to songwriters.

However, in instances in which the chorus is not exactly the same every time, it is important to let the singer know which special words will be used in each verse. This is called a *parameter*. I define a parameter as an extra piece of information that you pass to the function to customize it for a specific need. I share an example of what these definitions would look like in a simple song, such as "Old MacDonald Had a Farm." With the program's code written as plain text, the parameter might look like this: chorus(parameter1, parameter2). The chorus represents the function and the variety of animals represents the parameter. I ask student volunteers to sing the song with different animals as an example. I explain that I defined the chorus, I called the chorus, and the students sang the chorus. Then, I ask for complete silence in the recording studio as I play the song "The Greatest Show." The students have paper and pencil on hand too, so they can take notes. When the song is over, I ask the following questions:

1.   Were you able to identify the chorus when the lyrics changed?
2.   How might you use the same idea of calling a chorus when the chorus is different from verse to verse?
3.   Would you rather write lyrics over and over again, or define a chorus?
4.   Do you think it's possible to create multiple choruses for the same song?
5.   Does it make sense to create a new chorus every time it is needed in a song?

Now that they have a trained ear, they usually enjoy this activity so much that we repeat it with another song. Enrich the activity by asking students to go home and listen to their favorite songs and determine if they can recall the functions and parameters. This activity was inspired by an unplugged activity on Code.org's website, and it can be done with a variety of musical choices. Students can be challenged to become their own songwriters and write their own lyrics that incorporate parameters and functions. Music and coding make a winning combination.

Two other unplugged activities that we thoroughly enjoy for this age group that is also from Code.org's website involve math, cards, and cups. The card activity teaches students about conditional statements and nesting conditionals. If this occurs, then this happens, else something else happens. If I have my library card, I will check out a book. Else, I will have to wait to check out a book. Using decks of cards, students create games comprised of rules made of conditional statements. First, they identify the objective of their game. For example, the first player to accumulate thirty points wins. Then, they establish the rules in the form of conditional statements. If a player picks a card of seven spades, for example, he or she receives five points. Else, if the card is less than seven, the other player receives five points. Else, you receive one point. This is an example of using nesting conditional statements to establish the rules of the game.

By the end of the lesson, students have learned the definition and purpose of conditional statements, while doing quite a bit of math. The other activity that integrates coding and math is cup stacking. Here's how it works: Students work in pairs, in which one person is the robot and the other person is the programmer. The pairs are given a stack of images that have various arrangements of cups stacked on top of one another. The robot leaves the room, while the programmer picks one image to recreate in code using arrows, pencil, and paper. On the board, there is a symbol key to reflect what type of movement that each arrow means. For example, the up arrow means to pick up a cup, and the down arrow means to put it down. There are various arrow symbols for moving sideways and turning a cup upside down. Once the programmer has re-created the chosen image in a language using the arrows, the robot gets called back into the room (without being able to see the chosen image) and attempts to stack the cups based on how the arrows read. This is done in complete silence.

In the end, if the robot malfunctions, the partners work together to "debug" the program so that the robot can correctly re-create the image with the actual cups. Again, this is a fun activity involving computational thinking. Both the robot and the programmer have to calculate the number of movements required to place each cup in the correct spot. The learners are so immersed in the unplugged activities that I almost sense a tinge of disappointment in them when we announce that we will be exploring coding with the use of technology.

Unplugged activities are rewarding, but if there is an opportunity to train students as content creators through coding and curricular connections with technology too, then by all means, give learners that opportunity. One of my favorite fifth grade coding activities integrates food and JavaScript. Because we are a faith-based school, we take great efforts to expose our students to a variety of religions and cultures. Khan Academy has a strong platform for teaching students about functions, variables, and conditionals, and allowing them to apply these concepts when using

JavaScript, a text-based programming language. Through a series of videos and short challenges, learners can build upon coding concepts. In their "What's for Dinner?" activity, mentioned earlier in this chapter, students are challenged to code foods of their choice. They code foods found in a variety of cultures. The only problem is that we are all hungry after this activity. (It is best done right before lunch.)

Using this same teaching tool, students can code fractions. For example, the math teacher might ask them to code a pizza that has one-fourth of the slices missing. Students might code a pizza that has twelve slices total, but three pieces are missing. Another approach to integrating math into the coding curriculum is to ask students to design, build, and code robots that have specific numeric parameters. For example, we have a clear storage case where we keep all of our works in progress. I like for learners and visitors to see the evolution of the projects that we create. The space between the shelves is twelve inches tall, and as a result, I require that robots be no more than eleven inches tall. Working with the math teacher, consider establishing other parameters involving math challenges with preexisting robots, such as Dot and Dash or Sphero. For example, students must demonstrate that the robot can make a ninety-degree turn, move forward three feet, and be programmed with enough force to go up a student-made ramp and the students must calculate the percentage of the slope.

One of my favorite robotics tools is the Hummingbird Robotics Kit. The reason is that it encourages unlimited creativity, while inspiring students to learn sophisticated programming languages that will benefit them in other areas. The CREATE Lab Visual Programmer is awesome. It is free to download on the Hummingbird robot website. It teaches learners how to create an expression to build a sequence using LED lights, servos (motors that can turn 90 degrees in either direction), and sensors. When programming the servos, students can first graph the angle of rotation that will best suit their project. For example, one of my students created a girl demonstrating dental care by repeatedly brushing her teeth. As shown by scanning Figure 5.5, she had to calculate the angle of rotation to program the servo to ensure that the toothbrush's rotation would stop when it reached the robot's mouth.

Figure 5.5 A student-created dental patient robot made with the Hummingbird Robotics Kit.

Another coding tool that allows students to explore angles is called Pencil Code. When I introduced Pencil Code to my fifth graders, I had a hard time getting them to quit when the bell rang. Pencil Code gives learners experience with another text-based programming language known as Coffee Script. There are premade activities that relate to curricular goals that can be found at the following link: http://activity.pencilcode.net. Coders can also be challenged to draw complex, 3D shapes in Pencil Code. Pencil Code is free and can be used on any computer that has internet access. On their website, there is a section entitled "Coding Outside the Computer Science Classroom," which includes opportunities for additional curricular connections.

Coding as Character Development in Middle School and Beyond

Coding is a flexible learning tool. The subjects that are chosen to be merged with coding and the tools that educators choose to use allow fluctuation in the levels of complexity. Each of the lessons described in this chapter and the technology tools utilized can be adjusted to accommodate more sophisticated learning experiences. However, when we go beyond subject matter and use coding as an opportunity to teach students to be better, more inclusive, and empathetic citizens, everyone benefits. Middle school and beyond are excellent periods to integrate coding for the simple goal of "doing good." You may be aware of situations in which students have designed and programmed prosthetic limbs for individuals who were either born missing a limb, had to have a surgical procedure to remove a limb, or suffered from a combat injury resulting in the loss of a limb. There are a variety of scenarios in which coding can be a powerful force to improve someone's life. The next sections describe some examples that can also be modified to accommodate younger learners.

ADA Compliant Arcade. Cultivating compassionate coders means creating opportunities for learners to explore diversity in religion, culture, learning abilities, situational needs, family structures, socioeconomics, and humanistic qualities. Exposure to a wider world generates empathy and understanding toward individuals and situations different from our own. School librarians and teachers can create coding challenges for learners to tackle real-world issues via coding, while also thinking about others' diverse needs and life experiences.

The first time I challenged our middle school students to use a variety of technology tools that required coding to create an arcade, there was a lot of enthusiasm generated throughout the school for this project. Students used the Hummingbird Robotics Kit and the CREATE Lab Visual Programmer to program variations of the game of Skee-Ball made out of cardboard. They coded Scratch to create challenging mazes. An unanticipated outcome of all this activity was that faculty and students wanted to pay money to play the games. Students quickly set up cardboard coin slots next to their games for individuals to insert money if they chose. Unexpectedly, we raised enough money to make a small donation to an organization that offers free coding camps in the summer for underserved children. After some communication back and forth with this organization that hosted these summer camps, we had developed a relationship and were able to take a field trip to visit their facilities and learn more about the programs they offered. In turn, they became judges at our Technology Fairs. It morphed into a strong community partnership, and we all felt good about how our arcade "played out."

This got me thinking about how we can further leverage an arcade to consider accommodating other people's needs. Ultimately, we decided to create an arcade that was in compliance with the Americans with Disabilities Act (ADA). Students had to research ADA requirements, and in turn learn about physical disabilities in order to design and program games that were inclusive. Each game creator had to document the ways in which their arcade game accommodated others. They had to think about height requirements, range of motion accessibility, the ways in which instructions were communicated, sight limitations, and other issues. Homeroom classes came in and played their games through a simulated experience. For example, if a game was designed for someone in a wheelchair, the participants experienced playing the game in a wheelchair. If the game was developed for someone who was hearing impaired or visually impaired, they played the game with earplugs or blindfolds. The coders took their mission very seriously, and in the process, they learned so much about individuals with disabilities through empathetic coding opportunities.

Empathy in Entrepreneurship. Students can also be taught how to create websites from scratch using Hypertext Markup Language (HTML) and JavaScript in middle and high school. Rather than have them create websites of their hobbies and interests, challenge them to create websites that advertise a charitable organization for which they are the founder. A solid resource for any educator or student to familiarize themselves with the basics of HMTL is a website created by Jill Jeffers Goodell (http://www.goodellgroup.com/tutorial/index.html). Once the coder surpasses the skill level specified on this website, Jill provides links to additional resources, which we have found to be helpful as well.

It is always a good idea to establish requirements for students to meet. For example, they can be required to insert a "Contact Me" form, include a colored background, and add three or more images that are compliant with copyright laws. It is always fun to bring in business owners to assess the students' websites. They can share their expertise on what improvements they think could be made to the websites to inspire more donors to contribute to the causes.

Micro:bit to Maximize Communication. Using literature to inspire empathetic coders is awesome too. Our students love the book *Out of My Mind,* by Sharon Draper. We have used this book in upper-elementary book clubs, on middle school summer reading lists, as the subject for online book talks, as a suggested read-aloud in the upper-elementary language arts classroom, and as a book report option. What a great book to pair with a meaningful coding project! *Out of My Mind* tells the story of an eleven-year-old girl, Melody, who cannot talk or write due to cerebral palsy. By the end of the novel, Melody has discovered a machine that will allow her to communicate with others. It is life-changing. Challenge students to learn to program a tiny computer called a micro:bit so it can serve as a communication tool. I would encourage students to work in small groups or pairs, start with a design plan, and keep their ideas secret until the day of the project reveal. It is an interesting experience to see how groups tackle the same goal by taking different routes. It is a powerful opportunity for learners to see that there is more than one way to improve someone's life, even with the same intended outcome. Conclude this coding challenge by reading the picture book *What Do You Do with an Idea?* by Kobi Yamada; it reinforces that ideas are the origin for making people feel that they belong in a world that is anything but one-size-fits-all.

Coding to Lead. Everyone has value. Angela Maiers, author of the "You Matter Manifesto," which promotes the positive message that everyone matters, urges society to recognize that "all of us have the ability to begin changing the world by contributing our genius to solve the world's problems." Inspire students to code what they know as leaders, mentors, and teachers who can share their genius with someone else. Inspire them to consider the way in which coding can facilitate sharing their knowledge. Examples include coding a website that teaches someone sign language, coding a digital story in Scratch that educates others about a disease or disability with which they have personal experience, and integrating the micro:bit Global Challenge, a contest in which global leaders have chosen a series of goals for a better world, into a health and sciences class by challenging students to program the micro:bit to develop an invention that will address noncommunicable diseases. A teacher's guide for this last activity can be found here: https://microbit.org/en/assets/globalchallenge /ncd-innovation-lesson/ncd-innovation-lesson-teacher-guide.pdf.

Tap into students' personal concerns or areas of interest and allow the "coding to lead" approach to be relevant to their lives. Teach them to code with a purpose. Cultivate compassionate coders. Change the world, one coder at a time.

CHAPTER SIX

Sometimes It Is All Fun and Games

"I love learning with Breakout EDU because it encourages you to think outside the box."

—Chance, age 11

Gamifying the learning has been around for ages. The difference now, however, is that we have swanky technology tools that help make gamification more appealing to the facilitator while amplifying the participants' experiences from traditional game design. Sometimes, old school games are the best games and sometimes, innovative tools can up the game of gamification. In this chapter, we will explore areas of content in which gamification can be applied to motivate students, bring joy to the learning process, and keep the learners coming back for more. We will explore specific technology tools that school librarians can expose teachers to for the purpose of integrating gamification into the classroom. Just like my student who used the term "hard fun" to describe how he felt working with innovative technology to achieve a goal, author James Paul Gee describes gamification in learning as "pleasantly frustrating" in his book *What Video Games Have to Teach Us about Learning and Literacy* (2007). He goes on to compare the notion that learning in school is not necessarily considered good when it is hard but, when playing video games, hard is considered good. It's good, hard, fun, even though it is challenging. Applying the gamification approach to learning can alter students' feelings so that they experience hard learning as fun and rewarding.

Where to start? Similar to a Head Coach developing trust from their team, school librarians have to develop trust among colleagues to inspire teachers and students to be open to new approaches to learning. When trying to impart the value of gamification in the classroom, the school librarian can often succeed by integrating gamification into professional development. In this scenario, teachers discover implementation strategies while learning new content. Read on to discover strategies for gamifying professional development to demonstrate how gamification can be modeled in the classroom.

Get Your Game Face on for PD

Professional development (PD) can get a bad rap. What may flash through your mind is the image of teachers being required to "sit and get" for hours at a time with little interaction or engagement. Yikes. PD does not have to be this way and neither does student learning in the classroom. School librarians are at the center of a web. They work with all stakeholders in their school community, they evaluate and acquire resources that impact all of the school community, and they develop a variety of programs that reach every stakeholder. As a result of the school librarian's breadth of contacts and relationships within the school, their depth of knowledge as it relates to the curriculum, and their ability to organize and implement large-scale programming, school librarians can be central forces in revitalizing PD and transforming the learning culture. It does take some time to transition a school's culture from dreading PD to looking forward to PD. The trick to turning PD's rap sheet around and clearing the record is to create opportunities for choice in which participants can own their learning. Gamification as a teaching and learning model allows this to happen. The moment someone starts playing a game, they have to make their own decisions. As players in the game of learning are responsible for their choices, they become empowered as the leaders of their own learning journey. Findings compiled by researchers at Hanover Research firm (2014, 3), discovered supporting data that "by empowering students to exercise a degree of autonomous decision making, student choice makes students active participants in their education, thereby increasing levels of engagement. Notably, researchers highlight the fact that such autonomy is generally associated with greater personal well-being and satisfaction in educational environments, as well as in terms of academic performance." They go on to note that one mechanism for proving this theory was that standardized test scores improved when choice and voice shaped students' learning experiences.

Active Gaming

In gaming, when the mind is active, the physical body is not always active. While there are plenty of powerful game-based approaches to learning that keep us in a chair, there are quite a few that keep us moving. When learners have the opportunity to work their minds and their bodies, their memory muscles are stronger (Jensen 2005, 60). In a multisensory experience, we tend to be more astute in remembering the experience and absorbing the content. There are a number of tools that encourage active learning through gamification. We will explore how those tools can be implemented through professional development opportunities inspiring teachers to integrate these innovative gaming tools into their classrooms.

Breakout EDU

Escape Rooms are all the rage for entertainment purposes. Breakout EDU is a similar experience for learners. As the clock races, participants must solve clues to unlock a mystery. Breakout EDU is an immersive learning platform designed to transform the classroom experience. Breakout EDU kits come in both physical form and digital form or they can be combined together to create a blended experience. The physical kit is a black box that includes a variety of different locks, an invisible ink pen, clue cards, and more to create a mystery-oriented learning experience. The digital Breakout EDU games require internet access and include a scenario that has to be solved, clues that are embedded within a website, along with a timer that lets the players know how much time they have left to "open" the digital locks within the website. The Breakout EDU website, https://www .breakoutedu.com, shares three different pricing models. Once registered, Breakout EDU facilitators can access games that have been created by other users, the featured digital games, and Breakout EDU resources that include teaching users how to create their own digital game. There is also a platform access fee that is good for one year and costs $75.00, as of the time of this publication. With platform access, users can plug in content to generate their own digital game, rather than create a game template from scratch. It also provides access to subject pack games and allows for the creation of student accounts. A site-wide license can be purchased for $500.00 and provides full access for all teachers within one school. To purchase a physical kit, the cost is $150.00 and includes one platform access. There are discounts available for two or more kits. To set up a game with the kit, clues are physically placed throughout a room or a school, along with locks where learners have to use the clues to help them unlock it and move onto the next clue/lock. It's an exciting, heart pulsing, active race to be the first team to break out, also known as "the most resourceful." There are large signs the winners can hold up at the end that say "We broke out" or "Better luck next time." It's a fun, team-building experience that tests your knowledge and motivates players to strive to learn more about the game's subject matter. Any subject or content area can be used for a Breakout EDU experience. There is a Breakout EDU Facebook community with over 31,000 members. It is a virtual resource where people share original Breakout EDU games they have created, help each other solve difficult Breakout's, share new clue or lock features, and solicit subject areas for games that may have already been created by a group member to avoid reinventing the wheel. It is a strong resource and the fact that it even exists demonstrates that there is a growing network of Breakout EDU facilitators that have taken the concept and run with it in their own learning environments.

School librarians should consider using this tool first in their own class. Try it out. Get comfortable with it. Test it out on your students. The first time I used it was with a Technology Exploratory class on the topic of coding. I used the physical kit. Through an educational learning conference, I was able to get a coupon code soon after the launch of Breakout EDU and spent $99 on the kit for our school. It was well worth the investment. I hid the final clue in a corner of the library and the team that first uncovered all the clues won bragging rights with a giant sign that read "We broke out!" I also made a point of attending a couple of sessions at local conferences with teachers and school librarians that were already using Breakout EDU in their learning environments. As attendees, they walked us through our own Breakout EDU experience. Then, I created a digital version for my class. I found the digital versions to be easier to create in that I followed explicit directions on the Breakout EDU website. It is a little different now in that Breakout EDU has started offering online templates for game creators to plug in the information and the online platform is customized and generated for you. Previously, using Google sites, you could set up the scenario and "hide" the clues in hidden links throughout the webpage, along with an embedded Google form where learners could plug in the information that they thought would solve the clue. If they were correct, the form would allow them to move onto the next question. If not, they had to keep trying. While the digital version may have required the players to run around the room or the school to solve for clues, the game facilitator could sit at their desk and create an entire game without hiding clues around the building. Once you create one digital game, the rest comes easily. The first time you create a game, whether it is physical or digital, it is a learning curve. Learning to create Breakout EDUs is well worth the investment of time because it suits both large and small audiences and, therefore, can create engagement within a variety of learning environments.

Now, back to PD. After I had dabbled in both the physical and the digital version, I was given permission by my principal to roll out this innovative gamification tool to all faculty during our pre-planning week. We were launching our twenty-fifth anniversary year and, as a result, we had a lot of festivities planned throughout the upcoming school year. We were also beginning a large capital campaign to expand our school's learning spaces. Therefore, the chosen topic for the faculty Breakout EDU was the school itself. I would test the players on their knowledge of the school's history, its current mission and values, and the goals for what we were referring to as The Next Stage, our upcoming capital campaign. Because there were so many of us and I only had one physical kit, I decided to create a digital Breakout EDU and break everyone into groups consisting of six to nine people. Each group would meet in one classroom and use one computer to work together to solve the clues. The first group to break out would race to the library and get their picture taken with the bragging rights sign. Well, there was one group that had an unfair advantage. Naturally, the group with our Head of School won, as shown in Figure 6.1.

However, I felt like the real winner because everyone loved it! As each group broke out and came down to the library, I would give them an informative talk about the physical kit versus the digital version and tell them that they could check the kit out from the library and I would

Figure 6.1 The Davis Academy faculty that broke out during a Breakout EDU pre-planning activity.

happily help them set up a digital game to accommodate their curriculum or they could go online and explore the preexisting games. In no time at all, teachers were kicking off their school year with Breakout EDUs in their classrooms. In fact, we have since had to have one of our locks replaced in the physical kit due to excessive usage.

Using tools, like Breakout EDU, to solidify relationships and grow partnerships even beyond the classroom can also transform the learning. As Breakout EDU was becoming so popular, parents started to hear about it. We decided to facilitate a Breakout EDU experience for our Parent Teacher Organization meeting. It was an amazing way to demonstrate to our parents the type of innovative learning that their children are being exposed to in the classroom.

community [handwritten margin note]

As a faith-based school, we purposefully and with considerable planning expose our student body to cultures and religions different from our own. We invited another faith-based school to visit us for a day of learning and, as part of the experience, we created small groups of students from both our school and their school to work together and race against the clock to help the minister and the rabbi find the missing key to their shared place of worship. Students tapped into their knowledge of their different religious backgrounds to help each other solve the mystery. I created the game in digital format with the help of another school librarian, Jessica Osborne, and together we used our different religious backgrounds to create an educational experience for our students. To set the tone of the event, we played pipe organ music for the students as they filed into the room. Access the digital Breakout EDU we played during this interfaith day of learning by scanning the QR code shown in Figure 6.2.

Figure 6.2 Scan the QR code to access the interfaith day of learning digital Breakout EDU in which players help the rabbi and the minister find the missing key to their place of worship.

Think outside the box with gamification tools. Consider how you can expose and connect with larger audiences to the innovative practices happening in your classrooms to help you and your school grow the resources.

Digital Badges

I love the idea of gamifying learners through digital badges. The possibility for creativity is endless here. I use this model almost every year with professional development for our teachers. Here's how it works:

1. Commit to your content.

2. Create a point value system in which different ranges of points are worth a specific badge type.

3. Invent challenges that drive the learners to explore the content goals.

4. Ask participants to track the accrual of their points.

5. At the conclusion of the timeframe to earn points, have participants add up all their points and share their experiences in a group setting.

6. Provide participants with the digital badge that aligns with the number of points they accrued.

7. Celebrate their efforts and their success in being brave and tackling the challenges.

There are a number of reasons why I find this type of gamification to be awesome. First, it allows learners to choose their own adventure, giving them choice and voice in their learning. Second, it allows participants to actively learn at their own convenience and pace. Some may choose to do many challenges at once and some may choose to spread them out gradually throughout the course of time that you have given them. Third, with this gamification model, the learning can be differentiated so that participants not only choose their own pace but can also choose how deep they want to go with the content. Finally, it allows the creator of the content to customize the learning to best suit their learners while also holding learners accountable for their own professional growth.

The first year that I used the badge system, it was to encourage technology integration within the classroom. Inspired by Dr. Brad Gustafson's Digital Leadership Challenge (2014), I used a similar model for our teachers to challenge them to think more consciously about technology integration within their individual classrooms. Tying in a fun Star Wars theme for the teachers added a dose of creativity to the challenges, while also modeling that they could do the same for their students. Scan the QR code in Figure 6.3 for access to the Tech Scout PD.

Figure 6.3 Gamified professional development with a Star Wars themed digital badge system.

After teachers participated in these choose your own adventure technology integration challenges for the year, we held a participation ceremony the last week of school called The Tech Scout Grand Finale. Each participant was publicly congratulated for completing the Tech Scout Challenge, added up their points, and shared a technology integration revelation, moment, and/or lesson that they felt proud of during the year. The next year, it was back by popular demand. Some teachers decided to participate in the first version of the Tech Scout PD as they heard how great it was while others asked to do it again, at which time I created Tech Scout 2.0. I was able to customize it to those specific teachers' needs. For example, the music teacher was one such teacher that wanted to repeat a Tech Scout-style PD opportunity. As a result, I created a separate Google document that included customized challenges to specifically meet her technology integration needs in relation to her music classes. One challenge involved app-smashing. From this, she created an incredible activity for our students. She called it Davis Idol. Students could come up to the microphone, sing a song of their choice, or play an instrument. She would record it via the camera app with an iPad. Then, she would upload their performance video onto YouTube and their performance pictures onto the PicCollage app as one large collage. She would then use the image from PicCollage as her background image within the Thinglink app and embed each performance into Thinglink via YouTube. She would send the link to the parents in the class and they could view their child's Davis Idol performance on Thinglink. As a nice twist, she would give each performer a sticker for their shirt that said, "I participated in Davis Idol today." This was a great conversation starter between parent and child at the end of the school day.

This year's digital-badge gamification PD is *Become a Digital Citizenship Scout.* Teachers are being challenged to learn about digital citizenship, how to teach it, and then integrate digital citizenship into their lesson plans. The goal behind this PD strand is that if teaching digital citizenship is to be effective, it needs to be relevant to the core curriculum and not compartmentalized solely within the media center during library time. By offering a badge system PD model each year for teachers, often with variations, I am demonstrating the value of putting this play into practice. Each year, teachers are faced with a new group of students, each of which has different needs. By exposing teachers to the possibilities and benefits of crafting a gamified learning system that is built upon a badge system, you are supporting them in creating a versatile learning environment in which students' needs are very different, class sizes vary, and the abilities are diverse. Set them up for successful plays in the classroom and demonstrate that badge systems can be hosted on a digital platform or earned as physical badges that learners can adhere to their backpacks, laptops, or lockers. The gamification of learning through badge systems require that learners put themselves out into the world, try new approaches, and actively grow their expertise in one or more content areas.

Digital (or Not) Scavenger Hunts

Digital scavenger hunts can be some of the most simple and yet, creative ways to get students moving and learning at the same time. There are a variety of ways in which these can be done. There is the "go out and find format" in which learners are given a finite amount of time to go out and find specific objects and return to the home base to present their findings. The first group to return to the home base and who has successfully accomplished all of the tasks wins. This can be done with any mobile device that includes a camera. With teachers, kick off the school year with a values-based or mission-driven digital scavenger hunt. I love this activity as a reminder of what our school's mission stands for as we kick off a new school year and I love it for the ability to mix teachers up across teams that do not get to interact often throughout the year. It reminds teachers that they are all "on the same team" despite teaching different ages and different subjects. Provide each group with a list of words or values that reflect your school's mission statement. Send each group off to take pictures of objects that represent those words. For example, one of our values is "wisdom." Some groups took a picture of the rabbi's office, some took a picture of the library, and some captured an image of the brain in the Science lab. It is so interesting to come back together and share how each group chose to represent each word differently, and sometimes similarly. The same approach can be applied to specific content for teachers in which they may be undergoing training. For example, one year we were learning about improving communication skills and discovering a growth mindset by reading and discussing John D'Auria's *Ten Lessons in Leadership and Learning: An Educator's Journey* (2010). A great way to get teachers active and engaged is to send them on a scavenger hunt that asks them to agree on and capture a representation of something they learned in each of the ten lessons. The benefits of digital scavenger hunts are that they are less cumbersome to create, they allow the facilitator to customize the content based on their learners' needs and goals, and they get learners moving, which increases student engagement.

On the Field: Curricular Examples of Active Gamification. Breakout EDU can be used with just about any content area. Math, Language Arts, Science, Coding, Social Studies, Music, Physical Education, and any other topic you wish to share with your learners. The main component to consider with Breakout EDU, regardless of if you are using the physical kit, a digital game, or a combination of both, is whether or not the content already exists or if you will have to create the game from scratch. While creating one from scratch to use in either format may feel daunting, it is an awesome opportunity to grow your team. Offering to work with a teacher to help them customize their Breakout EDU so that it specifically meets their students' needs is a win-win. You are empowering them with a new tool for their toolbox by teaching them how to create their own games, you are working together on a common goal thereby improving your relationship, and you are creating something magnificent for your learning community. Over time, you cultivate a stronger team with these teachers and can take these partnerships on the road to showcase how you worked together to learn and share a new innovative tool. The potential to inspire other teachers and school librarians to team up should not be disregarded. Consider sharing these experiences at local conferences, via webinars or through professional publications.

Gamification through a badging system or through scavenger hunts can be used in any content area. With younger students, perhaps model badges after Boy Scouts and Girl Scouts with actual badges that look like the patches we have come to recognize so easily. The idea is to send them out into the world to learn specific content and accomplish a specific task related to that content. There are a variety of approaches to integrating a badging system or scavenger hunt, digital or not:

- In Reading, instead of having homeroom teachers send home a dreaded reading log to track their students' reading for twenty minutes each night, have them do a project that represents the last 100 pages that they have read and turn in the project for an "I read 100 pages" badge. The project can be an illustration of their favorite scene, a comic strip that retells the story so far, or a podcast summarizing the story at this point and ending with a hook to inspire others to want to read the book on their own, as some examples. Each time they read another 100 pages, the equivalent of 20 minutes a night each school night per week, they receive another badge that reflects the number of pages that they have read. Have a competition to see who can earn the most badges at the end of the school year.

- In History class, students can earn points for creating a propaganda poster that reflects what was happening during World War II for ten points.

- In Math class, award badges once students demonstrate that they have learned the different levels of their math facts.

- In Social Studies, award a badge for every ten states and their capitals that students learn.

- In Science, award a badge each time students demonstrate their learning of a human body system, whether it is through a song, a poem, or a test.

- In Kindergarten, divide students into groups of four. Provide each group with an iPad, assign a team leader to ultimately be responsible for the iPad but explain that everyone will be able to use it. Then, ask students to go on a digital 3D shape scavenger hunt. They have twenty minutes to take pictures of as many 3D shapes as they can. Upon returning to the classroom, they must be able to identify the shape name. Emphasize that each group member will get at least one turn to capture an image of a 3D shape. As added fun, you can ask the students to put all of their images into a digital collage using the PicCollage app and label the shape of each image with text.

Consider scanning the QR code of the Tech Scout PD strand shared earlier in the chapter, renaming a new copy of the Google document and save it as your own to modify the content and make a badging system that works for your learners. There are different approaches to modifying scavenger hunts to accommodate different group sizes and learning spaces. For example, when there are multiple groups sharing the same space, students can be given an envelope with a clue that they have to solve to figure out where to go to set them on their digital scavenger hunt course. At each location, if they make it to the right spot in the correct order, the next clue (marked with a clue number and their group color) is waiting for them. This is best done when you scramble each group's clues so that not every group is traveling to the same clue at the same time. If there are multiple groups but they do not have to share the same space, use the same clues but set them out in different parts of the building. For example, team one works on the first floor, team two on the second floor, and so on so that each group is solving the same clues at the same time and their experiences are identical but there is no chance of them running into each other. In our middle school, for example, we have three levels, all of which contain a water fountain, a back stairwell, a specialty teacher's classroom (art, music, PE, theater, media, and foreign language, for example), a front stairwell, lockers with even and odd numbers, and more. Finding similarities in different parts of the building for each team to work separately can simplify the setup, which is helpful for the game creator. The starting clue may read, for example, in a middle or high school Social Studies class learning about Mesopotamia, "What goes up must come down. Find this spot to discover the birth of something big." Upon arrival to the base of the stairwell, students find a puzzle piece with an image of a cradle with a number one on it. On the back of the puzzle piece is the second hint or clue: "When you discover what this place is the cradle of, it will take you to a whole new world. When you think you know it, go to the place that starts with the same initial." If they guess the cradle of civilization, then they will know it is Mesopotamia where civilization was born (hence, the cradle image). Mesopotamia starts with an M so you hope they will head to the music room (or some other room that starts with an M in the building). Depending on your school's physical set up, this could be the math class, the media center, or the mailroom. You decide. When they arrive at the correct room, another clue (marked number two), will be waiting for them in which M is the letter in common. This is a fun, active way to test their knowledge of a particular subject as a unit review.

The school librarian can support the teacher to use these gamification models in a scrimmage, or rather as a warm-up activity to introduce a new unit. It is a nonintimidating approach to assessing student knowledge before beginning a new unit. Preassessments and the introduction of new units can be gamified in a variety of ways. In addition, gamification can create powerful plays in partnering with homeroom or subject-specific teachers to introduce content and improve research skills. For example, introduce a unit with a giant word search that takes students around the building while also teaching them about the school's research databases. With Mesopotamia as the example, have students divide into three groups, advise that each group is responsible for finding two to three letters. Hand each of the three groups an envelope. In one envelope is the following clue: This letter is the first initial of the longest river in Western Asia. Students are required to use the library's research databases to identify the information. Be sure to explain that this is not to make the search more challenging but rather to ensure that what they find is factual. Once they discover that the correct answer is the Euphrates River, they are now searching the building, media center, gym, or whatever space(s) are available for the letter E. Perhaps the E is hidden in the elevator. Get creative. Once all the teams return with their respective clues after doing their online research and letter finding, they spread the letters onto the floor and scramble them until they identify the word. In this case, it would be "Mesopotamia." Not only have they learned some facts about the unit that they will begin but they kept moving and had fun working in collaborative teams while doing so. Not only does gamification allow school librarians to focus on one core curricular subject by teaming with one teacher at a time, but they can go multi-sport pro and team up with several teachers (great for middle or high school librarians) and integrate library navigation and research skills into a variety of curricular topics. For example, approach the math teacher to create a series of equations for their students to solve that coincide with what they are learning. Ask the math teacher to provide you with the answer key. When students have found the correct answer, they take their answer to the school librarian who then checks it with the answer key provided by the math teacher. If correct, the school librarian gives them a new clue that involves using the library catalog. For example, what math did you use to solve this equation? Find a book in our library catalog with that word in its title. Once you find that book, you will find your next clue. If they used arithmetic, then they may identify the book, *The Devil's Arithmetic* by Jane Yolen in the library cata- log. Their second clue is hidden in the front of that book, once they locate that book on the shelf. They have to use the call number from the library catalog to do so. Their second clue is another math equation but perhaps this one is a word problem that gives them a four-digit number as the answer, such as a specific year like 1934. Using the library's research data- base, they have to identify the significance of this date to their current novel study in Language Arts. What happens in 1934 in *To Kill a Mocking- bird* by Harper Lee, for example? The teachers will love that you are part- nering with them to integrate their curriculum into learning research skills and navigating the library. To gamify the learning is to create fun for learners of all ages. Alter the content and the level of technology usage to best suit your learners, your goals, and your specific content areas.

Don't Overdo It: Remember It's a Warm-Up. Here's the thing about gami- fication: Once you walk your teachers through the process in a safe, fun environment, they gain the confidence to implement this strategy into their own classroom. It's messy, fun learning that makes the content memorable. Since the launch of Breakout EDU, our teachers have created their own versions of gamifying the learning using puzzles, game boards, and dice. Our sixth-grade Language Arts teacher, Michelle Stein, has a year-long game going so that any time students find vocabulary words outside of class, they get to move forward on her in-class gamification board. Different models work best for different teachers and different learn- ers. Some games are best suited within one class period, some involve year-long tracking systems, some are digitized, some are "no tech," and some are a combination of all of the above. By introducing teachers to gam- ification strategies through professional development, the school librarian is modeling an innovative learning strategy for teachers to gain confidence to emulate.

Moving into the Red Zone

There is a lot of innovative equipment available to help the school librar- ian acting as the quarterback help move the running backs, or other edu- cators, across the field and into the red zone to score winning plays in education. Not all gamification strategies, however, require significant calo- rie burn. The gamification tools that I will share below encourage focus. These tools add value to the learning with increased student engagement, clearly defined goals, and by encouraging students to create their own content. Get ready to rumble.

Passive Gaming

Don't let passive scare you off. Have you ever noticed that serious topics for kids, such as understanding cell structure and function, are often animated? Why is this? Well, typically it is to make the delivery of the subject matter so enticing that the child will be riveted by every word and the content will stick in their minds and they will be all the more intelligent. The same objective can be applied to the motivation behind game-based learning, even those that are passive experiences. There is the goal of wanting to creatively share information so that it is learned. People are so enthralled in the game that they forget that they are learning. It's a fine strategy for making school a more appealing experience. A school day equals a fun day. We will explore a variety of gamification tools that don't necessarily translate into physical movement but are enthralling, nonetheless. We will continue to explore strategies for educating teachers about gamification opportunities, and the ways that you, the school librarian, can support teachers in their quest to gamify their classroom experiences with specific curricular connections.

Catch the Game Craze with Kahoot

If you have not experienced Kahoot yet, you are missing out! If you have used Kahoot before, I will offer some novel approaches to using Kahoot. For those readers who are not familiar with Kahoot, I will start with the basics. Kahoot is a free game-based learning platform that can incorporate any subject, in any language, and for any age. In order to use Kahoot, technology is needed. Creating a game on Kahoot requires a computer or a mobile device. If using a mobile device, the free Kahoot app will need to be downloaded. There is a library of premade Kahoot games but so much of the fun is in creating your own games. There are four different game formats. The first is a jumble in which the question is a sequencing question (another connection to coding!) in which participants have to put the answers in the proper order. This is a great tool for a history test review in which students have to remember a timeline of events in their proper order. When the game creator creates the question, they put the answers in the proper order but when the game is played, Kahoot automatically jumbles up the answers for the players. The game creator can set a time limit up to 120 seconds for responses to be submitted. Images and links to YouTube videos can also be embedded into each question. Another function of Kahoot is to create a survey to generate feedback. This is a great tool to check students' confidence level on a particular subject without publicly asking their feedback so that they feel comfortable. Kahoot also offers a discussion tool in which a topic can be shared with a class to generate conversation. For example, if students are learning about financial literacy, the teacher can simulate a real-world situation in which students are given a finite amount of money, specific jobs, circumstances that impact their living environment, such as needing new roads, and once all of the facts and economic conditions are laid out, can generate questions, such as "Do you think there should be a tax increase to repair the roads?" Respondents can answer yes or no and the results can lead to a strong discussion about the role of government and being fiscally responsible.

The most commonly used feature of Kahoot is the quiz feature. Questions can be asked with four potential answers and a timer can be set so that each question has to be answered in a specific amount of time or players forfeit their response. Once each question is answered, if it is before the time limit is up, the players and facilitator can see that all answers have been submitted and move onto the next question immediately. Players can play the game individually, requiring everyone to need their own device or they can play in groups requiring one device per group. To play, an individual or group nickname must be submitted. Teachers can require that students use their real names to assess their learning or they can allow them to select an unidentifiable username when wanting to assess their knowledge without the pressure of identification. Between each question, Kahoot will share the usernames of the top five players that are in the lead. With the Kahoot app, games can also be created on a mobile device, not just on a computer. A great feature of Kahoot is that if one teacher creates a Kahoot for a test review, other teachers on their team can use it too.

According to the Kahoot.com website (2018), there are more than seventy million active Kahoot users each month. That's a lot of Kahoot! If you are already familiar with Kahoot, consider changing the ways in which you use it. Don't underestimate the value in building up strength in brainpower by having students create their own study guides. While Kahoot is fun just to play in the classroom, encourage teachers to assign students to be the creators of their own Kahoots as homework or during class time. Students can challenge their peers to play each other's games as content review. After creating their own games and playing their classmates' games, they are more likely to grasp the content. Additionally, with the new homework challenge feature, teachers can assign a Kahoot to students with a specific deadline. Students can play the assigned Kahoot at home on a mobile device. The teacher can download a report that shows how each player performed. Once our entire school community had been infused with a love of Kahoot, we started using Kahoot in a variety of creative ways. On Grandparents and Special Friends Day, our fifth graders played "Are you smarter than a fifth grader?" They played in teams so that each child and grandparent or special friend was competing with the other children and their grandparent or special friend. It was a great team building experience for grandparents and their grandchildren that brought the class together. On Back to School Night, our third-grade teachers have the students make a video sharing all the important information that the teacher needs parents to know. For example, dates to remember, field trip uniform requirements, big projects, and more. The hope with this approach is that the parents will be more interested in watching a video of their children share the information as opposed to listening to the teacher stand up and talk for a long time. Then, the teacher asks the parents to get out their mobile phones, download the free Kahoot app, and tests them on their listening skills with a game of Kahoot. The teacher projects the questions on the Smartboard. The questions are comprised of the content from the student video. The game begins and parents play on their mobile phones. The winner receives a bag of chocolate. It's a fun way to ensure parents are receiving important information for the school year ahead. We also use Kahoot to close out our Field Day. The entire school has a representative in each grade level on every team color that comes up to a stage and sits in one of four spots that have an iPad on a table. Next to the stage is a giant screen that projects a Kahoot question. Each team representative answers a trivia question that relates to their grade levels curriculum and then goes and sits down and the next grade level representative for each color and grade level comes up to the table on the stage and does the same. Once every grade level has been represented, the color of the team that scored the most Kahoot points gains Field Day points. It's a fun way to close out Field Day. We also use Kahoot on special programming days as a rotation. For example, we have a day in which we celebrate the birthday of Israel. We have a rotation in which students are asked trivia questions via Kahoot all about Israel as part of their celebration. If your teachers are already using Kahoot, then you know that it is a great tool for test reviews in just about every topic and is suitable for all ages. We have had teachers so enamored with this gamification tool that they have used it for fun at their family holiday celebrations quizzing family members on their knowledge of the family tree. Kahoot is extraordinarily user-friendly. Once a game is created at Kahoot.com, players input a unique game pin to enter a specific game. It is best suited when the facilitator can project the questions on a larger screen for all to see the questions and results.

It is worth noting that there are different versions of Kahoot-type experiences. One example is Socrative. Some of our teachers like to use Socrative instead of Kahoot when they wish to take some of the playful air out of the learning experience and create a more serious mood while still using gamification as a learning strategy. Socrative is a website and a mobile app. Socrative lacks the bright colors that you see in Kahoot and it is geared toward generating assessments. There are different forms of responses, such as multiple choice, short answer, or true/false. Socrative can also be used as an exit ticket to test students understanding of that day's lesson before they walk out the door. Results can be saved and can help the teacher plan for the next day or see where there are still knowledge gaps. Another alternative to Kahoot is Quizlet. Quizlet allows teachers or students to generate custom flashcards and then they can quiz themselves through multiple choice games, matching games, or a gravity game in which students have to type in the correct answer before the planet is hit by an asteroid. Our Hebrew teachers create vocabulary lists in Quizlet for students to practice their pronunciation and understanding of specific words and then the students take a quiz within Quizlet to test their learning. They require that students achieve a certain percentage before having considered themselves masters of that particular word list. It's extremely motivating for students to compete against themselves and try to improve their scores. All of these options are powerful tools to implement in a variety of situations.

In order to get teachers started with Kahoot, I suggest helping one teacher on a teaching team create a Kahoot for a test review, have that teacher share it with the other co-teachers, and then have that same teacher teach the other teachers on the team how to create their own. Create a pyramid of teachers and learners. This way, each teacher on one team can take turns creating Kahoots to coincide with different unit reviews. We now have some teachers who have been using the same Kahoots for a few years when specific unit reviews come up because they have built up their own library of Kahoots to coincide with their grade-level curriculum. The same approach can be taken with Quizlet or Socrative, both of which have sharing features for co-facilitators.

Class Dojo

Class Dojo is a fun one too! Class Dojo also requires technology, either a computer or a mobile device. It allows teachers to set up avatars for their students (some teachers let students choose their avatar) and teachers can reward with points throughout the day. Class Dojo has behavioral categories built into their point system so many teachers use it as a behavior management tool. However, teachers can also customize the categories in which students can achieve points. For example, our middle school Judaic Studies teacher Samara Schwartz set up her classroom so that it was discussion-oriented. Students engaged in debates, discussed philosophical topics, and shared personal stories. She used Class Dojo to reward students for class participation. Every time a student chimed in on a topic, they were awarded a point. It is quick and easy to tap a button on a student's avatar to denote the point addition. Some teachers display the Class Dojo point system for the entire class on the Smartboard so that the students can see where they stand for that particular day. At the end of the week, parents can receive an email reminding them to check their child's Dojo account to see a report of their weekly rewards. Our Physical Education teachers enjoy using Class Dojo because they see entire grade levels at one time and this tool can help them manage behavior. I have used it on lunch duty in conjunction with a classroom teacher who is on duty with me. When the kids eat and talk to each other at a respectable noise level, they earn a Dojo point. When a student reaches a certain number of Dojo points, they can pick a prize out of a treasure chest. Class Dojo can be modified to fit just about any situation or goal. Educators can get very creative with the ways in which they label the Dojo categories. For example, our middle school Judaic Studies teacher would use names of Jewish heroes as her reward system. For example, students could earn points in being strong like a Maccabee in conversational skills. Teachers can also add co-teachers to award points to students that are set up within a class. I can set up a class for a specific second-grade teacher and assign her the rights to award points. I can use it for her class when they visit the library and she can use it when her students are in homeroom with her. It is transferable across the building among different teachers. Another strong feature of Class Dojo is the digital portfolio option. Teachers can push assignments to students or classes and require that they complete specific activities by turning in a video, text, image, or a drawing. Their work can also be published to the parents so they can see their child's submission. The digital portfolio tool adds another layer of engagement with the ability to share student work and progress.

Classcraft

Classcraft was initially created to manage classroom behavior for older students. Now, however, Classcraft has developed into an online gaming platform meant to turn lesson plans into quests using video game mechanics. It's pretty awesome but it does require a more significant investment in time than the tools mentioned above. Similar to World of Warcraft, players are immersed in a shared alternative world in which new rules are in place. Establishing and learning those rules can be quite detail-oriented. With an educator who is devoted to implementing Classcraft into their learning environment, middle schoolers or high schoolers can really get into Classcraft. By entering a new reality, students can escape into education. There are preexisting lessons in Classcraft and teachers are also encouraged to create their own. Creating a quest, or lesson plan, can take some time as there are many facets to this multiplayer world. Teachers launch a quest, students can level up and move forward as part of a team, yet everyone is accountable for the learning. In order to assign the subject-specific quests that have already been created and that are available in the marketplace, the cost is $8.00/month for unlimited student access and unlimited classes. With the free version, Classcraft can be used as a classroom management tool. Players can interact through a web browser on a computer or mobile device. School librarians probably have certain teachers that may take to this gamification tool more than others. Therefore, exposing teachers to Classcraft as one option can be worthwhile. Some teachers may be very interested in gamification, in general, and therefore more open to trying out this tool in their classroom while others may be fans of fantasy universe games and may love the opportunity to integrate this type of game into their classroom.

Minecraft

The beauty of Minecraft is that you already have players on your team that have bought into Minecraft in a big way and on their own time. Therefore, Minecraft as a learning tool already has brute force behind it. This is a tool that can really transform the learning. Described as a game that is about placing blocks and going on adventures, there are different modes such as creative mode, survival mode, adventure mode, gameplay mode, spectator mode, hardcore mode, and a mode in which players make their own rules. There are some differences among the various modes. For example, in creative mode, students can tap into unlimited resources or those resources that the teacher makes available to them, to build anything they can imagine. In survival mode, players have limited resources and must feed, defend, and arm themselves in order to survive. Then, there is the option in which you, the teacher, can establish the rules and create the setting. Fortunately, there is an education edition in Minecraft, which can be used via a computer or a mobile device. This edition is not free but volume licensing discounts are available through Microsoft. The education edition has starter kits that include lesson plans for Language Arts, Science, History and Culture, Computer Science, Math, and Art and Design. Pretty awesome, right?

The lessons can be searched and sorted by subject and grade level. For example, Lynne Telfer, an Australian educator, has created a library of lesson plans available on Minecraft's website. One lesson is entitled "Join an Ant Colony!" This lesson inspires players, suitable for ages six and up, to collectively create an ant colony and, in doing so, learn about the food they eat, the land they inhabit, how they communicate, and how they protect their food and look after the queen. Minecraft Education also awards educators digital badges for their lesson plans. I can see that Lynne has earned a Minecraft Certified Educator and a Global Mentor badge. I can also search for lesson plans under specific educators' names if I like the quality of lessons that certain educators produce.

School librarians can make Minecraft easy for teachers to implement into their curriculum. Carve out specific times for their students and the teacher to hold class in the computer lab or in the classroom if you work in a 1:1 environment in which every student has their own device. Ask students who are already very comfortable with Minecraft to do a quick review of the major commands and function keys, as shown in Table 6.1. Then, establish a multiplayer world with a specific goal in mind. For example, in Math, drop various objects into the multiplayer world and have students calculate the perimeter, the area, or the volume. Using the */say* command, educators can send all of the people in their shared world a

Table 6.1   **Basic Minecraft Commands**

Command	Function
A	Move left
D	Move right
S	Move backward
W	Move forward
Left-click on mouse	Destroy blocks
Right-click on mouse	Place a block down
T in a multiplayer world	Enables chat feature
CTRL	Sprint
Spacebar	Jump
E	View inventory

message with specific directions so that text pops up on their screen. In this way, you can give them virtual math challenges. If you would rather start slow, you can make Minecraft a single player world and have students work independently to demonstrate their learning. For example, in our school second grade learns about landforms. They can recreate the landforms and their characteristics in Minecraft. The same can be done to demonstrate different habitats. Our sixth graders were challenged to create a game in Minecraft that taught players the different parts of speech. Players hopped in the mine cart and they would encounter signs that asked them questions, such as "What is a verb?" If they thought the answer was on sign A, they could go to the left and proceed to the next question. If they thought the answer was on sign B, they would go to the right and have further verb review creatively demonstrated via Minecraft. By creating a roller coaster ride in a Minecart, these students simulated a learning journey for their peers to reinforce the concepts they were learning in class. Students can recreate scenes from novels or use Minecraft as a storytelling tool to write about their creations. Our first graders learn about historic landmarks. They can recreate these in Minecraft and provide educational information about their landmark to "visiting travelers" that journey through their Minecraft world. This can be done as a multiplayer activity or as a single player activity in which each "architect" presents their creation to the class. To ease into Minecraft, another approach is to set students up in a single player world but tell them that they can earn the ability to do activities in a collaborative multiplayer world.

Reinforcing digital citizenship components throughout the communal use of Minecraft is a strong play to integrate digital citizenship into the core curriculum. The ultimate goal is to make it so that the teacher feels comfortable building Minecraft into the lessons independently knowing that they can call on the school librarian when help is needed or questions arise. Often, when teachers realize that they have Minecraft experts (all it takes is one) within their student body, they feel more comfortable navigating a brave new world with their students.

Google Slides

Google really has its own language unto itself. As the school librarian working to create and support a winning culture of innovative educators, it is critical to ensure that all teachers, regardless of their years of experience, have the opportunity to learn the language of Google. Otherwise, they will be left on the bleachers and won't understand the rules of the game. I've seen it happen. Help them learn the language of Google. It is increasingly becoming a tool that innovative teachers depend on for its interconnectivity and flexibility with work being stored in the cloud, allowing students to sign into a variety of tools with their Google account, and with its ability to seamlessly share content back and forth between educators and students.

One strategy for teaching educators the language of Google is to facilitate a lesson with their students in which Google allows the students to incorporate gamification into the curricular content. When I encounter a teacher that is not comfortable with Google Slides, I equate it to PowerPoint, even though the argument could be made that Google Slides and PowerPoint are actually very different. More than likely, reluctant teachers have some familiarity and comfort level with PowerPoint. This typically eases some of the anxiety. With Google Slides, students can create interactive "choose your own adventure" style games. By creating a series of slides and inserting hyperlinks from one slide to another depending on the path (or link option) that the player chooses, an interactive game is born. Students can create their own version of a game centered around specific content and take turns playing their peers' games. Even though the content area is the same, the games will have their own unique creative details. For example, in fifth-grade Social Studies, our students learn about the Civil War. Rather than memorize facts about the Civil War from the textbook, over the years, I have partnered with the teachers so that students learn about the Civil War by taking their class notes (and their textbooks, if they choose to do so) and creating interactive games for their peers in which they reimagine themselves as a person alive during that time having to make difficult decisions relevant to that time period with accurate historical data. As the quarterback on the field, you can launch the lesson with an example, such as the one shown in Figure 6.4, and explain the technical component of how to link slides together within one presentation, how to cite sources, and how to share the completed project. As the running back, the teacher will carry the lesson the rest of the way down the field inserting the content expertise and outlining the expectations as indicated on the rubric, such as the one shown in Table 6.2.

Figure 6.4 Fifth-grade student example of Civil War choose your own adventure style game.

The first year that I worked with our fifth-grade Social Studies teachers on this project, I did not push too hard on what the bibliography should look like but I did integrate a lesson in copyright as it pertains to using images for

Table 6.2   Interactive Civil War Project Rubric Combining the Teacher's Content Expertise and the School Librarian's Requirements to Avoid Plagiarism and Copyright Violations

Due Date_____	
Slide 1: Introduction	
Your Name	1
Title	1
Slide 2	
Years of the Civil War	2
2 Factually Correct Differences between the North and South during the years leading up to the Civil War	6
User selects if they are a Union or Confederate solider	1
Slide 3	
2 Important and Correct facts about Union	6
User selects from 2 battles	1
Slide 4	
2 Important and Correct facts about Confederacy	6
User selects from 2 **different** battles	1
Slide 5: Battle A	
Year	1
Location	1
Winner	1
Why this is considered a major battle	3
Click to Conclusion link	1
Slide 6: Battle B	
Year	1
Location	1
Winner	1
Why this is considered a major battle	3
Click to Conclusion link	1
Slide 7: Battle C	
Year	1
Location	1
Winner	1
Why this is considered a major battle	3
Click to Conclusion link	1

(continued)

Table 6.2   *(continued)*

Due Date_____	
Slide 8: Battle D	
Year	1
Location	1
Winner	1
Why this is considered a major battle	3
Click to Conclusion link	1
Slide 9: Conclusion	
Who won	1
Where the surrender happened	1
Who were the people at the surrendering	2
Slide 10: Citations	
Used at least 2 sources	2
Harcourt Social Studies the United States: Civil War to Present	
Ebsco Database	
Used Correct MLA format	3
for help creating your citations, use:	
http://www.easybib.com/mla8-format/website-citation	
Sources listed in alphabetical order	1
Complete sentences	10
Correct punctuation, grammar, spelling	10
Includes at least 5 pictures related to the Civil War	5
Be sure to use Creative Commons search to locate your images	
Links work	5
Font is easy to read	2
Slides are neat and organized	2
Turned in on due date to your Social Studies teacher	3
Total	**100**

the game with a lesson in plagiarizing. When I received push back on certain areas, such as bibliographic formats, I chose to wait until the next year to focus more heavily on this as I recognized the need to be flexible to ease the teachers into this type of project. It is important to pick up on the signals that teachers are sending you when they are being brave enough to try something new. Eventually, they will get more comfortable and will agree to tighten the parameters during the next play.

Seesaw

Believe it or not, Seesaw, the digital portfolio platform mentioned in Chapter Four, can be a gamification tool. Seesaw as a gamification tool can also support the flipped classroom model allowing teachers to prepare video instructions for students to access on their own time. Seesaw can be a vessel for students to show what they know and demonstrate their learning on a particular topic. When teachers establish goals for students to achieve and to showcase their achievements, students can create videos of their work directly within Seesaw using the camera app. Each time a video of their work is submitted to the teacher's liking, they earn a reward. If necessary, the teacher can set up multiple classes in Seesaw making it is easy to organize challenges by class. The teacher can view the submitted videos, share their feedback, and students can resubmit improved versions of their work, if necessary. For example, our music teacher, Michelle Gimpelevich, uses the Recorder Karate method from Plank Road Publishing to incentivize students to practice and improve their recorder skills, as shown in Figure 6.5.

Students are given a recorder challenge via an instructional video that is hosted on Mrs. Gimpelevich's WordPress blog alongside key bullet points for students to remember as they record themselves practicing the recorder. Once students feel ready, they access the class' Seesaw page and record a video of themselves playing the recorder challenge. The teacher will leave a comment advising as to whether or not they have earned the next color bead

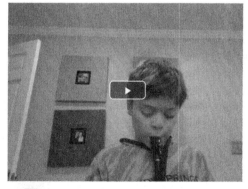

Davis Academy Music Ok, I can see you're playing with left hand this time! You earned yellow. Work on that tonguing at the beginning and not putting the finger down after the tongue. The end sounds great, just like that.

Figure 6.5 Using Seesaw's digital platform, students upload video of themselves practicing the recorder at home and the teacher provides feedback on their performance.

for their belt or if they need to go back and correct a few items and resubmit their video.

The school librarian can introduce students to Seesaw during their library visits. Then, they can share with teachers how Seesaw can gamify the classroom and improve the flow of communication with their students while reassuring the teachers that the students are already familiar with the tool. In this way, the school librarian is encouraging other teachers in the building to use it within their own classes. Once students have a Seesaw account, they can toggle back and forth between their different Seesaw classes making it easy for them to showcase their work and earn rewards accordingly.

Bloxels

Bloxels is a tool that allows learners to build their own video games. Using a tactile board with small color-coded cubes, game creators can design their own backgrounds and characters for their games. The colored cubes signify different characteristics of the game. For example, white blocks are story blocks that allow the game creator to type messages for the player to see when they reach that particular block. Yellow blocks are coins and can be collected throughout the game. The game creator decides where and how players can access each block. Bloxels provides both a tactile and digital experience. Bloxels can be used as a digital storytelling tool to create a narrative. For example, students can be given a writing prompt or a visual cue and they are tasked with building a game around that prompt or cue. Bloxels were created with ages six through thirteen in mind but older learners can use them too. Within the Bloxel Educator handbook, there are a variety of lesson plans. Educators can create a username and password for a thirty-day trial that outlines specific lesson plans with implementation strategies and goals. Examples of lessons include retelling a story through a specific character's point of view. This is a great lesson for teaching perspective. Other lesson plan ideas include building a game that walks a player through the parts of a cell, a journey through the branches of government, recreate an ecosystem, represent a historical event, learn about the solar system, or create a virtual world that represents a specific culture. Again, the school librarian is the quarterback punting innovative tools for teaching to the running back, the teacher. Introduce the big play, or the teaching tool, and allow the running back to incorporate the content. When students can have some exposure to tools prior to working with their homeroom teacher, this is helpful too. For example, our students did a fun activity to celebrate the upcoming Jewish holidays by creating animated representations of the holidays using Bloxels. Scan the QR code in Figure 6.6 to view student examples.

Any opportunity for students to create their own content is a powerful play in learning. Add the concept of video game creation into the equation and students are excited to learn. Lift up your team by supporting the use of these fun and innovative tools in the learning experience.

Figure 6.6 Students use Bloxels to animate apples and honey, the blowing of the shofar, and the Israeli flag in recognition of the upcoming Jewish high holidays.

Gamestar Mechanic

Gamestar Mechanic was awarded a top website for teaching and learning by the American Association of School Librarians in 2012. Since then, its usage has only grown. It is free to create a Gamestar Mechanic account, which provides access to designing a quest, making and publishing games, and accessing the larger Gamestar Mechanic community resources. In order to use Gamestar Mechanic, access to the internet and Adobe Flash Player is required. There are some awesome lessons that have already been created by other educators that focus on core curricular areas, such as the water cycle, rocks and minerals, and cell division. There is a teacher section on the Gamestar Mechanic website that provides informative tutorials for creating games. Students can offer feedback on other students' games reinforcing proper netiquette and there are elements of drag and drop programming for students to use in order to design their games. Gamestar Mechanic was designed with fourth through ninth graders in mind. However, in 2015, another edition of Gamestar Mechanic Jr. was released under the umbrella of PBS Kids. It's a simplified version of the original Gamestar Mechanic but designed for younger players to be able to create games and play quests created by others. Both versions support learning patterns and sequences in Math and motion and physics in Science. There are quite a few teaching resources available on Gamestar Mechanic's Twitter page @GamestarMech.

From the Sidelines to the Field

There are a number of strategies for inspiring other educators to embrace innovative equipment on the field. First, as the school librarian, exposing students to new tools before integrating them into the classroom teacher's core curriculum can reassure the teacher that the stress and frustration will be minimal. Second, highlight how students and/or other teachers are already using some of these gamification tools, even if they are outside your school community. Sometimes we need a visual picture of a tool's positive impact. Third, spend time with the teachers to launch innovation within the classroom. Avoid starting by showing them a new tool and then running off expecting them to implement your ideas. Make it known that you will launch the play and be there to support the subsequent usage of these tools. Ultimately, they will gain independence but don't expect that in the beginning. Plan to carve out enough of your time to support them. This may mean doing less in other areas in the beginning but, in the long run, you will have cultivated players who can hold their own and you can spread your resources elsewhere. Finally, encouragement is critical. Highlight powerful plays that they are already making and build from there. Gamestorm together to figure out the best entry points for gamification in their curriculum. Finally, consider targeting teachers that have challenging classrooms as it pertains to behavioral issues. Often, these teachers are looking for novel approaches to engaging their students and appreciate the offer of building a team together to positively impact their learning culture. Gamification can look very different across a variety of classrooms. Consider that there are multiple gamification strategies to establish new rules to gamify the learning.

CHAPTER SEVEN

Engineer the Learning to Be Awesome

"Engineering a weather vane was hard but it was cool. It was fun to see it all come together."

—Laurie, age 9

Engineering encourages significant creativity while having a huge effect on the learning culture with a high level of success assured. Engineering can lead to celebrating mistakes. When we discover mistakes, we are doing something right. We can create a culture that allows us to grow forward and improve. The engineering design process reinforces this concept. As Tom and David Kelley, authors of the book *Creative Confidence: Unleashing the Creative Confidence in All of Us*, write "early failure can be crucial to success in innovation. Because the faster you find weaknesses during an innovation cycle, the faster you can improve what needs fixing" (2013, 41). Before I start any engineering activity with students, I ask them if the engineers of the world have always had a blueprint or a map to follow before they start building. Obviously not. That's why engineering in education and learning by design means discovering issues or problems in a safe environment. Teaching students the value of developing prototypes, similar to the value of developing an outline before beginning a research paper, is a great habit to adopt. Marina Umaschi Bers, a co-founder of KinderLab Robotics, breaks down the engineering design process for early learners into a series of steps. These steps include:

- Ask
- Imagine
- Plan
- Create
- Test
- Improve
- Share

She notes that students can effectively enter into this design process at any phase of the process (Bers 2018). As learning coaches, school librarians and teachers can feel comfortable having their students work within this model, given the fluidity of the process.

The degree of structure that educators build into the engineering design process can vary depending upon the age of the learners. Beginning with this simplified engineering design process model, school librarians have the curricular expertise and the flexibility to develop an engineering culture that supports innovation.

The Fifty Yard Line: Meet in the Middle

There are a variety of entry points for engineering across the curriculum. I launched a makerspace in my school, which has become an innovation hub and will be discussed more in Chapter Nine. What I noticed, however, was that there was a high level of enthusiasm for makerspace activities that incorporated engineering. If this has been the experience in your school, then you already have a winning strategy upon which to build. Approach teachers to cultivate a partnership to engineer the curriculum. While some teachers are going to be more invested in the planning process than others, highlighting the growth of a library makerspace can demonstrate the effectiveness of giving students the opportunity to design and build their content. Students construct meaning when they think with their hands (Cleaver 2019). In the next sections, I will break down core subject areas and engineering opportunities within each of the content areas. The activities can be modified to accommodate different age groups. I have also discovered that creativity is sometimes stronger when fewer resources are available. Therefore, do not be discouraged by having limited supplies or materials with which to build. When it comes to engineering, less becomes more as it is a learning opportunity mimicking real-world scenarios in which resources are limited. Ultimately, what affects the effectiveness of a play is a strong partnership between the school librarian and the teacher. While some teachers may come around quicker than others in their willingness to innovate with engineering opportunities, student feedback and responsiveness eventually wins them over. Do not forfeit the game if your ideas are not immediately accepted. Eventually, they will meet you at the fifty-yard line.

Rising through the Ranks

One benefit of incorporating engineering into learning is collaboration to improve social-emotional growth. There are multiple potential solutions to one problem and when learners work together, their individual ideas influence the process in unexpected ways. As different ideas come together to form new solutions, each engineer can recognize that they have value in the process, which positively affects self-esteem. When one teammate appears to be on the outskirts with the rest of the group, it is an opportunity to fortify them with communication techniques to help them get back in the game. Additionally, students learn resilience when faced with failure. They develop coping skills that will train them to continue forging ahead as opposed to giving up when obstacles are encountered. The role of the school librarian is to reassure the students that when mistakes are made, that is an opportunity to ask more questions. In modeling this encouragement, all learners, the students and the adults that are present, begin to accept that facing challenges is an intentional component to the learning.

While it feels uncomfortable at first, it is important to embrace the obstacles and practice resilience with coping skills. One strategy for sending this message is that before beginning any engineering activity, remind students with their teacher present that they must first put on their "patience hats" before entering into the learning space. This piece of equipment, although invisible to the eye, is critical. Without these hats, we forget that not knowing all of the answers is necessary to reaching success. When putting on the patience hats becomes routine before the start of each activity, learners start to do this independently without your prompting. There are benefits to accepting the engineering design process as a learning strategy. Research shows that when students are not exposed to STEM-related activities prior to middle school, they are less likely to pursue a career in Science, Technology, Engineering or Math (Milgrom-Elcott 2018). Read on to discover elementary engineering activities, all of which can be modified to accommodate older students by infusing more curricular content and more sophisticated equipment, as described below.

littleBits Challenges: Fuel for the Imagination

Creating littleBits challenges centered around curricular content is one of my favorite engineering activities. littleBits are small magnetic circuits that snap together to create simple to complex inventions. Depending on the level of difficulty, an invention consists of some variation of a power source, an input bit, an output bit, and accessory bits. Bits can be purchased individually or there are a variety of littleBits kits available with a five percent educator discount at the littleBits website at https://littlebits.com/education. I recommend purchasing the kits and adding on individual bits when needed. littleBits allow for versatile logistical situations. littleBits challenges, in which students solve problems directly related to their curriculum, can be arranged so that multiple students can work together at one time, even with a limited supply of bits. I recommend limiting group sizes to four individuals. This ensures that each groupmate can work with at least one bit at the same time. The littleBits are easy to move around and take apart quickly. For example, if your school has enough littleBits to support two groups working at one time to complete a challenge, the other groups can participate in a different activity and then rotate to the littleBits station. Now, onto the actual challenges.

Consider the different unit studies for the early elementary students in your school. Ideally, this involves a conversation with the teachers in which they provide curricular goals and work with you to brainstorm meaningful challenges. In my experience, the intersection of creativity with specific content areas makes it fun to create engineering challenges with littleBits. It becomes a challenge in and of itself to create meaningful inquiry-based learning opportunities that support the curriculum. However, when relevant challenges are created, a moment of "This will be so great!" happens. The learners will pick up on your enthusiasm when you introduce the challenges. Involving students in older grades to help craft the challenges is another strategy to channel resources, get collaborative input, encourage student leadership, and demonstrate to other educators the value of collaboration. If, at first, some teachers are more reluctant to invest the time in co-creating challenges, perhaps you have a curriculum map or a "Year at a Glance" sheet available to help guide you in the content. Once other educators see the challenges at work, they will get into the game. Our class periods are fifty minutes long but I have done these challenges with students in twenty-minute blocks when necessary. When time is significantly limited, I create an outline that students see upon entering the learning space. For example, with a twenty-minute time limit, students are first put into groups of four. This is done quickly or it can be done by the teacher beforehand. Each group is assigned a table where the challenges, supplies, and blank paper and pencil for planning are ready and waiting for them. I give the groups five minutes to brainstorm and sketch. The design blueprints can be created on paper or on a whiteboard with dry erase markers. Teachers can help in these efforts as sometimes it is difficult to keep learners from wanting to jump into engineering before they plan out their ideas. Each group has ten minutes to build (this is why teamwork is so important). I set a timer on the Smartboard so they can pace themselves accordingly and manage their time. The last ten minutes are spent presenting and reflecting. When possible, I carve out space to display their finished work. I tend to give each group a different challenge so that during the presentations, the learners are exposed to different subtopics.

Here are some of my favorite challenges:

- Zoo Animals, shown in Table 7.1.
- Rocks and Minerals, shown in Table 7.2.
- Summer/end of school year, shown in Table 7.3 with an example shown in Figure 7.1.
- Novel studies, as shown in Table 7.4.

It can be fun to embed QR codes into the challenges to deepen the learning. For example, in one of the above rocks and minerals challenges, students can scan the QR code to view a YouTube video of cave explorers studying different rock formations.

Table 7.1   littleBits Zoo Animal Challenges Inspired by Zoo Atlanta

Design a lion cage that will light up when the door is opened.

Hint: You will need to use the light sensor.

Design an alarm for the zookeeper that she can control with a button to alert the zebras when she is nearby for feeding times.

Design a traffic light for a busy pedestrian road at the zoo so visitors don't run into each other.

Design a cooling system for the panda bears living space.

Table 7.2   Rocks and Minerals littleBits Challenges

 A quarry is a big manmade hole where rocks or minerals are taken from the ground and used for building materials. Create a shovel that will help the workers dig up rocks out of the quarry. After completing your design, compare what you engineered to the machinery that is used at this quarry.

Engineers use rocks, soils, and minerals when they design buildings, roads, foundations, electronics, bridges, cars, appliances and many types of objects. Design and build a structure out of littleBits that are constructed out of a mineral in real life.

We use certain materials for certain jobs. Why don't we use concrete for airplanes? Why don't we build pencils out of sand? Why don't we build windows out of clay? Why don't we build schools out of diamonds? The properties of the material determine what we use and where we use it. When building, engineers must pick the correct rocks, soils, and minerals so that their design will work, is safe, and is not too expensive. Engineer an object that is made out of the best rock, soil, or mineral for the job.

Sedimentary rocks are formed when soil deposits become compacted over time and eventually cement together. What are some items that can be made out of sedimentary rock? Build a prototype of that item.

 Extrusive, or volcanic, igneous rock is created when magma exits and cools above (or very near) the Earth's surface. These are the rocks that form at erupting volcanoes and oozing fissures. The magma, known as lava, can reach the surface. It can cool and solidify almost instantly when it is exposed to the relatively cool temperature of the atmosphere. What do you think this looks like? Build a prototype of a volcano erupting using littleBits to demonstrate the process of the formation of the igneous rock. When you are done, watch the video here to see an igneous rock formation in action.

A mineralogist is a type of geologist that studies minerals. One of the tools that they use is a chisel to chip away at materials that are covering the minerals discovered in the earth. Ridding minerals of debris helps mineralogists get a better, cleaner look at the mineral that they wish to study. Design a chisel that a mineralogist might find useful.

 Caves form naturally from the weathering of rock. Cave explorers encounter different types of rock formations. However, there is no electricity in the caves. Invent a device that cave explorers can wear to light up their path as they explore. After you complete this challenge, scan the QR code to watch these cave explorers in action. Notice the different rock formations in the caves! What type of rocks do you see?

Table 7.3   Summer/End of School Year Challenges

Summer is for reading! Invent a device to help you read. You decide what that is!	Create a device that you can use at summer camp.	You love to draw in your free time and summer offers more time for that. Create a drawbot.	Summertime is for visiting the park. Make a moveable playground activity.
Sipping cool lemonade on the porch is a summertime activity. Create a rocking chair to enjoy the breeze and some lemonade.	You love to joyride in the summer. Create a scooter to do just that!	Stars and Stripes is fun to visit in the summer. Create an arcade game that you can play.	Make a swing to enjoy at the park this summer.
Stone Mountain is fun to visit in the summer. Create a fireworks show set to music.	We love to visit the aquarium in the summer! Create an underwater scene with a swimming fish.	We have more time for entertainment in the summer. Invent something that entertains.	We get to enjoy more time with our pets over the summer. Invent something that is useful for a pet.
We love visiting Six Flags over the summer! Create an amusement park ride.	Summertime means more sunscreen. Invent a sunscreen dispenser. Use your imagination!	The nature center is awesome in the summertime. Create a beautiful spinning butterfly that you might see there!	We have to keep our room clean over the summer. Create a contraption that can help you with this. Be creative!

Natural Resources

The study of natural resources and the production of renewable energy can be fascinating through the lens of an engineer. Learning about water scarcity challenges students to consider their responsibilities as global citizens. Introducing them to water as a resource that drastically affects the degree to which a society can thrive encourages empathetic engineers.

Figure 7.1 An example of a summer-themed littleBits challenge to create an object for relaxation.

Your teachers probably have a preexisting lesson in which early learners are taught about the water cycle. They may recreate the water cycle through a hands-on activity using craft supplies or technology tools, such as Scratch, as mentioned in Chapter Five. School librarians can partner with teachers to take this learning beyond the classroom by reaching out to one of the many organizations that work hard to improve water conditions in developing countries. Often, these organizations will video chat with learners to help educate the larger community about their mission and to inspire social action.

Through an internet search, for example, I discovered Splash.org, a social justice organization headquartered in Seattle that works to provide children around the globe with access to clean water. As shown in Figure 7.2, they shared

Table 7.4   Students Chose Harry Potter-inspired Scenes and Characters

Recreate the book cover for *Harry Potter and the Cursed Child*.	Create a moving version of Dobby.	Recreate the scene in which Harry Potter sees his parents in the enchanted mirror.
Recreate the scene in which Moaning Myrtle haunts the restroom.	Create Harry Potter's home.	Create a Hippogriff inspired magic trick.
Create the scene of escaping the dragon's cave.	Create a young Harry Potter, scar included.	Create the scene when Harry Potter time travels through the sink.

a powerful presentation with our early elementary students and introduced them to same-age children in other parts of the world that suffer from being in communities that lack access to clean water and the ramifications on their quality of life. Through this exercise, our teachers were also inspired to take the study of water to the next level, reinforcing the value of collaboration.

After learning about the effect of a water shortage, students worked in small groups to design and build water filtration systems. As part of this lesson, we walked through a myriad of different water filtration systems that had already been invented and the

Figure 7.2 First graders in the United States learning about the Hygiene Club in India to support clean water efforts.

materials that went into making them. I created a Google slide presentation so that students could see the variety of approaches to solve this crisis. They learned about water filtration systems that include special straws, pitchers, buckets, and discovered the variety of machinery that has been invented to tap into clean water within the depths of the earth. They could see that so many individuals and organizations have committed themselves to solve the water shortage crisis. In turn, they were motivated to contribute their own efforts. Each group received a piece of poster board, straws, Popsicle sticks, pipe cleaners, paper, glue, tape, markers, Q-tips, and scissors. Their process was to brainstorm, sketch, prototype, and present. Each group was able to improve upon their designs by listening to the other groups share their ideas. Interestingly, our community had experienced a water boiling advisory the week before so one group took it upon themselves to build a heating system into their prototype. Another group engineered a contraption that could be used in higher elevations to expel clean water from cloud condensation. After their presentations were complete, we put their water filtration systems on display in our innovation and design studio.

In addition to building a water filtration system, another low-cost, high-impact engineering opportunity that focuses on access to clean water includes building a water well out of a pulley system. With craft sticks, straws, a Dixie cup, and string, challenge students to design and build a water well. Add another layer of science and incorporate simple machines by asking how many they can identify within their design. Both of the above examples were appealing because they presented engineering opportunities within the confines of the supplies that were available to our learners at that time. In the second example, more time can be spent on the process of excavating water from the earth. Brainstorming and exploring opportunities to incorporate engineering into the learning experience allows school librarians and teachers to pool their resources together to extend possibilities.

Once this partnership is established, additional opportunities arise. For example, the following year, we purchased the book, *The Water Walkers* by Joanne Robertson, which tells the true story of one tribe's cultural tradition to respect water as a valuable resource. From this story, we were inspired to join the global community of junior water walkers and adopt a body of water, a portion of the Chattahoochee River, to protect and preserve. To learn more about this initiative, information can be found at the following website: https://mrcssharesease.wordpress.com/junior-water-walkers.

In addition to joining the junior water walkers and as a symbol of the water cycle, we decided to bring the theme of water full circle within our larger school community. We participated in a one school, one read novel study of *A Long Walk to Water* by Linda Sue Park for our sixth through eighth-grade students. We planned a special morning of learning that incorporated a deep-dive discussion, creative writing, additional engineering challenges, and an art project into a meaningful collaboration between the school librarian, the administration, and the teachers. One engineering project can lead to a multitiered learning experience.

Another natural resource that presents powerful plays in engineering opportunities is air. Challenge students to brainstorm, design, and prototype a wind turbine to produce energy. The supplies can vary here as well. Our students used straws, paper, craft sticks both large and small, duct tape, wine bottle corks, paperclips, scissors, rubber bands, molding clay, straight pins, and wooden skewers. It was interesting to see significant variations in each groups' designs. I brought in a small fan so that groups could test their wind turbines. In order to have measurable data, fans (a hair dryer works too) should be set at the same speed and the wind turbines should be the same distance from the fan when testing each group's wind turbine air output. Groups were able to go back to their tables and make changes to their designs according to the amount of wind they were able to produce during their testing phase. Reflection for improvement is a key component of the engineering process. Prior to presenting their projects, students should reflect as a group. Reflection questions to consider include the following:

- Did you change your original design? Why?
- Are there any materials that you did not have available that you think would have worked better and if yes, which materials and why?
- Did you alter your product during the building process so that it is different than the original design that you sketched? If so, how?
- What are the pros and cons of wind turbines as a renewable energy source?
- What were the benefits of working within a team?

When our students presented their projects to one another, we were inspired by the variety of different solutions to this challenge. This engineering exercise also provides an opportunity to introduce students to Newton's laws of motion. A helpful teaching tool can be found here: https://go.nasa.gov/2F08XGH. With older students, creating wind turbines that measure the wind velocity using a DC voltmeter is possible too. These can be purchased for less than $15.00 at SparkFun.com, a website devoted to electronics literacy. To deepen the learning, connect with the American Academy of Environmental Engineers and Scientists (Moulden 2019) to arrange a videoconference lesson with your students on the engineering process to conserve natural resources.

Simple Machines

Regardless of your school environment, simple machines are more than likely an early component in your school's math and/or science curriculum. Some students are not fans of learning about simple machines but, interestingly, engineering simple machines can help win them over. Consider which grade level(s) have simple machines woven into their curriculum. Then, think of the grades before that one and consider introducing those learners to the concepts behind what makes simple machines work. Because simple machines are a part of so many everyday objects, it is possible to do a year-long curriculum to generate interest before it is mandated by standards. With LEGO, craft supplies, and Pinterest, the possibilities for understanding and creating with simple machines are endless. Early learners do not need to memorize the specific names of simple machines but exposing them to what they look like and how they work supports a more complex understanding as the year progresses. For example, gears are interesting mechanisms in that they are made of a simple shape that has the power to create energy when merged with another gear. To understand this concept, students who are ages four and up can use Play-Doh, water bottle tops, and either toothpicks or Q-tips to create two gears that turn when meshed together, as shown in Figure 7.3. Hands-on learning at its best.

When challenged to engineer a roller coaster, early learners can grasp the concept of an inclined plane. One of my favorite ways to launch a learning-by-design challenge is to incorporate a brown bag of mystery goodies, otherwise known as craft supplies. Given a marble, straws, paper and/or cardstock, scissors, and tape, students can build elaborate roller coasters that incorporate Newton's law of gravity. If working with older students, more complex mathematical concepts can be integrated including maximum velocity, slope, angle, and speed. Former middle school teacher and current college professor and author, John Spencer, has created amazing maker resources that include engineering challenges. Check

Figure 7.3 The littlest learners creating gears out of craft supplies and household items.

out his roller coaster challenge here: https://bit.ly/2s4E7nI. John Spencer's videos help launch creative engineering challenges. The challenges can be modified to suit different ages, the resources available, and different time constraints.

Wheels and axles present unique curricular connection opportunities as well. LEGO Engineering sells a LEGO robotics kit for educators especially designed for kindergarteners through second graders. The LEGO Education WeDo Software, available for download on a computer, allows learners to program the LEGO robots. They have a robust curriculum that incorporates force, friction, simple machines, and other target areas within science as outlined by the Next Generation Science Standards. The curriculum guide can be found here: https://bit.ly /2IMQBWV. In order for students to grasp the importance of design as it relates to functionality, one strategy is to start by having students create a robot that is outlined step by step in the curriculum guide. Ask them to point out the simple machines that are used within the design. Then, challenge students to create their own unique robot, not from the book but from their own imagination, that integrates a specific content area and includes a wheel and axle, or a different simple machine (see example in Figure 7.4).

Figure 7.4 Students integrated Judaic studies and created Noah's Ark that moves through the "water."

Engineering activities educate learners about how simple machines work and can connect with other content areas. For example, the creation of the water well within the above natural resources section incorporates a pulley system. The creation of a chisel among the littleBits rocks and minerals challenges uses a wedge. The water bottle tops used to create the gears referenced above are turned into screws. Building with one simple machine can involve incorporating the study of multiple simple machines.

Laws of Motion

Learning about Newton's Laws of Motion at a very early age may be overreaching a bit. However, exposing students to the concepts behind Newton's Laws of Motion is valuable in building an early foundation in science through engineering and design. For example, crafting a marble run offers an explanation about Newton's First Law of Motion. The marble will remain stagnant until the player tilts the box to create a force that moves the marble. Because the marble is small and lightweight, it only requires a small amount of force to create movement, demonstrating Newton's Second Law of Motion. Newton's Third Law of Motion states that for every action, there is an equal and opposite reaction. When the marble hits the side of the box, it is forced to move in the other direction to expel that energy. Marble runs can be made to be simple or complex. To start simple, use scotch tape, scissors, cardstock to build a shallow rectangular open-air box, plastic straws to tape to the bottom of the box to act as bumpers, and one marble to construct a portable marble run. The littlest engineers can learn about the concepts behind Newton's Laws of Motion through active learning.

Students love thinking about zip lines! In my experience, integrating zip lines into the learning generates excitement among students of all ages. Challenge students to build LEGO zip lines. The supplies needed include a box of LEGO and a length of rope that will work within your space. For upper elementary students and older, consider having them build a pulley system. Sound familiar? Be sure to point out the repetitive use of simple machines across the curriculum and across the grade levels. In the version that does not include building a pulley system, learners can build a platform surrounded by four walls. The two side walls can be connected with a bridge-shaped LEGO piece. This is the place through which the rope will run to create the zip line experience. If LEGO figures are available, place one inside the cart. If one is not available, have students craft a figure out of available supplies: Play-Doh, Q-tips, and/or construction paper, can suffice. When students work in groups of three, one student is at the base of the zip line, one is at the highest point, and one is responsible for creating force with the initial push. Ask students to consider the following questions that in addition to Newton's Laws of Motion also incorporate math:

- How does the angle of the slope affect the speed of the cart?
- What is a strategy for slowing down the cart's movement?
- What can slow down the gravitational pull that the cart experiences when force is applied (Newton's First Law of Motion/Inertia)?
- How does the tension, or how tight the rope is pulled, affect the cart's travel?
- How would you describe the friction that the LEGO cart experiences when traveling the zip line?

Zip lines can be constructed with different approaches depending upon the supplies available, an example is shown in Figure 7.5.

Pom-pom launchers make for great engineering challenges that incorporate Newton's First Law of Motion. An object (the pom-pom) will remain at rest until acted on by an unbalanced force (a tap of the finger). This challenge can be approached with a mystery bag too. Supplies can include Popsicle sticks, pom-poms, masking tape, a spoon, large marshmallows, a paper cup, scissors, and plastic straws. It is also helpful to have a ruler on

Figure 7.5 The library becomes a zip line adventure park.

hand. There are different variations of a pom-pom launcher that can be created from these supplies, one of which is shown in Figure 7.6.

Questions to consider:

- How far did you launch your pom-pom?
- What do you think affects the distance of your pom-pom launch?
- What do you think affects the height of your pom-pom launch?
- How can you rework your design so that your pom-pom travels further?
- How does working within a small team affect your engineering process?
- How did your original design idea change from your completed pom-pom launcher? Why?

Middle or high school teachers who teach physics can partner with school librarians and have their students design a catapult in Tinkercad while taking force and trajectory into consideration to maximize the catapult's effectiveness. The school librarian incorporates research into the design process so that students research different types of catapults, how they have evolved, and designs that have proven to be effective. Students will need to also consider how the mass of the object they plan to launch will affect the distance that the object flies. If your school has a 3D printer, once students have committed to a catapult design, the catapults can be 3D printed and put to use. Consider having students build a model out of craft supplies prior to creating their 3D print design in a 3D modeling

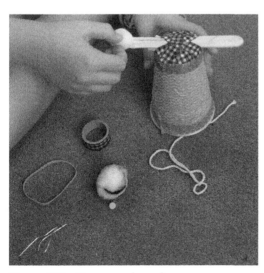

Figure 7.6 Pom-pom launcher.

software, such as Tinkercad. Each layer of prototyping that goes into the catapult design will result in changes to improve its effectiveness. Ask students to track the changes that they make throughout the iteration process. They can gain a broader perspective of the evolution of their projects and an appreciation for each phase of the design-build process.

Sphero structures present numerous opportunities for students to demonstrate

Newton's Laws of Motion. Sphero is a small round robot that can be programmed to move, change colors, and execute programs created on a mobile device. Sphero structures are structures built out of cardboard and other materials to influence the ways in which Sphero interacts with the world. Examples include a multilevel house or a building accessible by an elevator or ramp, a chariot to improve Sphero's mobility, or an obstacle course for Sphero to demonstrate programming challenges. Each Sphero structure can incorporate the Laws of Motion. See the Sphero challenge examples shown in Table 7.5.

Newton's Cradle is a source of fascination for students. Inexpensive versions can be purchased on Amazon.com to demonstrate Newton's Laws of Motion. Challenge students to engineer their own Newton's Cradle. There are a variety of building materials that can be used. In our case, we used string, Popsicle sticks, cardboard platforms, marbles, plastic straws, and masking tape. How does Newton's Cradle demonstrate the

Table 7.5 Sphero Robotics Challenges That Incorporate the Laws of Motion

Newton's Laws of Motion	Explanation	Sphero Challenges
Newton's First Law of Motion	An object at rest tends to stay at rest, and an object in motion tends to stay in motion, with the same direction and speed. Motion (or lack of motion) cannot change without an unbalanced force acting.	Build a chariot for Sphero. How does the chariot affect the force required to move Sphero forward ten centimeters within five seconds?
Newton's Second Law of Motion	The acceleration of an object produced by an applied force is directly related to the magnitude of the force, the same direction as the force, and inversely related to the mass of the object.	Build a ramp as part of an obstacle course for Sphero. How does the angle of the ramp affect the force required to propel Sphero up the ramp and the acceleration?
Newton's Third Law of Motion	For every action, there is an equal and opposite reaction.	Create a home for Sphero. What happens if Sphero runs into the wall? How does this relate to Newton's Third Law of Motion?

conservation of momentum? How is the energy of one ball converted to kinetic energy? How does Newton's Cradle demonstrate Newton's First Law of Motion? Does the string have to be the same length? Why? Do the marbles need to be the same size and weight? Why? Does the base on which the Newton's Cradle sit have to be flat? Why? These are all questions for the groups to consider. Reflection allows each group to learn new knowledge from one another.

Climate

Climate, as defined by *Merriam-Webster*, is the average condition of the weather at a place over a period of years as evident by temperature, wind velocity, and precipitation. Engineering and climate can be approached through the back door. Consider focusing on skyscrapers, which tend to have an air of mystery and appeal for learners of all ages. Something that towers over others casting deep shadows from high in the sky is fairly fascinating. What is even more fascinating, however, is how engineers have to consider the climate in which they build skyscrapers so that the skyscrapers can sustain the elements over long periods of time.

I first considered this when exploring the Skyscraper app created by an award-winning app developer, Tinybop. Tinybop creates high-quality, educational, animated mobile device apps that cover a variety of topics including weather, skyscrapers, simple machines, the Earth, and space. The apps are $2.99 and are available for both iOS and Android devices. Under the education volume licensing discount, twenty or more of the apps can be purchased for $1.49. The Tinybop website has free educational handbooks to accompany each app that provide teaching guides and questions for consideration. If funds are available to purchase the Skyscraper app, for example, it is a powerful learning tool to explore foundational requirements and building materials in relationship to climate. Within the app, users can change the weather conditions to include wind, lightning, or an earthquake to explore the effect of these changing weather conditions. Engineers of skyscrapers must also consider the materials and structural shapes that will best suit different weather conditions. A skyscraper built in Dubai may require very different building materials than a skyscraper built in Chicago. Users can explore the materials that sit under the foundation of the skyscrapers, such as dirt and fossils. How does the earth affect how skyscrapers are built? In connection with the natural resources mentioned in an earlier section, how must engineers consider access to water in how they construct the pipes and the flow of electricity for all of the building's tenants? All of these questions are interconnected. Challenge students to engineer their own skyscraper that takes each of these questions into consideration. How can they design a skyscraper that will respect the planet while meeting its tenants' needs? Supplies can vary but may include Play-Doh or modeling clay, straws, pipe cleaners, Popsicle sticks, package tape, cardboard, cardstock, scissors, construction paper, and markers. If using cardboard, investing in a few pairs of cardboard scissors can be helpful. We use the CANARY cardboard scissors, which are available at Amazon.com for under $18.00 per pair.

Much of the engineering process is driven by questions. What if a building had to exist in an arctic climate? How would the arctic climate influence its structure? What type of building materials would be necessary to withstand significant amounts of snow over long periods of time? How can the shape of the structure help deflect the weight of the snow? Challenge students to consider these questions and with twenty toothpicks and both large and small marshmallows task them with building a structure that can withstand snow. Test their snow forts by chugging a series of large marshmallows at the completed structures. Which group's structure withstood the pressure of the "snow"? How was their structure different? How did they build their foundation? What shape was their structure? What would they do differently next time? Why?

Using the same factors, such as climate conditions, residents' needs, and available building materials, inspire middle school or high school students to be empathetic global citizens with a similar challenge. As members of the Red Cross disaster service team, challenge them to simulate the building of a disaster-proof housing structure working within the confines of a budget and available resources. This engineering challenge integrates financial literacy, geography, science, math, and research skills. They select a climate disaster to research, such as a hurricane, flood, or windstorm. As part of their research, require that they specify areas where these particular disasters are more likely to occur. Based on their research, they should select a geographic location as their focus. Provide them with a budget, a price list for a set amount of supplies, as shown in Table 7.6, and challenge them to build disaster-proof housing for a family of four in their chosen geographic area. They will need to consider the supplies accessible in that part of the world and the environmental conditions, all of which can be learned through their research process.

For the Love of Libraries (and Math)

Take hold of that new teacher in your building! Help them. Make yourself a friend. Most importantly, cultivate a relationship to partner with

Table 7.6   Sample Price List for Building Material Supplies to Accompany an Engineering Challenge

Price List	
Pipe Cleaners (Insulation)	$1.00 per square foot
Plastic Straws (Bamboo)	$2.50 per foot
Popsicle Sticks (Wood)	$2.50 per square foot
Clay (Clay Bricks)	$2.00 per square foot
Rope (Steel Binding Wire)	$1,000 per ton
Masking Tape (Nails)	$11.00 per 3,000
Cardboard (Drywall)	$2.00 per square foot
Duct Tape (Cement)	$5.00 per square foot
Scissors (Hand Saw)	$10.00 each
Foam Sheets (Sheet Metal)	$11.00 per 2 × 2 ft

them. We gained a new middle school math teacher and, as part of his role, he teaches eighth-grade advanced math. After some discussions early in the school year, we decided to brainstorm effective math projects for his students that would benefit others, incorporate engineering and math skills, and encourage creativity. The creative component is important. Tony Wagner, author of the book *Creating Innovators: The Making of Young People*, notes that creativity can be nurtured to produce innovators when given the opportunity (2012, 16). The first year, we worked together so that the students would invent helpful tools for the teacher. The second year, however, we became a bit bolder. I love libraries and he loves math so it was a perfect partnership to brainstorm the creation of a Little Free Library. Free resources are available at the Little Free Libraries website to guide students as they tap into different subject areas across the curriculum to design and build a Little Free Library for the middle school campus. They can be found at the following link: https://littlefreelibrary.org/build.

Using Tinkercad software with the school librarian, students design and print a replica of a little library as a prototype for their larger project. Using the blueprints available from the Little Free Library Sharing Network, students measure the materials needed during a field trip to Home Depot. Measuring the materials so that they are accurate in size is critical to the process and is supervised by the math teacher. Then, with the assistance of the art teacher, students design a unique outer display for the walls of the library that includes the school logo. The collaboration among content-specific teachers and a group of advanced math students results in a touchdown, a fabulous addition to the school community for all to use and enjoy.

Holidays

As a Jewish school, we follow the Jewish calendar of events recognizing, learning about, and celebrating Jewish holidays. There are a variety of approaches to incorporate engineering into holiday celebrations or learning about areas that are not outlined in national curricular standards or teaching manuals. For example, our school celebrates Shabbat, which is considered a day of rest to recognize God's day of rest on the seventh day of creation. The Judaic Studies teacher was looking for ways to encourage students to understand what it means to rest on the Sabbath. In brainstorming together, we developed a lesson in which students were partnered in groups of four that included two kindergarten-prep students and two fourth-grade students. We are constantly looking for opportunities to encourage student leadership roles. Each small group was given a mystery bag that contained a marble, plastic straws, Popsicle sticks, paper, tape, and scissors. You may have noticed that the craft supplies overlap from project to project. I employ this strategy to keep the budget down. Just as the content drives the engineering process, the materials on hand influence the specific projects we choose to tackle. In each bag, students also found a small piece of paper that included the following message:

> The entire week is about constant motion. Shabbat is about ceasing the movement to conclude the week we have just had. It is a day of rest. Using the materials in your bag, please create a contraption from your imagination that demonstrates movement and then an abrupt cease of motion. Think creatively and work together as a group. You will find all of the materials that you need in your brown bag but please share the tape in the classroom. There are multiple solutions to this challenge. In your small group, please discuss the answer to the questions below and be prepared to share with the larger group:
>
> 1. How does the contraption that your group built represent the movement that takes place in your daily life?
> 2. How does the obstacle that you created to cease motion represent our observance of Shabbat?
> 3. What would have made this activity easier? For example, would it have been easier working alone, in a larger group, with other supplies? Please explain.
> 4. Does this activity make you think differently about how you will observe Shabbat? Why or why not?

Figure 7.7 Community of tiny houses built of craft supplies and LED lights.

A timer was set and students were tasked with engineering a contraption as referenced above to demonstrate the observance of Shabbat. As you can imagine, the conversation was rich, the inventions were unique, and the sharing of each group's final product generated deep reflections on the ways in which we understand and recognize Shabbat each week.

The Judaic studies teacher also has the curricular goal of teaching students about Pirsum Ha'Neis or publicizing the miracle. It is the guiding principle for lighting the menorah and showcasing it in a window so that it is visible to those that pass by in the community. She and I worked together to engineer the students learning to create a community of light. Students built tiny houses or buildings made of paper. They were given a paper template as a blank canvas to contribute to their community of light. Their community included many details. Not only did they build power lines but they included identifying characteristics of our own community such as the local bagel shop and a synagogue.

For this activity, I provide the lesson in circuitry teaching students how to build a simple circuit out of copper tape, an LED light, and a coin cell battery. The Judaic Studies teacher provides the Judaic content in conjunction with the curricular goal. We are very proud of our little community. A video of our creation the first year that we did this project can be viewed by scanning the QR code in Figure 7.7.

Our middle school students have been learning about the Jewish New Year, Rosh Hashanah, since they can remember. As an innovative twist to merge their understanding of Rosh Hashanah's cultural traditions and the engineering design process, students were challenged to build a Rosh Hashanah-themed cantilever. Most students had not heard of a cantilever before this activity. Cantilevers are beams supported at one end that carry a load at the other unsupported end. We brainstormed examples of when cantilevers might be useful and where we have seen them in use. We also talked about the traditions that we enjoy during Rosh Hashanah, one of which is eating apples and honey for a sweet new year. Students were challenged to build a cantilever to support an apple. The rules were as follows:

1. The structure must be at least 9 inches in length from the edge of the table.
2. The ruler may only be used for measuring, not as part of your cantilever.

3.   The apple must be at the very tip of your structure.

4.   The apple may not be punctured. It must remain intact.

5.   You will have twenty-five minutes to plan and build your cantilever.

Middle schoolers love a good competition and it quickly became a race to see who followed the rules and reached success. It was a fun approach to recognize the holiday in an inventive way, teach the students a new vocabulary word (cantilever), and consider gravitational pull to create support for their apple.

Engineer to Assess

Lesson planning is similar to the engineering process. Teachers scaffold lessons that allow students to learn about a particular topic and apply their learning to situations that generate a deeper understanding of a subject matter. Ensuring that the content has been retained is important in the lesson planning process. According to Indiana University's Center for Innovative Teaching and Learning (n.d.), student assessment serves as research for the educator to evaluate the effectiveness of their teaching strategies and if students can demonstrate their learning. Engineering-infused activities can serve as an alternative assessment strategy. The benefit to engineering-based assessments is that students are given the opportunity to show their learning, as opposed to telling their learning. There is an opportunity for collaborative interactions, increased engagement, creative application, and guided inquiry. Each of these components is a part of the American Association of School Librarians (AASL) standards framework for learners. The domains and competencies within the framework include think, share, create, and grow (AASL 2018). Engineering to assess also increases communication between the educator and the learner. Rather than returning a graded test with red marks on it, educators can engage in meaningful, rich discussions with their learners about their engineering designs and the thought that went into modeling their learning. This type of assessment lends itself to deeper relationships and additional practice of social interactions in professional settings. School librarians are well positioned to challenge educators to rethink their assessment practices and provide the support to innovate the long-standing practice of traditional assessments that include quizzes, exams, and research papers. Each of the skills required for these traditional forms of assessment is still integrated into the practice of engineering for assessment.

Educators witness the application of knowledge, as opposed to the regurgitation of knowledge.

What the Research Says

Not all school librarians employ assessment methods into their teaching practices. This can be for a variety of reasons. These reasons can include not being expected or granted permission to grade their students, assessments were not a formal component of their library training, or perhaps it is viewed as taking the joy out of library visits meant to instill a love of reading. Engineering offers opportunities to assess student growth and demonstrate the school librarian's value in student instruction, without learners feeling the scrutiny that can come with traditional assessments. Judi Moreillon, former school librarian and retired school librarian educator, notes that evaluative techniques hold adults accountable for improving learning communities, resources, and outcomes (Moreillon 2019, 6). When assessment data is used to demonstrate value, make positive revisions for improvement, or grow a school's resources, it becomes a beneficial tool. Regardless of whether or not assessments are a common practice in your school library, school librarians should consider adopting and influencing the assessment process when working as instructional partners with other educators.

Engineering for assessment falls within what is considered authentic assessment. Authentic assessment is defined by *Merriam-Webster* as "a set of methods or techniques for assessing the academic achievement of a student that includes activities requiring the application of acquired knowledge and skills to real-world situations and that is often seen as an alternative to standardized testing." Indiana University's Center for Innovative Teaching and Learning offers tangible strategies for crafting authentic assessments that can be applied to engineering challenges in order to demonstrate the learning. Their list of strategies for evaluating active learning can be found on their website at https://citl.indiana.edu/teaching-resources /assessing-student-learning.

Because school librarians are trained to improve information literacy skills, we work against ourselves when we avoid partnering with other educators to formulate meaningful assessments. Learners can and should be held accountable for the twenty-first-century skills that librarians work so hard to instill. Innovative assessments model the type of iterative thinking that school librarians can encourage other educators to adapt to better connect with and relate to their students. Students are going to school on the internet learning whatever it is they wish to learn with the click of a mouse. One role of the school librarian is to help an educator evolve too in assessing the changing ways in which their students' are learning. Because there have been significant iterations in the learning process, assessment practices should reflect these iterations with collaborative authentic assessment models, including engineering. Research shows that not only do students benefit from school librarian and teacher partnerships but so do the teachers and the school librarians themselves. Teachers learn more about how to teach the inquiry process and critical thinking skills while school librarians learn more about the specific curricular content (McNee and Radmer 2017).

Assessment in Action

Developing authentic assessments to evaluate projects that learners engineer to demonstrate their knowledge can be broken down into four main tasks. The first is to consider the curricular goal or the objective of the learning. For example, a curricular goal may be to determine reading comprehension. The next task is to mimic a real-world scenario so that students have to participate in an authentic task. For example, if students read the novel *Bubble Boy* by Stewart Foster, a coming of age story that focuses on diseases and disabilities, readers can be challenged to build a prototype of a protective suit for the eleven-year-old boy, Joe, so that he can leave his hospital room and go out into the world without being exposed to germs and/or illnesses that can complicate his preexisting medical condition. Integrating math can require that prototypes be proportional to his size (scale factors can be used to represent larger dimensions). The next step is to develop criteria for the task. One approach to developing criteria is to consider what a poor prototype would look like and flip the language so that positive expectations are specified. For example, if one concern is that the students will not present a descriptive view of the setting as part of their oral presentation, require that students integrate a minimum of three descriptions of Joe's hospital environment to reflect their understanding of Joe's restrictions in such a controlled environment. Finally, create a rubric that reinforces the above requirements. The rubric, as shown in Table 7.7, outlines the ideal standards for the engineered design and the presentation in a collaborative setting.

The Authentic Assessment Toolbox published by the National Education Association (NEA) provides a step-by-step guide for creating authentic assessments that can be applied to design-build projects intended to demonstrate student learning (Nast 2017). This resource can be found at the following link: http://www.nea.org/tools/lessons/57730.htm.

Table 7.7   Sample Rubric for Authentic Assessment of Engineering a Novel Study

Criteria	1	3	5
Planning the Prototype	Did not sketch out a design or consider available supplies before building	Began building without a plan but considered the supplies available	Sketched a design prior to starting and took the available materials into consideration when creating design sketch
Effectiveness of Suit	Did not integrate Joe's specific needs into the protective suit prototype	Oral presentation included some of the reasons for specific features constructed within Joe's suit however, sizing needs were not taken into account	Oral presentation included the reasons for the features built into Joe's protective suit and was built to a scale representative of the average size of an eleven-year-old boy with Joe's condition
Collaborative Efforts	Not every team member contributed equally to different phases of the project	Little communication so that most project tasks were done within a silo making it difficult for the end product to come together in synchronicity	Each team member put in equal amounts of work and communicated openly and effectively throughout the process resulting in a well-organized understanding of one another's roles
Understanding of Main Plot Components	The oral presentation did not address at least two of the following: Setting Supporting Characters Moral Dilemma(s)	The oral presentation described only two of the following: Setting Supporting Characters Moral Dilemma(s)	The oral presentation described the role of two supporting characters within Joe's life, described the setting of the story, and demonstrated the moral dilemma(s) that the characters faced within the novel. Total Points: / 25

Huddle Up to Excel at Engineering

In order to excel at integrating engineering into the learning process so that it is valued as an innovative tool within the classroom, school librarians need to know the skill sets of the other players. By taking an inventory of the current knowledge base, school librarians will have a better understanding as to which areas may require more training and guidance while out on the field. It is important to consider that while you may not have specific training in engineering, chances are neither do the teachers. As the school librarian, however, you are resourceful in putting together the pieces of information that you need to create powerful plays in learning. Consider that other educators are looking to you to be the expert. Often, being the expert simply means being the support system, a teacher, and a partner throughout this process. In fact, research shows that teachers would be more inclined to integrate STEM into their interdisciplinary subjects if they had more resources and technology support, more planning time with colleagues, and more professional development training. The school librarian is the key to each of these components. School librarians are resourceful and can offer technical support, school librarians can leverage their schedules to plan with colleagues, regardless if on a fixed or a flexible schedule, and as connected educators, school librarians can serve as leaders in professional development (Shernoff et al. 2017). Embrace the opportunity to be a guide and support educators to engineer the learning.

Supporting Teammates

There are a number of strategies to support different teachers with cultivating their resources for engineering, helping them plan, and offering professional development. I have yet to encounter a school in which the resources are infinite. Take inventory of what you currently have. Once you have a list of the supplies that are currently available, create a WANTED poster of those educators you would like to collaborate with on a joint project to engineer the content. Convince them of your value by sharing that they will have someone with whom to share the work, assist with classroom management, brainstorm ideas, and to help teach the content, to name just a few of the benefits. Together, make a list of the supplies that you will need to collaborate on this particular project. Let them know what resources that you have available to contribute and ask them to share what they have available to contribute. If you fall short, I am a big fan of the mass email to other educators in the building asking for supplies. If I don't think I can replenish the supplies, I make that known in my initial ask. Otherwise, I let them know when they can expect to have the supplies replaced or returned as these factors will influence their willingness to share. I am often surprised by not only how many educators (and sometimes individuals in the business office) respond to these requests but I am surprised too by which educators respond. It is often someone unexpected so if I had not made the initial larger request, I would have never known that they would be so willing to share their supplies. It is nice to build a culture of sharing and support. If there is no luck from colleagues in gaining the resources that are needed, my favorite word to get administrator buy-in for acquiring new or additional resources is "pilot." This is an example of what I might say to my boss:

> The Judaic Studies teacher and I would like to pilot a new program in which engineering and design challenges allow our students to work collaboratively to broaden their knowledge of the Jewish faith using criteria that focuses on inquiry, critical thinking, evaluating information, improving oral presentation skills, and that also integrates math, science, engineering, and art. I would also like to invite the marketing director to the student presentations as they may want to advertise the benefits of this collaborative process at our innovative school.

It works. Trust me. I googled my name, my school's name, and the word innovation and sure enough, I counted seven articles alone on the first two pages of my Google search that reference collaborative work with other teachers. Don't discredit the value of inviting an audience to garner support that will ultimately translate into more resources. I shared this strategy with another colleague who voiced disappointment in having to go through these efforts to gain additional resources. I urge you not to look at it in a negative way. Even when we have support, sometimes we need more. I choose to look at this approach as a win for all. By bringing others into our learning spaces, we grow our networks and our support base.

Sometimes, planning can be trickier than acquiring resources. If working on a fixed schedule that does not allow for common planning time with a teacher, it is worth considering if schedules can be moved around a bit. For example, I have traded an afternoon carpool duty so that I can be free to meet with a homeroom teacher after school when they do not have carpool. I have offered to meet them in their classroom at the start of the school day when their students are getting unpacked and settled. I ask a responsible fifth grader to oversee the library in my absence, with their teacher's permission. This at least buys me thirty minutes with a teacher to come up with a plan of action. A lot of communication happens over email. I also love the tool Voxer, which is a walkie-talkie application. Voxer is a free digital platform that can be installed as an app on a mobile device or used via the internet to communicate back and forth in real time or on your own time. Voxer takes some of the mystery out of email communication in that you can hear the other person's tone and they can express themselves freely through verbal communication.

Middle and high school librarians tend to have more flexible scheduling. Prioritizing the time to meet with subject-specific teachers is critical. Whether it is over lunch, during their planning period, before or after school, carving out the time to run through a plan is worthwhile. Again, being able to demonstrate the value in these collaborative partnerships is critical to gaining support from administrators to reserve collaborative planning time as a routine part of the school librarian's role. As a result, the need for creative efforts on the part of the school librarian may dwindle when others start to recognize the value in this planning time.

School librarians are so fortunate to have a wealth of support via Facebook, Twitter, Instagram, and through professional associations, online webinars, face-to-face educational conferences, and from informative books. Leveraging these resources often means that we *are* the professional development for other educators. We go out there and gain new knowledge, curate it, alter it to make it work for our school environment, share it, and work together to implement it. Innovation doesn't happen in a silo. We are responsible for being the change we wish to see. Gaining credibility to offer professional development among our colleagues sometimes means pointing out that we have a unique vantage point. Chances are you are only one of a few faculty members that have an experience similar to that of your administrators *and* the other educators. You work with everyone on your campus: all faculty, all students, all parents, all staff. Everyone. This is similar to administration. Plus, you are "in the trenches" teaching alongside the teachers. This vantage point gives school librarians power to make suggestions that have credibility simply due to our unique lens. Media and technology specialists can leverage this position to create growth in school culture, which often leads to growing resources. It is up to us to demonstrate that we have a unique lens when it comes to community needs and areas for growth. It isn't necessarily obvious.

Resources for Engineering in Education

There are quite a few useful resources to support school librarians in their efforts to craft meaningful engineering experiences for students. In addition to the Future Ready Librarians Facebook group, there are a number of online resources that outline the design process, provide high-quality integration ideas for inspiration, and that educate the non-engineer on effective engineering strategies.

- Novel Engineering (http://www.novelengineering.org): Novel Engineering offers an innovative approach to integrate engineering into literacy in elementary and middle school. High school teachers, however, can gain ideas for inspiration and approaches to engineering in literacy. Check out the section entitled Classroom Books to get ideas for how novel studies can translate into engineering activities.

- Engineering is Elementary (https://www.eie.org): A project of the National Center for Technological Literacy at Boston's Museum of Science, EIE develops curriculum to integrate engineering into different subject areas. They offer professional development and provide research to support the benefits of engineering in education.

- The Stanford d.school (https://dschool.stanford.edu): The d.school offers resources to support the design thinking approach, a creative method, for individuals to solve real-world problems.

- PBS Kids Design Squad (https://pbskids.org/designsquad): This portion of PBS Kids provides an online library of engineering activities and guides by topic for the youngest learners to high schoolers.

- TryEngineering (https://tryengineering.org): This organization, a suborganization of the professional technical organization for the advancement of technology, offers resources, lesson plans, and activities for educators to implement innovative engineering activities into the learning.

- eGFI (http://teachers.egfi-k12.org): This organization's name stands for "engineering, go for it." Their website shares powerful lessons to promote and enhance efforts to integrate STEM and engineering into educational practices.

Each of the above resources offers great launch pads to get started with engineering in the curriculum for students in preschool through high school. Keep in mind that activities can be modified to accommodate curricular goals, time constraints, and variations among age groups. Browsing these resources will certainly provide the inspiration to get started, which is often just what is needed.

CHAPTER EIGHT

Leveraging a Love of YouTube

"Sharing my projects on YouTube allows other people to believe they can code and lets other people know they can create something meaningful."

—Zoe, age 10

Most kids today are intrigued by or want to be their own YouTube star. This may be difficult for us to understand, or maybe not. Despite our personal opinions, YouTube commands power in the eyes of young learners. There has been an evolution in how kids gauge popularity. Some kids view YouTube as a gateway to a higher status. No more are the days in which verbal chatter and perceptions of face-to-face encounters are the primary influencers of how kids rank themselves among their peers. Instead, students judge their status by how many virtual views and how many likes they receive. Add into the mix the fact that this is all very public and kids feel the pressure to matter digitally. If so much stock is placed on how far-reaching one's digital persona is, then it is sure to infiltrate other aspects of growth, including education. This chapter will explore how school librarians and other educators can innovatively leverage YouTube to transform a learning culture so that the learning experience feels relevant and critical to today's students.

Any Given School Day

You may be familiar with the 1999 hit movie, *Any Given Sunday*, directed by Oliver Stone and featuring Al Pacino, Cameron Diaz, Jamie Foxx, and a host of other stars. The premise of the movie is that when given the field, or a place from which to shine, unlikely characters will sometimes emerge as the stars. In the film, a third-string quarterback is called into the game with little warning due to injuries suffered by the starting quarterback and the second-string quarterback. The third-string quarterback rises to the occasion, ultimately becoming a star player throughout the season and leading the team to victory. The injuries of the other two star players presented this third-string quarterback with unexpected opportunities allowing him an audience with whom to share his talent. YouTube is appealing for this reason. It provides a stage on which anyone can share their talents. We could be discussing any number of video hosting sites but YouTube has cornered the market. YouTube's website notes that users view over 1 billion hours of video each day with over 1,000,000,000 users, representing one-third of the internet (2019).

Patricia Lange, author of the book *Kids on YouTube: Technical Identities and Digital Literacies*, notes that some video creators on YouTube are motivated by the ability to commercialize their ideas while others are inspired to use YouTube as a way to connect with a small group of close friends. Despite the differences in the motivation behind YouTube usage, the common wish is to share individual experiences, thoughts, or ideas (2016, 16). Learners can share their content knowledge with a preexisting or a developing fanbase on the digital field. This digital field allows learners to develop their media literacy skills in an educational setting that with guidance can positively influence how they craft their digital tattoo.

The Digital Field

Uploading content to YouTube signifies reaching the end zone and scoring a touchdown. It's the final stage in the creation process. It's crossing over into the next zone to share a victory with a larger audience. When students have an audience to share their work with and gain instant feedback, as well as an audience to collaborate with, they are motivated to create learner-generated content (Ramsay 2014, 57). There are a number of examples to support this notion. The biggest piece of evidence to support the value that people feel when they gain an audience is the existence and wild success of social media tools. Individuals would not spend as much time on social media as they do if they did not value this form of digital interaction. Common Sense Media reports that tweens ages eight to twelve average six hours of media usage per day for entertainment purposes (Rideout 2015, 15). Celebrities, strangers, family, friends, and colleagues feel closer to us when we can peer into their lives and interact with them through social media. Instagram, Twitter, YouTube, Facebook, and Snapchat, for example, all thrive as a result of society's desire to share and interact. There are benefits to creating a learning culture in which students share their own content. These benefits include the following:

- Receiving instant feedback
- Gaining satisfaction from sharing work with larger audiences
- Creating opportunities to make personal connections
- Collaborating beyond classroom walls
- Developing digital skills for media literacy
- Establishing expertise in content areas
- Learning to manage the dissemination of information

Now that we have outlined some of the benefits, let us consider how we can get teachers to create a digital field for their students.

A Crash Course in YouTube

The primary obstacle that teachers may face in leveraging YouTube usage in their learning community is feeling like they do not have the necessary comfort level or know-how to keep their students safe or the ability to navigate the digital nuances of the tool. This is where school librarians come into play. Sometimes, teachers need individual attention with a tool like YouTube to get them started. A little personal attention and encouragement can go a long way. For example, there have been countless times where I have popped into a teacher's classroom to see awesome student work that could be transformed by sharing their content on a digital platform to access a larger audience. It allows teachers to receive positive feedback from parents and sometimes other educators. Students feel additional pride in their work for the ability to share beyond the class. The school librarian can break down the barriers of fear or the lack of knowledge to get teachers actively creating and participating in an innovative culture of sharing. Approach YouTube teacher training step by step:

1. As outlined previously, make sure to demonstrate the value of sharing student work on a global platform.

2. Help teachers create a log in. While this may seem like an easy step for them to accomplish, you might be surprised by how often this step is a primary obstacle. One common reason is that teachers do not want to merge their personal Gmail accounts with their professional lives. Help teachers by walking through the process of using their school email address as the email

address to log into YouTube when using it for school purposes. To do this, teachers need to be logged out of all Google apps. Then, they go to YouTube .com and click on the sign in option. From there, they will select *Use another account* and then select *Create account*. Now, they will be at the page that allows them to input their first and last name, an email address of their choice, which can be their school email address, as well as a password to create their Google account that will allow them to post on YouTube.

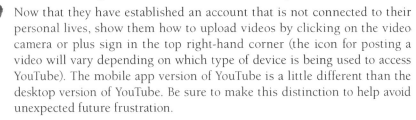

3. Now that they have established an account that is not connected to their personal lives, show them how to upload videos by clicking on the video camera or plus sign in the top right-hand corner (the icon for posting a video will vary depending on which type of device is being used to access YouTube). The mobile app version of YouTube is a little different than the desktop version of YouTube. Be sure to make this distinction to help avoid unexpected future frustration.

4. Demonstrate how to edit titles of videos so that they are labeled accurately. Because YouTube automatically generates its own video titles, this is an important step to ensure that videos are well organized and easy to identify and locate.

5. Very importantly, explain how the privacy settings work. Be sure to educate teachers on the difference between public, private, and unlisted. As a rule, we establish our privacy settings as unlisted so that those people that we share the link with can access the videos. While this does require that we are more thoughtful about where and how we share the links, unlisted as the privacy setting has worked well for us.

6. Finally, be sure to review how to share the link to the videos. Again, this may feel obvious but in my experience, it is not intuitive nor is it obvious to someone who is truly sharing via YouTube for the first time.

When educators feel that you are on their team by running the field with them, you are building trust and earning credibility to be partners in innovation in future endeavors. It starts with the relationship.

Practical Applications of YouTube

There is value in YouTube when it comes to usage in formal education. First, YouTube can be one application among a series of other apps that are used to create and to share a meaningful project, otherwise known as the process of app-smashing. Second, YouTube can also be used to win students over by building enthusiasm for sharing content that they are responsible for creating. This added responsibility provides a sense of ownership, flexibility, independence, deeper interest, and higher self-esteem (Kearney and Schuck 2005). Third, uploading content on YouTube allows learners to improve their technical skills and their ability to navigate the nuances involved in sharing content. How restrictive will the privacy settings be? Will there be efforts to reach larger audiences, such as subtitles to accommodate the hearing impaired? Will the YouTube videos be shared on other social media platforms? There are quite a few questions to consider when sharing content via YouTube. When videos shared on YouTube inspire engagement through conversation, comment sharing, and watching content at one's own pace, then active learning is occurring. Active learning helps us interpret and retain information (Allocca 2018, 164). As a result, YouTube is a universal tool that can be valuable across the curriculum. There are so many digital tools that allow learners to create interesting, relevant, important content while having fun. However, the ability to share the content varies significantly. YouTube allows content from a wide range of digital tools to be shared universally. Let's evaluate strategies for improving the learner experience through the power of YouTube.

Be Anyone, Go Anywhere, and Do Anything with DoInk

If you have had the opportunity to play around with green screen technology, then you know it does not have to be complicated. If you have not had the opportunity yet, you will realize that it is a simple yet powerful learning tool, especially when paired with a video hosting platform. I like the Green Screen app by DoInk because it is easy to use. This app is compatible with Apple mobile devices and costs $2.99. The app can also be purchased for $1.49 when twenty or more apps are purchased under the volume licensing agreement for education. DoInk allows students to drop in any background of their choice to make their learning come to life. There is no need for a fancy green screen. In addition to painting a section of a wall the color green, there are a variety of inexpensive green screen hacks. For example, green butcher paper, green fabric, cardboard painted green, and green poster board all work with the DoInk app to create a custom background. If you are limited in space, consider painting the inside of a pizza box in green to create miniature movies. This is also a great strategy for allowing multiple learners to film at once. Pizza box green screens make for a great way to create stop-motion animation, puppet shows, or headshots with unique backgrounds. If working with an Android device, consider the WeVideo app, which now includes a green screen feature.

Figure 8.1 A fifth grader sharing the weather report for Chitungwiza, Zimbabwe.

A green screen app adds another dimension to the learning. For example, in Earth Science, our fifth graders learn about weather, climate, and atmosphere and how each varies significantly by geographic location. To demonstrate this, students choose a different place in the world, research the weather, climate, and atmospheric pressure for that particular place on that specific date and create a weather report that includes a background that is representative of that location. Backgrounds might include a map of the region, a landmark found in that area, or a newsroom with scrolling news that is relevant to that location. The students can choose how they want to demonstrate additional knowledge of that particular location through the use of green screen technology. It involves researching the area, learning how to give a weather report with pertinent information, and the technical skills associated with filming, editing, and creating the green screen effect. Scan the QR Code shown in Figure 8.1 to see a sample weather report created by one of our students:

Together, DoInk and YouTube allow students to recall key learning points throughout the week. By reflecting on the week and the major learning highlights, students are synthesizing information to educate others about what they have recently learned. Sharing this content as part of a news anchor team has several benefits. The process of selecting a backdrop relevant to the content that they have learned encourages them to make connections that deepen their understanding through a visual representation. They must consider how to show what they know. Additionally, student-generated news highlights from the week offer teachable moments in digital citizenship for both learner and educator. School librarians can seize this opportunity to educate the students about retrieving images that are not restricted by copyright. The DoInk's FAQ section on their website provides helpful information such as where to locate copyright-free images and recommended paint brands and colors to create a homemade green screen. Regularly created news videos also provide additional practice in presentation skills. Without a video hosting platform, these weekly news reports would lose some of their luster in that they would be confined to the classroom. By app-smashing DoInk and YouTube, students become content creators who can share what they have learned while strengthening their media literacy skills as well as strengthening the connection between school and home.

Video Creation as a Marketing Strategy

As the saying goes, timing is everything. One of the great wonders of YouTube is that it creates on-demand learning. Another is that it makes it so easy to publish videos when the timing is just right. For example, are you in the midst of hosting a book fair and hoping to gain serious foot traffic? School librarians can work with teachers to leverage YouTube as a marketing tool. Film the students as they are browsing the fair and ask them what looks intriguing. Allow students to give an impromptu book talk. Do the same with teachers asking them which books they are requesting on their classroom wish lists. Share these timely book talks via the morning broadcast, on Twitter, or ask teachers to share them as part of their morning routine with their entire class as highlights from the book fair. Get students excited about the opportunity to be on camera to share their favorite reads. As stated, timing is everything. Consider the affect that walking around with a mobile device while recording has on bystanders. Humans are curious creatures and the act of filming others generates excitement even before publishing to YouTube.

Show What You Know with Spirited Songs

If your school subscribes to Flocabulary.com, a website that supplies educators with educational rap videos to help make content stick, consider inspiring a use of YouTube for learners to create their own Flocabulary videos and sharing them with others. This activity is great for learners of all ages and incorporates content curation, writing skills, and musical production. When our students learn about the Roaring Twenties, they can bring the learning to life through the use of sharing their new knowledge in the form of rap videos using the free rap music beats provided on the Flocabulary website. The website even provides instructional guides for students to successfully engage in creating their own raps, all the way from improving one's rap skills, using a rhyming dictionary to help make the content stick, and how to effectively use hip-hop metaphors. Host Flocabulary-inspired music videos on YouTube for all to learn from while discovering new musical talent.

Bring on the Red Carpet with TED Talks

Does your school embrace learning in the form of TED Talks? If not, consider suggesting that TED talks become a part of your larger learning community. We have been hosting TED movie night for at least five years.

TED Movie night is actually a faculty meeting in disguise. You can host your own TED movie night and, before you know it, teachers will be sponsoring their own TED-Ed clubs with their students. Middle and high school students are the perfect age for TED-Ed clubs but faculty members that teach all ages can benefit from TED movie night. First, we select a group of approximately six educators from a variety of grade levels and subjects to curate TED Talks. They are tasked with selecting eight TED talks from a list of about twenty-five that have been published within the last three years. We focus on talks that relate to teaching, learning, communication, faith, innovation, and any topic that inspires thoughtful discussion and that might affect our teaching practices. We schedule the one-hour movie night so that each faculty and staff member can view two TED talks and participate in a discussion after each viewing. It is our own version of going to Hollywood. We roll out the red carpet and serve popcorn, candy, and sodas. We select faculty members that were involved in the curation process to facilitate the discussions after each viewing. There is some psychology that goes into which faculty members are selected. It is a combination of those faculty members who are quick to innovate and those that may benefit from being on the other side of making change and trying to sell innovative ideas to a roomful of peers. Different faculty is chosen each year but the school librarian is the constant. Having the opportunity to tap other faculty members to lead this evening of learning (okay, faculty meeting) helps forge relationships and grow teacher leaders. Now that our faculty is comfortable with TED talk night and the rich discussions that come from this, they support and lead TED-Ed club groups within our school. The TED-Ed club website provides helpful resources for launching TED-Ed clubs in a variety of different formats at the following website: https://ed.ted.com/student_talks. The concept of student-generated TED talks is similar to that of a video essay. Students select a topic that is meaningful to them, they do the research to challenge or support their big idea, they formulate their ideas into a talk, and they share it on the big stage. Parents are invited to the school as part of a live studio audience but the talks are also captured through video and shared via YouTube. Like adults, students have big ideas too. Giving learners the stage from which to share their ideas highlights the power that they have in shaping the world.

You Matter and YouTube

YouTube is proof that you matter. We all matter. Kids matter. Teachers matter. Relatives matter. Friends matter. Strangers matter. Everyone matters. YouTube offers evidence of this. When educators work together to create miniature celebrations of who we are and showcase them on YouTube to share the joy with others, they reinforce Angela Maier's "You Matter Manifesto." This manifesto reminds everyone that they have influence, genius, contributions to make, and a gift that others need. These reminders can be silly or serious. While some schools have moved away from acknowledging Mother's Day or Father's Day, if recognizing these holidays is still a part of your school's practice, consider using video creation to acknowledge these holidays. Once our teachers were comfortable with YouTube and had established their own professional YouTube channel, they came up with a fun idea to poll the parents or a special friend of the children in their class. These individuals were asked specific questions and provided their responses privately to the teacher via email so that the children could not see their answers to the questions. Then, teachers filmed each child being asked these same questions and sharing their responses. During the editing process, they gave the video subtitles (using their editing skills that the school librarian helped them acquire) that included the adults' actual answers. Watching the child share their verbal response while seeing the adult's actual response always makes for a hysterical film screening event. For example, one question might be, "What is your mom's favorite drink?" The mom might write back to the teacher that her favorite drink is Diet Coke, which is what is included in the video's subtitles, but on camera the child says whiskey. Invite all of the parents or special friends into the class to watch the video of each child's interview clip. It is a fun approach to building community. Another innovative approach to sharing an appreciation for those we care about is to build a digital cookbook that can be shared via YouTube. Invite mothers, fathers, or special friends to submit their child's favorite recipe to the teacher. Film each child sharing why it is their favorite recipe (while wearing a chef's hat of course) and include an image of the handwritten or typed recipe within the video. Compile each student's video clip into a video editing tool, such as iMovie and upload the movie onto YouTube. Now parents have a digital cookbook that includes personal stories that allow families to learn about each other while building community through a shared love of good food.

The Big Picture

YouTube is a tool that helps learners reflect and improve. When we learn a concept, demonstrate that learning via video, and play it back, we consider how deeply we have absorbed new information. We have the opportunity to evaluate our ability to demonstrate our own learning. It offers a mirror into the growth process. Learners can consider what they would change in the ways that they share their new knowledge, how they can better connect with their audience, and what they would add or delete within their shared content. Video creation with the intent to reflect on our academic progression reinforces the value of learning. Many schools continue to block YouTube but perhaps, with specific learning goals in mind, school librarians can convince administrators that YouTube can be embraced as a digital tool to connect our students to their learning. If this is not likely, however, digital tools continue to evolve to allow video file hosting directly from within apps and bypassing YouTube altogether. While these alternatives to YouTube do not always allow audiences to search for discoverable videos, they do allow content creators to share their videos with target audiences. Alternatives to hosting videos on You-Tube include websites and apps like Padlet, TouchCast, Animoto, Google Drive, and Thinglink, which is $35.00 a year for the educator's version that allows users to upload a video file of 25 MB.

It is important to keep in mind that children learn from the people they love. For this reason, replacing a personal relationship between teacher and learner with video instruction does not necessarily translate into a meaningful learning experience. Learners engage with content through their emotions and without the connection between teacher and student, the learning can fall flat. Therefore, leveraging the concept of video as a creation tool in which school librarians support other educators to gain comfort with the skills necessary to support their students to become their own content creators is a touchdown on the digital field.

CHAPTER NINE

Making Connections with Makerspaces

"In Maker Monday, you get to be creative, explore cool technology, discover what is out in the world, and expand your mindset of critical thinking."

—Clayton, age 12

Makerspaces aren't magic. Makerspaces are the result of dedicated facilitators, often school librarians who are devoted to providing learners with an experience that focuses on exploring to learn. Implementing makerspaces can feel daunting but be assured, it can actually be quite simple to create a maker culture. It is not about the sophistication of a space, it's about the making. Kristen Swanson, co-founder of EdCamp, notes that it is up to educators to provide the white space for learners to explore and develop their passions. She mentions that this is the exact reason why so many educators rediscover their hobbies over winter break. When allowed the time and freedom to explore and create, we discover our interests (Swanson 2015).

Ultimately, experience in making is what will lead learners to establish resilience in problem-solving. The persistence and patience to navigate the unknown and problem-solve translates into valuable skills in the workplace. While some makerspace facilitators relish the freedom to create a space of exploration, others can feel hindered by not having a roadmap. There are no rules, required protocols, specific supply lists, or preestablished guidelines. There are, however, a multitude of excellent resources to support school librarians in launching makerspaces in the library that can then overflow into the classrooms through collaborative partnerships.

Makerspaces in school make me think of the phrase, "If you build it, they will come," the phrase made famous in the 1989 movie, *Field of Dreams*. This is true for makerspaces in school libraries. There is much research to support that turning a section of the library into a makerspace can transform a library's culture, changing the perception of the library to be one of a dynamic learning space. This is especially true for middle and high schools where, historically, students feel too overwrought with schoolwork to view the library as a place of creation, and instead view a visit to the library as a passive experience for the consumption of knowledge. Makerspaces allow patrons to interact and engage with content. Maker activities can be related to curricular goals, connected to a school's mission, and/or offer students practice in identifying goals and working diligently to achieve them. Because makerspaces tend to have fewer constraints than traditional learning environments, learners feel empowered to make their own choices through a discovery process. Personal investment allows learners to enter a state of flow, or the ultimate state of intrinsic motivation, in which they feel value in being able to succeed and in which they feel personally invested in the activity (Borovay et al. 2019). The true value in a makerspace is the freedom to discover, craft, and tinker to elevate one's understanding of the physical and digital world. Let's explore how this can initiate from within the school library to positively affect the school community.

A Method to the Making

In learning, as in sports, there are tried and true methods to shape the implementation of developing skills based on past experiences. In a maker culture, however, the makers create the blueprints, often from scratch. This is part of the joy. Having the freedom to explore and chart one's own path is a powerful play in learning. However, school librarians that initiate makerspaces typically start with a guiding force to help shape their makerspace.

Consider the Starting Line

In my own experience, we had a vacant space that needed to be relegated to create a meaningful learning opportunity. We decided to call this space the Idea Lab. We painted the walls with an apple green paint color to create a green screen effect, added a wall-sized whiteboard, and added fun, movable cushions to accommodate a flexible learning environment.

There were vacant shelves well suited for storing old electronics, a suitcase of littleBits, and a container of Spheros that a parent had generously donated to us. I also added some colored paper, a box of markers, scissors, pencils, pipe cleaners, pompoms, feathers, and glue sticks. A makerspace was born. On Mondays during recess, I would invite each grade level into the Idea Lab to make things. In order to manage crowd control, I set up four to six stations around the room, listing the day's menu choices on the whiteboard so that students could quickly identify which station they wanted to start exploring. Stations included a crafty corner, tinkering with electronics, a littleBits bar (set up on top of the shelf space), and a programming challenge with iPads and Spheros. Students loved what became known as Maker Monday. In fact, in order to implement further crowd control, I started asking our school's part-time IT Help Desk Coordinator to come in and work with the students at the electronics station. Students dissected old computers, took apart broken Kindles, and discovered the hardware inside a digital camera. It was helpful to have an extra set of hands for safety and education. Eventually, my colleague from the IT department had to stop working in the makerspace due to increased IT-related demands within his department. I again decided to shift my approach, which is always a good thing to do when you are already achieving success. I started to hone in on one project or focus at a time. As a result, some of the choice went away but I was able to announce to students ahead of time through their teachers what the maker activity would be for that week so that they could decide if they wanted to attend. While I scaled down in choice, I made sure to create a variety of different projects from week to week so that different students would be inspired to rotate in and out as their interests directed. As popularity for Maker Monday grew, teachers started responding to their students' enthusiasm for the program. Some teachers began to create their own version of a makerspace in their classrooms, and our school committed to supporting and building a new innovation and design studio to continue nurturing a maker culture. If you build it, they will come (and hopefully, the support and the resources will grow). Once I had an established space for students to explore and tinker, I became much more purposeful in my end goals. For example, because we are a faith-based school, I saw this as an opportunity to incorporate educational experiences about other cultures and religions. I also saw this as an opportunity to bring the concept of windows and mirrors into maker education. Students should not only see themselves in projects they are being inspired to create but should also learn about the wider world through their creation process. Additionally, curricular connections became increasingly important to model the value of maker education within the mainstream classroom and seize the opportunity to partner with the teachers. Each of these goals began to shape future acquisitions for the makerspace. Cultivating a makerspace is an evolutionary process. You may start out at one place and ultimately find yourself somewhere very different from where you started. This mimics real-world scenarios in which the only constant is change.

Evaluate the Playing Field

My initial method was driven by a space vacancy. What will be the guiding factor to get you started in your makerspace? Here are some questions to consider when setting up your makerspace:

- What craft supplies are available?
- Are there enough craft supplies available to leave them out while you are otherwise occupied doing other activities or does your makerspace need to be established during set days/times to ensure necessary materials are available?
- What hardware, if any, is currently available to add to your makerspace, either permanently or temporarily?
- Is there a current budget to grow items that you can include in your makerspace? If so, what purchases will allow for the most longevity and generate excitement for usage?
- Will your makerspace include digital tools, such as iPads and computers? If so, how does this affect where your makerspace is situated?
- Will your makerspace be high tech, low tech, or a combination of both at the same time or at different times? What will variety look like in your makerspace?
- How often, if ever, will you change the materials available in your makerspace with which to create or will the same materials permanently reside in your makerspace?
- When do students have the most flexibility in their schedules to visit the makerspace so that you can prepare for peak activity times?
- Is it possible to establish makerspace visits as formal learning opportunities within your school?
- Will you establish maker challenges or will students be given a blank canvas to drive their exploration?
- Will your makerspace need to be staffed and, if so, who is available to do this? Student leaders? A paraprofessional? A parent volunteer? The school librarian? An intern? Alumni?

How can you highlight the value of your makerspace? Is there room for students to publicly display their creations? Is there an opportunity for students to share their learning at a faculty meeting, a board meeting, or at a PTO meeting? Will students offer testimonials and where are the most effective places to feature these testimonials?

What unknown talents will you discover that your students have and how can you leverage these talents to empower these students to become leaders within the maker culture?

How will you track the traffic within your makerspace to help demonstrate its value and gauge student interest?

How can creating a makerspace redefine your role?

How can creating a makerspace influence your collaborative relationships with other teachers?

These questions will shape how you launch your makerspace. The answers to these questions will change over time as will your maker culture. As educators, we love to focus on the growth mindset or the understanding that abilities and intelligence can be developed (Science Impact 2017). Makerspaces support the growth mindset in that if learners put forth the effort and have designated time for exploration, they can discover new knowledge.

Establishing the Rules of the Game

There are a variety of driving forces that shape a makerspace, as is evident from the questions to consider in the previous section. These forces will inevitably fluctuate over time causing a change in how learners experience your makerspace. I will share how my approach to makerspaces evolved as my goals changed. In doing so, I will outline specific projects that I consider to be my biggest wins. These makerspace activities generated positive feedback, high levels of participation, significant engagement, and repeat requests.

How Much Time Is on the Clock?

Time is a significant factor in makerspace implementation. In our school, student schedules are fairly structured. Our open times for creative programming include thirty minutes before classes start in the morning and recess time. Our lunch program requires that students eat and remain in the dining hall so lunch is not an option for creative programming. The thirty-minute morning time slot is reserved for math club, book clubs, comic club, tutoring, Torah practice, Jewish music, and more. In other words, that precious thirty minutes in the morning is oversaturated. This left recess to create a maker culture. Not a problem. Recess it was! I started launching Maker Monday during each grade levels' recess as an experiment. I set up a menu of different stations so that a large group of each grade level could be accommodated at once. After a short while, however, I decided to regain focus and scale back on choice. I migrated to a tinkering station that allowed students to dissect old electronics and have one other maker activity going on at the same time. Sometimes, I would scrap the tinkering option and just go with the one activity. Our recess is in twenty-five minute increments so creating meaningful maker opportunities within a limited time constraint was my initial challenge. However, as with anything, practice means improvement and, over time, I became better at crafting meaningful activities with limited time. While Maker Monday still exists, I have cultivated a larger platform for maker integration within our new innovation and design space as well as seen the integration of maker-spaces into the classrooms. Each of these models translates into different curricular connections and different time allocations. To start, I will share some of the crowd favorites that fall within the twenty-five minute time-frame, some of which involve technology usage and some of which do not.

No Tech

- **Publishing a 3D Book:** Supplies include a set of 3D glasses with cyan and red lenses (available in bulk on Amazon.com), red and blue Sharpies (possibly borrowed from classroom teachers), white letter-size paper, and colored construction paper. First, have students outline a story that includes a title, beginning, middle, and an end. Second, have them write and illustrate their story with the blue Sharpie on the white paper. Next, have them trace their writing and drawings using the red Sharpie so that there is a small white space between both the red and blue lines. Have them decorate a book cover on the colored construction paper and include the title, using the red and blue Sharpies in the outline format. Staple the pages together to create a booklet. Finally, have the students view their stories with the 3D glasses and they will be surprised to see the 3D effect as their writing and illustrations jump off the page. The science behind the 3D effect is as follows: By creating an object in red and blue, the eyes see an illusion of two different objects that are at different angles, known as parallax. When viewed with glasses that have one red lens and one cyan lens, the brain fuses the lines together to create one image. One side of the glasses filters out one color and the other side of the glasses filters out the other color. This creates stronger depth perception. Presenting different images independently to each eye creates what is known as an anaglyph. As a high-tech version of this activity, especially suited for middle schoolers and older, direct learners to create an image in Adobe Photoshop and superimpose a duplicate of the image as an additional layer. Rename the first layer as left and the second layer as right. With the right layer selected, right click to go to blending options, advanced blending, and uncheck the red option under RGB channels. Do the same for the left layer but uncheck the green option instead. With the left layer selected, use the grab tool to move this layer about eight spaces to the left and do the same with the right layer moving it to the right. Leftover edges can be cropped out. Students can put on their glasses to see their images in 3D.

- **Meditative Making with Zendoodles:** Some students are stressed out. Let's be real: Teachers are stressed out too. That might be why this particular maker activity, as shown in Figure 9.1, was a huge, although unexpected, hit at my school. Set the mood with low lighting, aromatic scents, and soothing music. Provide black Sharpies and white paper. Offer a brief introduction to zendoodling, which is doodling to create a structure or a pattern that puts the doodler into a relaxed state of flow. Let them create! Set up a museum of their work. I am not sure what this says about our anxiety levels but be forewarned: There will be requests to do this activity again and again. Make this activity part of a faculty training on the topic of mindfulness.

Figure 9.1 Meditative Maker Monday creating zendoodles.

- **LEGO Pop-Up Book Character Interactive Museum:** This is a fabulous activity to inspire well-read makers. Simply put out as much LEGO as you can locate and ask students to build a LEGO figure inspired by a book character. Then, take all of the completed book characters and set them up on a shelf in your library. Number each character, put out sheets that are number lined with the same amount of book characters that you have set out, and provide pencils, as shown in Figure 9.2. Challenge library visitors to identify as many of the

Figure 9.2 Pop-up LEGO book character museum as a center activity.

Figure 9.3   Robot made out of recycled materials.

book characters as they can. At the end of the week, the visitor who identified the most book characters correctly wins an advanced reader copy of a book. Some of our teachers allow this to be an independent center activity for our younger students. These students come to the library with a timer to complete the activity within the timeframe that their teacher has allowed.

• **Recycled Robot:** The recycled robot is a powerful activity in demonstrating to the littlest learners that there is a difference between humans and machines. We talk about how machines have to be built and programmed to create artificial intelligence while human beings are born with intelligence. This is an opportune time to explore the difference between materials used to create robots and the epidermis as the natural outer covering for humans. Brainstorm the materials that robots are made of and you may hear responses such as plastic, metal, and glass. Challenge students to build their own robots made of craft supplies and repurposed objects, as shown in Figure 9.3. Ask them to compare and contrast their robots to their human selves. This activity is well-paired with *Wodney Wat's Wobot* by Helen Lester.

More Tech

• **Throw Pottery (Digitally):** Let's Create! Pottery HD Lite is a free app that encourages creativity, incorporates financial literacy, and educates learners about pottery-making. As with each of these activities, I am met with a few surprises. With this particular activity, I was pleasantly surprised to discover that the enthusiasm among all participants did not support gender stereotypes. With a mobile device and the free Let's Create! Pottery HD Lite app downloaded, an entire gallery can be established and with no mess at all. Learners tap on create, shape their digital clay, fire it in the digital kiln, decorate and paint the exterior, and sell it on the market. Coins are earned for creativity and can then be used toward additional art supplies. Makers have to decide how to manage their money and spend wisely to achieve their creative goals. This activity is well-paired with the book *Dave the Potter: Artist, Poet, Slave* by Laban Carrick Hill.

• **Grow a Garden with Stop Motion:** This activity pairs well with *Strega Nona's Harvest* by Tomie dePaola. Supplies include Play-Doh, a piece of brown construction paper, and a mobile device with a camera, such as an iPod, iPhone, or iPad. Be sure to install the free Stop Motion Studio app by Cateater, LLC onto the device. Have students lay the brown paper on a flat surface and select a vegetable to construct with Play-Doh. Each time they add a piece of

Play-Doh to their vegetable to make it grow, they snap a picture within the Stop Motion Studio app. Once their vegetable is fully grown, they can hit the playback button within the app to view their movie. Their movie can be directly imported into iMovie, Instagram, Seesaw, Google Drive, the Book Creator app, and Dropbox.

- **The Silent Film:** One of the most rewarding maker activities has been the art of creating a silent film. This activity involves collaboration, writing, creativity, and technical skills. Divide learners into groups of up to six people. Provide each group with a storyboard template. Give each group five minutes to brainstorm and draw each scene, consisting of no more than six scenes. If necessary, this allows each group member the chance to craft one scene. Then, provide each group with a mobile device that includes the Silent Film Studio app by Cateater, LLC. This app costs ninety-nine cents and is well worth the investment. It is possible to carry out this activity using only one device for multiple groups. Have a box of props on hand for added creativity. One person films each group's scenes from within the Silent Film Studio app. This can be a group member, a member of another group, or a student volunteer. I use a student leader who has a passion for film-making. Each video is created in black and white with fun antique editing options, such as a static-effect, a projector noise, old-timey frames, a countdown feature, and Roaring Twenties-style background music. When played back, it is condensed to become a short silent film with features that make viewers feel as though they have gone back in time. I give younger students a framework or topic to focus on and with older students I allow more open-ended choices. This approach is driven by the specific curricular goals and the time constraints. Younger students will take longer to settle on an agreed upon topic. With five minutes left in the activity, we all sit back for a movie screening at which time we view every group's silent film. Because they are condensed within the app, each group's movie is typically thirty seconds to one minute long. I use Apple TV to project the videos onto a white wall directly from within the app. The videos can also be uploaded onto YouTube to share externally. An example of a group's silent film can be seen by scanning the QR code in Figure 9.4.

- **Lantern Parade:** Some cities host lantern parades. These are colorful evenings in which people gather together to march and showcase their creative homemade lanterns. In my city, this is an annual event along an outdoor path known as The Beltline. Our city is proud to support a full-time lantern maker who creates commissioned lanterns all year long for a spectacular evening of lights. She also hosts workshops to teach aspiring lantern makers of all ages.

Figure 9.4 Students' silent film entitled *Why We Love the Media Center.*

Figure 9.5 A paper lantern lit up with the school logo.

Regardless of whether or not your area has an official lantern parade or even a lantern maker, there is absolutely no reason why you cannot create your own. This particular maker activity incorporates circuitry, creativity, and community. The supplies used include paper, markers, scissors, coin cell batteries, tape, and light-emitting diode (LED) lights. Ask students to cut a thick strip about an inch long off the top of their sheet of paper. Have them decorate the remaining sheet of paper on one side with unique drawings. Then, have them fold their paper in half lengthwise. On the fold, they can cut slits across the top, about an inch long. After unfolding their paper, have them refold the paper in a circular tube-like shape and tape the ends together. Now, they can tape an LED light to their coin cell battery and using more tape attach the battery with the LED light onto the inside of the lantern. The long strip of paper that they cut earlier can be connected to each side of the top of their lantern as a handle, as shown in Figure 9.5. Voila, there you have a lantern that is permanently lit up until the battery gives out, which can take up to a month. Our students were inspired to take their lanterns outside and march together for a beautiful showing of community, light, and learning.

- **Brushbots:** I love this activity for its simplicity and depth. Assembling brushbots makes for an engaging twenty-five minute maker activity that can be implemented with five year olds to fifteen year olds. Challenge students to build their own pet robot, otherwise known as a brushbot. This again demonstrates the difference between machines and living beings. I created a slideshow for young learners to break down the brushbot process, which can be viewed by scanning the QR code in Figure 9.6. With older students, add a layer of difficulty by challenging them to create a brushbot that can go forward. They will have to figure out how the weight distribution affects the brushbot's movement. My older students also like to create a game of Brushbot Wars where they construct a small arena out of pipe cleaners and see which brushbot can move within the arena longest without toppling over. The Brushbot Wars get pretty heated!

Figure 9.6 Google slides outlining the brushbot creation process.

Home Versus Away

While shorter maker activities are excellent entry points to gaining momentum in makerspaces, once you have caught the attention of the players and the spectators, you are ready for your next big play. Big plays can mean more time, more space, and more resources. This is where partnering with other educators to establish makerspaces within *their* learning space becomes part of the game. My suggestion is to start small. Identify one teacher, if they have not already approached you, to pilot the creation of a makerspace within their classroom. The in-class makerspace has two big advantages: Tying the creation process in with their specific curriculum and providing a creative outlet for exploration within the class. Other advantages include a makerspace being in close proximity to the learners, a safe space to integrate innovative tools to gain additional comfort with these tools for all learners, an additional learning option/station for students to discover in the classroom, and additional student-created projects for students' to share both within the class and beyond. Working with teachers to create a maker experience on their home turf will help accommodate learners who enjoy the maker experience on their home base territory and/or throughout their other classes.

Embracing the Home Team Advantage

Demonstrating the value of the in-class makerspace can be done by tying maker activities into the curriculum. In our school, our second-grade team led by the grade level chair Tamar Levy paved the way for the infusion of makerspaces into the classroom. After seeing the students' enthusiasm for maker activities on Maker Monday, she committed herself to establish an in-class maker corner for her students. My role in this was to be supportive and enthusiastic. When we discussed the different approaches, I made a point of being encouraging. She was intrigued by the idea of turning the makerspace corner into a place for literacy enhancement. She identified picture books that supported her curriculum and used those as a launch pad for maker projects. We worked together to identify the curriculum units that might mesh well with a maker project and to establish a materials list to get her started. She was comfortable asking parents to bring in supplies, such as empty cereal boxes, toilet paper rolls, paper towel rolls, old magazines, and newspapers. An important role of the school librarian throughout the process of supporting teachers to create their own makerspaces is to be their number one cheerleader. When she expressed an interest in wanting to ask our principal if she could spend some money on additional craft supplies, I helped pave the way by reaching out to the principal in advance of her request to help explain the value of what she was wanting to launch within her classroom. Because no other teacher had yet created a formal makerspace in their classroom, this was new territory and needed as much momentum and support to help get it started in implementation, ideas, and resources. As the school librarian, being enthusiastic about the teacher's efforts to grow a maker culture is critical for teachers to feel validated in their efforts.

In examining curricular entry points, we identified several areas of interest for launching maker projects that the students would be able to carry out independently. One project included building rocket ships out of toilet paper rolls in conjunction with their unit on space. The picture book that Tamar chose to connect to this activity was *Margaret and the Moon* by Dean Robbins. Students also created digital versions of their rocket ships using the free SketchBook Motion app created by Autodesk Inc. The students had so much fun creating physical rockets out of recycled materials, as well as digital rockets, that we also explored rockets with augmented reality. We printed out the Quiver augmented reality moon worksheet for students to color and scan with the Quiver app using the iPads. They were able to see rocket ships orbit the moon while also bringing their own homemade rocket ships into view making their homemade version a part of the digital world. As an added bonus, this maker activity coincided with an author visit from Stuart Gibbs to promote his *Moon Base Alpha* series books, generating even more excitement for the unit. Layer by layer, enthusiasm for the makerspace grew.

Another curricular focus for these students was learning how to demonstrate sequence. In fact, the following year they went on to create and present a How-To project. Therefore, these next two maker activities involve sequencing and writing skills. One activity was inspired by the book *The Bear Ate Your Sandwich* by Julia Sarcone-Roach, in which students were challenged to make a sandwich and create an advertisement for their sandwich describing what makes it delicious. Another activity was centered around the book *This Moose Belongs to Me* by Oliver Jeffers. Students made their own pet in the makerspace and then taught other students how to make their pet using the whiteboard app Educreations. Again, this involved sequencing the steps for others to be able to recreate their unique pet. Maker projects are sent home via the class digital newsletter, which is created with Smore.com. Pictures of the projects are linked to the newsletter through Google photos and shared via Twitter with the grade-level Twitter hashtag. The newsletter also includes videos of one to three students providing a news report of the week with highlights that include describing and showcasing their maker projects from that week. Using a variety of formats to share these projects generated communal enthusiasm beyond that of the school librarian and classroom teacher. The teacher was then able to steer her entire team through the process so that each teacher on her team had a makerspace corner. Once the maker-space was an established part of their grade-level experience, I asked the teacher to share her success at a Fall faculty meeting. The slides that she shared can be viewed in Figure 9.7.

Ultimately, the maker craze spread into other classrooms. Creating with paper circuits can bridge curricular connections and making. Some examples include collaborating with the Hebrew teacher in which students created paper circuit flags in celebration of the Jewish holiday, Simcha Torah. These flags were made out of letter-size white paper, straws, and decorated with colored pencils. Inside each flag, students installed LED lights with coin cell batteries to light up their celebration as they danced around the Torah. Near the holiday of Yom Kippur, the makerspace became a greeting card factory. Students made paper circuit greeting cards for their loved ones to express their penance for the previous year's sins. The LED lights added flair to their cards, as shown in Figure 9.8.

Figure 9.7 Second-grade teacher Mrs. Levy's slideshow highlighting her approach to building a classroom makerspace during a faculty meeting.

One of my favorite Judaic Studies-themed maker activities involved a concept that is known in Hebrew as Bikur Cholim, or the act of visiting and extending aid to the sick. For this particular project, we decided to light up someone's day with illuminated pillboxes. We used the following supplies:

- Lithium batteries
- LED lights
- Copper tape
- LilyPad button board
- Small boxes
- Markers
- Stickers
- Scotch Tape

I purchased packs of twenty LED lights, conductive adhesive five-millimeter-wide copper tape, and the button boards from Sparkfun.com. The CR2032 volt coin cell lithium batteries were purchased from cheap -batteries.com. I purchased Beadaholique Kraft brown cardboard jewelry

Figure 9.8   Yom Kippur greeting cards made of paper circuits. An LED light is placed in the middle of the heart.

boxes in packs of sixteen from Amazon.com. I discovered some old stickers in our library cabinets and brought in a large box of washable markers to spark creativity. Students decorated the boxes with craft supplies. Then, using a precut paper template outlining how the circuit could be assembled, students built their circuit and embedded a button switch to allow the light to turn off and on, as shown in Figure 9.9. The template ensured that the circuit easily fit within the lid of the pillbox.

We were able to deliver the pillboxes to residents at an elder care facility near our school. We arrived during breakfast and the residents could

not have been happier to see us. The students handed out the pillboxes, explained the technological component, demonstrated how to turn on the lights, and visited with the residents.

Another in-class maker activity that incorporates a science lesson on the topic of light encourages learners to demonstrate their learning and create a light-saber paper circuit using a

Figure 9.9   In order to ensure the batteries would not drain, we incorporated the LilyPad switch so that the lights within the pillboxes could be turned on and off, as needed.

template provided by Makerspaces.com. Makers use the same supplies listed previously that they used to create the pillboxes, as well as solid colored straws. In this activity, students learn that light is a kind of energy that moves in one direction very fast. Light travels in waves and is transmitted when the waves pass through a medium. Objects transmit light differently and are therefore classified as transparent, translucent, or opaque. Learners and makers discover that when the light hits the straw in this activity, the straw is translucent allowing only some of the light to pass through, as shown in Figure 9.11.

Figure 9.10 Pill boxes made with love.

Moving beyond circuits, consider supporting the launch of in-class maker projects centered around curricular themes. For example, there are numerous points within our curriculum in which water, ocean life, and habitats are areas of study. The grade level influences the degree of focus but there is overlap

Figure 9.11 Paper circuit lightsabers created with a template from Makerspaces.com.

in the general subject matter. For this reason, we decided it was worth the investment of purchasing eight of the Ocean Pets virtual aquariums invented by Pai Technology. These virtual aquariums cost $25.00 each and were purchased from the Pai Technology website. Using modeling clay, a variety of fish templates, and an iPad with the free Ocean Pets app downloaded, learners can create a variety of different types of fish and, using augmented reality, these fish come to life within the ocean habitat while interacting with other living organisms found deep in the sea. This activity merges the tactile creation experience with the use of technology to take learners on an underwater adventure. We use this tool with our students working in small groups in kindergarten, first grade, and second grade. In second grade, we ensure this activity coincides with an annual field trip to the Georgia Aquarium.

The study of other religions and cultures is another curricular entry point for learning through making in the classroom. Connecting this to the school's mission statement and/or values offers one strategy for an approach. For example, one of our core values is respect. We intentionally integrate other cultures and religions into our curriculum to cultivate empathy and respect for others. Here are some sample projects that school librarians can help classroom teachers launch within their classrooms to support learning that exposes students to a world perhaps different from their own.

- Global Soda Making Factory: Mix, make, and market. Inspired by the Coca-Cola Museum in Atlanta, Georgia, this particular activity was definitely a big hit within our community. From the slime craze, I knew that students loved to mix and make with a slew of ingredients. Cashing in on that inspired me to recreate why kids love visiting the Coca-Cola Museum so much: The Tasting Room! We shared an interactive presentation that highlights countries all over the world and their most popular sodas. I described the taste and the ingredients of each of these sodas. Then, students moved into the lab area where they were able to choose from a variety of ingredients to concoct their own soda. Ingredients included flavored extracts, seltzer water, simple syrup, and a variety of flavored juices. Students could mix their own soda, taste it, create a brand name, and a logo for their soda can using the free Doodle Buddy Paint Draw app on the iPads. This activity inspired makers to imagine themselves in another place where Coke and Pepsi are not necessarily the norm. Instead, participants were able to reorient themselves in another geographical location and consider how the culture and ingredients influence taste around the world.
- The Story Behind the Structure: Love is the universal language. In celebration of this, our students learned the history behind India's architectural achievement, the Taj Mahal. After all, learning about different cultures grows our ability to empathize and understand the wider world. We watched a short video about the history of the Taj Mahal, and using the DoInk Green Screen app, in conjunction with a mini-copyright refresher and exposure to Creative Commons Search, students made finger puppets out of straws, paper, and colored pencils. We researched Indian dress to create puppets that were

accurate in appearance and discovered a variety of customs and colors associated with Indian attire.

Students filmed scenes in front of pizza boxes painted green to create the green screen effect retelling the story behind the creation of the Taj Mahal. Using Creative Commons Search, they dropped in backgrounds to coincide with the stories shared in their movies.

- Code a Buddha: Although we are a Jewish school, in the interest of exploring other religions, we have a responsibility to nurture an understanding of other cultures and religions. This is an area of growth for us as our curriculum continues to evolve. In fact, our seventh-grade curriculum now includes a class on world religions. That being said, I had to get special permission for this particular Maker Monday project. In order to circumvent any controversy, I creatively framed the activity. Because our rabbi is highly respected within our community, I asked him to provide a quote to introduce a maker activity focused on Buddhism. Our school rabbi, Micah Lapidus, stated the following: "We are an observer more than a participant when studying other ways of life and religions." This quote was prominently displayed on the big screen as students filed into the space. The goal was for students to understand that they were exploring to learn. We watched a short introductory video on Buddhism. Students were asked to select a Buddhist-inspired saying that spoke to them and use that saying as the backdrop for animating a Buddha in ScratchJr. Some of our more advanced coders used the web-based Scratch version but most focused on the coding as secondary to the lesson in Buddhism. As a result, Scratch Jr. proved to be sufficient.

- Day of the Dead on the Small Screen: After the Disney/Pixar movie *Coco* came out, students were tapped into the Mexican celebration known as *Día de los Muertos* (Day of the Dead). This movie highlights an interesting cultural tradition that is celebrated all over Latin America. As a maker activity, challenge students to research this cultural holiday and share their learning through puppetry. They can create skull figure puppets out of popsicle sticks, paper, and colored pencils, as shown in Figure 9.12. Then, using pizza boxes painted green to serve as mini green screens, students can film skits that highlight cultural traditions associated with the Day of the Dead using their puppets. They can film their skits using the camera app on the iPads and then upload their projects into the Green Screen app by DoInk. Using Creative Commons Search, they can select backgrounds that are associated with the holiday. Sharing these short movies is rewarding for students to celebrate their creations and showcase their knowledge of this cultural celebration.

Just Do It

Whether makerspaces happen in the classroom, in the library, or elsewhere in your school, meaningful maker projects can ignite curiosity that

Figure 9.12   Pizza boxes painted as green screens and finger puppets used to create *Dia de los Muertos* mini-movies with the DoInk Green Screen app.

results in positive change. Supporters of a maker culture are motivated by developing empathetic problem-solvers, collaborators, and creators that will be a positive force in the world. Maker activities can be approached through a design thinking process of identifying, synthesizing, exploring, prototyping, and testing for desired iterations.

When infused into the learning environment, making is the ultimate approach to cultivate a growth mindset. Learners experience power in thinking with their hands to identify and implement solutions. In doing so, there becomes an awareness that positive change can happen when there is a demonstrated investment in the value of exploration through making. As the school librarian, consider that at first it may be necessary to spark a maker culture in isolation but be assured that the passion for learning through making will soon catch on and become an expectation. Latch on to student interest to propel other teachers forward to integrate makerspaces into their learning environment. Be their supportive coach, best cheerleader, and willing teammate as they strive to spread the maker culture.

CHAPTER TEN

Socialize Learning with Social Media

"Using Twitter in class became a fun experience while still being safe and appropriate."

—Madison, age 12

Social media has completely altered the rules of the game. Social media is everywhere. It is hard to identify an adult who does not have some type of social media presence and it is becoming harder to find a nine-year-old who doesn't interact with some form of social media. I happen to love the use of social media and the positive connections it can influence and the bridges that it can build, no matter the distance. However, in education and in parenting, there is one aspect to social media that is not discussed as often as it should be and, for me, it represents the door stop. It's the point where we consider if and how fast we push through the door into the next space. The point is this: Legally, young kids do not have permission to use many of the mainstream social media platforms. Instagram users need to be at least thirteen years of age. However, I can think of countless children who are using Instagram that do not meet this age requirement. To further complicate our global embrace of social media, kids are often using social media platforms without having received any formal instruction on how to navigate a digital landscape. We would never put someone who is under the age requirement mandated by law behind the wheel of a car without a formal driver's education. So, why do we allow students to put themselves out there digitally without having first provided them with formal training and practice to navigate the digital highway and in consideration of the legal age requirements? I can think of several reasons. First, this is still somewhat new territory for parents and educators who do not always feel like they have an instruction manual. Second, it requires commitment or an added layer of educating kids when we don't always feel like we have the time or the resources to do so. Third, we see so many well-respected and trusted parents and educators turning their underage children loose on social media that we feel it cannot be so bad. There is much to be said for allowing children to navigate the digital world at an early age so that they can make mistakes and learn from them before the repercussions feel so extreme. We have all heard the mantra, "Little kids, little problems. Big kids, big problems." Why not let young kids stumble and fall on social media at an early age when the mistakes have fewer consequences?

This chapter will explore the ways that we can steer learners in positive directions as they interact with social media but in a manner that is thoughtful, age appropriate, and impactful. We tend to gloss over the age factor and yet, we can use this parameter as a guide to direct how and when social media is integrated into the learning. This is where the school librarian becomes a consultant. School librarians can leverage themselves as social media gurus, inspiring teachers to use social media as a tool to teach relevant content while cultivating strong digital citizens in the classroom and in the larger community.

The Officials and Their Stance on Social Media

School librarians are key players in evaluating and influencing their school's relationship with social media. Understanding how the school community interacts with, responds to, and views social media will guide how school librarians can integrate responsible social media usage within the classroom. These are questions to consider in advance of advocating for social media usage in school.

- Are teachers using social media and, if so, how?
- Does the school connect with current and prospective families via social media and, if so, what platforms are being used and what type of information is communicated?
- What opportunities can social media offer to students in your school?
- How can social media help fulfill your school's mission?

- What are your school administrators' attitudes toward social media?
- Which educators in your school are connected to other educators via social media and how does it benefit them?
- How can you, the school librarian, demonstrate the value of being a connected educator to the rest of the school community?

The answers to these questions will help shape the necessary areas of focus to build a framework for students to learn social media usage within the classroom.

Get in Formation

The school librarian is in a strong position to influence the ways in which social media is used throughout the school. Demonstrating the power of connections and the opportunities that can arise from these connections, school librarians are sharing good data to support a more inclusive approach for using social media in educational settings. The school librarian has a responsibility to highlight the number of curricular connections made via social media, as well as the responsibility to feature these opportunities via social media platforms, as shown by scanning the QR code in Figure 10.1.

Figure 10.1. Use of Piktochart to create an info-graphic for social media visuals and for school officials highlighting the effect of the school library on the learning culture.

Leveraging the data that demonstrates the powerful connections that social media encourages, partner with school officials to create a strategic plan for how social media can help achieve schoolwide goals, as reflected in Table 10.1.

As mentioned in Chapter One, school librarians have a unique vantage point in that they work with all stakeholders connected to the school community. This allows us to see areas of growth from an aerial perspective. The examples listed in Table 10.1 are just a few of the ways in which social media can support the growth of a Future Ready School. Once the importance of your role in relationship to social media usage in the school community has been established and schoolwide goals have been identified, all players have skin in the game. Let's explore how investing in social media as a learning tool and as a way to strengthen a community can bolster programming opportunities.

Table 10.1   Ways in Which Social Media Can Help Achieve Schoolwide
              Goals

Schoolwide Goals	Social Media Aids
Improve school-to-home communication	Require that all teachers create a professional Twitter account.
Demonstrate innovative learning	Create grade-level hashtags
Showcase high-quality teachers	Share teacher spotlights on Twitter, Facebook, and Instagram
Strengthen professional development	Host faculty Twitter chats and encourage faculty to bring an educator friend from outside the school community
Expand resources without growing costs	Use Twitter and Skype to arrange video chats with subject-matter experts
Expose students to places outside their area	Access YouTube's virtual reality video library to journey to destinations related to curriculum
Grow library resource circulation rates	Host student book talks via Instagram, Facebook, and Twitter
Teach learners to think critically about the resources they access	Allow student bloggers to evaluate and report on current events and critically analyze their news sources as part of their writing
Curate high-quality learning tools	Select student leaders to explore and review digital tools and share their feedback via a schoolwide teacher resource YouTube channel

Grow Your Fan Base with Social Media

Social media create platforms for not only showcasing the great learning happening in your school community but also generate programming opportunities that are inspired by the popularity of social media usage. These are some examples of strategic plays to positively leverage social media usage to create awareness and learning opportunities for all stakeholders:

- Host a student-led digital citizenship townhall for parents and educators in which a student panel share the ways in which they use social media in school to deepen their learning, share the pitfalls of social media usage and how they have grown from these experiences, and what they would like their teachers and parents to know about how they interact with social media.

- Co-host with student leaders community workshops for parents and grandparents, teaching them how to interact with your school through social media platforms. At the same time, a workshop of this type allows participants to experience the innovation happening at your school. We did a workshop for grandparents teaching them how to interact with our school via Twitter. The first half of the workshop highlighted some of the great work our students are doing using technology tools and the second half of the workshop taught attendees the technical skills needed to use Twitter. The presentation can be viewed by scanning the QR code found in Figure 10.2. Student leaders served as floaters to provide technical assistance to facilitate getting the grandparent community active on Twitter.

Figure 10.2 Sample grandparent lunch n' learn workshop highlighting the ways in which grandparents can interact with the school via social media.

- Generate an iHelp job chart that allows each student to rotate in and out of specific class jobs that teach them how to use social media responsibly. Under a teacher's class social media account, students can take turns posting on social media under the guidance of the teacher and a peer whose weekly job is to be the proofreader before the post is published. Some students are regular bloggers, some are Insta users, some are Twitter lovers, and others are not. Their comfort levels using different social media platforms will vary depending upon their individual interests, parental controls at home, and previous exposure to social media. Giving each student the opportunity to rotate in and out of a job that encourages them to represent their peers publically via social media allows the teacher to guide them within a safe framework and grow digital citizens that make smart choices. Through these jobs, shown in Figure 10.3, learners are encouraged to think before posting, consider how they represent themselves with grammar, spelling, and word choice, and evaluate what information is considered too personal to share. This creates healthy habits for the time when they are no longer under the guidance of a social media savvy teacher and peer editor.

Figure 10.3 iHelp job chart.

- Lead a TED-Ed club in which students share powerful messages about the ways in which social media impacts our world. Encouraging students to research the role that social media plays in the lives of others cultivates thoughtful social media users inspired to think before they post. Through the development of a TED talk, learners consider how they want to shape the digital representation of themselves.

I love the way that social media can be leveraged to recognize student experts in which they demonstrate their knowledge to a larger audience. We have shared countless student creations via Twitter with the makers of the tools that we are using, which has afforded us unexpected opportunities. For example, we love to create inventions with littleBits, the magnetic circuits that snap together to create an action. Students blog about their littleBits inventions and through a class Twitter account, we tweet the blog posts to the makers of littleBits. In turn, the maker of littleBits has shared some of our student works with their own social media audience, allowing us to become a chapter school for littleBits, and giving us access to littleBits challenges that have resulted in free littleBits kits to grow our resources. All of these opportunities are a result of students sharing via social media platforms under a class Twitter account and a class blog via Blogger. Our class blog tagline is "Written by students for students," because while it gives others a window into our classroom activities, it helps us generate more resources and additional learning opportunities.

Gaining Experience and Improving Momentum

Social media usage in the classroom provides experiential learning opportunities. The more that educators incorporate social media use into everyday curriculum, the more savvy we all become in navigating these platforms. If your students are under the age of thirteen, allowing them to interact on social media with the teacher as the buffer allows students to gain real-world experience under the confines of the law and with the safety of an adult. If students are over the age of thirteen, consider incorporating the thoughtful use of social media into assessment practices. Build a social media component into a rubric requiring that students share their work on a social media platform and to reflect on the outcome of doing so. The more we encourage students to think about the ways in which social media shapes their growth, the more they will consider its impact and use it for good.

Social media evokes emotion. When we watch videos, read a tweet, or listen to a podcast, we have a human response to that content. In turn, this human response helps us remember what we learn. In this way, leveraging social media to create experiential learning opportunities is another powerful play in learning. Next, I will share some of my favorite lessons, projects, and activities that have brought the learning to life by harnessing the power of social media.

Facilitate Awesome

As a school, we actively explore resources that will help us craft powerful learning opportunities for our community. One example of this is our eighth-grade Social Studies teacher, Matt Barry, and his use of Twitter and video chat technology, to reenact the Second Continental Congress. His invitation states the following:

> Friends and U.S. History Teachers alike! It's almost time for the Second Continental Congress Meeting! This September 30th from 8am–11am EST, my 70 8th grade students and I will reenact the Second Continental Congress meeting in Philadelphia! In years past, we have skyped with a few classes and are opening up that chance again. We are also going to live tweet the event and use Periscope! If you are interested in tweeting with us or watching and asking questions to our class, reach out to me at mbarry@davisacademy.org #davis8 #sstlap #tlap.

Students arrive to school in full costume ready to assume the identity of the delegates. Using their culminating knowledge learned over the course of the weeks leading up to this event, students are ready to actively participate in a live Twitter chat and Skype session with other students from around the country. In character, students ask questions and respond appropriately back and forth in front of a live audience of parents, students, and other educators. This event fittingly takes place in the library that has been transformed by Matt to resemble a different era. We like to say "it's not your mama's media center." It's a place that comes alive by the unique experiences that our learners bring into it. Matt sets the stage with the following notice: "Fifty-six delegates from thirteen colonies meet in Philadelphia to determine whether the actions of the British Parliament and the Crown are justified. It is May 1775 and the Battles of Lexington and Concord have taken place and our natural rights have been violated. We will meet to determine where to go from here . . .". It is one of our most highly anticipated days of the year.

Each year, specific classes in different parts of the country are regular participants while others come on board as newbies. Further inspired by Dave Burgess' model of Teach Like a PIRATE, Matt has helped develop a following of other educators who facilitate their own experiential learning opportunities to increase student engagement (Burgess 2015). In the interest of motivating others to create simulations of historical events and interesting hooks in the classroom, Matt has led professional development strands that focus on the power of Twitter in education and Dave Burgess' Teach Like a PIRATE approach to learning.

Speaking of pirates, Twitter became a stage for our kindergarteners to connect with @Mathspirates in New Zealand to participate in engineering and math challenges between our two campuses: one being in the United States and one being in New Zealand. Other classes signed on too from Canada and Australia. In fact, we discovered at times that there was a language barrier that made for some interesting outcomes, even within the English language. For example, we would take turns initiating engineering and math challenges to one another and filming our process and outcome. In one such challenge, we were to build the tallest tower using biscuits or cookies and large marshmallows. Our New Zealand pirate friends were using biscuits, which in New Zealand is not the same as biscuits in the United States. In New Zealand, biscuits are more like crispy cookies or crackers and here in the United States biscuits are fluffy and doughy. When it comes to building a tower with biscuits, the outcome would be very different depending on which version of the biscuits were used, just based on the weight and stability alone. Until we realized the difference in meaning, we were scratching our heads. It was another powerful learning experience that carried us around the globe allowing us to participate in active learning and discover differences in semantics in the United States versus New Zealand. We were able to challenge them to a dreidel building and spinning activity, teaching them about a religious symbol important to our student body. The cultural connections made via Twitter for our kindergarten students and their teachers resulted in an awesome ongoing learning opportunity infusing math skills, design skills, lessons in semantics, and relationship building.

Social media allows educators to create learning opportunities that inspire civil discourse and promote social action. Missy Stein, a sixth-grade Language Arts teacher at The Davis Academy, required that her students read *The Watsons Go to Birmingham* by Christopher Paul Curtis, which takes place during the Civil Rights Movement, as a summer reading assignment. Upon our return to school at the time in which students were discussing this novel in Mrs. Stein's class, Ferguson, Missouri, was ignited in fury over the death and shooting of Michael Brown, Jr., an eighteen-year-old African American man, who was fatally shot by a white police officer. Through Twitter, our sixth-grade Language Arts classes were able to live tweet with educators in the vicinity of Ferguson and engage in dialogue that explored how the present mimics the past: "As we are currently evaluating the characters in the book, the post-traumatic stress that the main character endures, and how the bombing changes everyone we will talk about (a) What has and has not changed since 1963 (b) Do we have enough facts to take a side in the Missouri case and (c) How do we examine this situation with our lens of righteousness (this is one of our five core school values)?" (Stein 2014). Students in Atlanta, Georgia, were afforded the opportunity to learn more about social injustice in Ferguson, Missouri, from individuals experiencing these events firsthand. Embracing the Twitter hashtag #TogetherWeCan-Change to document and share the conversations made for a day of learning that will resonate with our students for years to come.

As social media users get younger, the stress and anxiety that parents and educators feel to bring back some level of control when it comes to social media usage among children is growing. Ben Halpert, Founder of Savvy Cyber Kids, offers a variety of free resources for parents and educators to "get the tech talk started and never stop." The Savvy Cyber Kids, Inc. blog notes that the best parental controls are parents themselves (2017). With this in mind, one of the most powerful lessons using social media was dubbed ProTech the Ones You Love. In this lesson, fifth-grade students created a lesson on digital citizenship based on tips that they had learned at home. They made a short film specifying each tip and role playing these tips in practice. They debuted the film with our five-year-old learners and, together, using the tips the fifth graders shared, the five-year-old students cowrote a blog post alongside a fifth-grade mentor highlighting what they had learned and demonstrating how to be better bloggers while protecting their privacy online.

The study of entrepreneurship presents active learning opportunities for positive uses of social media. I facilitate a sixth-grade course that focuses on the role of technology in entrepreneurship. Each of the students dream up an invention to solve a problem. They grow their business idea by crafting a business plan in Google documents, a budget in Google spreadsheets, a 3D prototype in Tinkercad, and finally a marketing campaign using a variety of social media platforms. In addition to developing an app in iBuildapp.com, they learn HTML to create their own websites from scratch to advertise their product. They use Piktochart to create an infographic highlighting their inventions' benefits. They blog about their process using Blogger.com because, as with most experiences in life, it's about the journey as much as the destination. Documenting and publishing their process offers practice in reflection and discovering areas for growth.

Passive Approaches to Learning with Social Media

There are a variety of technology tools that school librarians can introduce into the classroom that offer a safety net between sharing on the internet and gaining experience using digital platforms. Classtools.net is a robust resource that is updated regularly with new tools that mimic social media platforms to simulate the experience of interacting via social media. Below is a list of explicit examples and the ways in which these tools can be used:

*   Ifaketext.com is a text generator simulation tool. There are multiple creative ways to engage learners with this tool. Examples include practicing vocabulary so that "texters" have to use the vocabulary word in context, recreating a scene from a novel in text format, describing how to solve a technical difficulty, or any other use that involves demonstrating knowledge. As opposed to just using the tool, build in a peer review process in which students evaluate how they are representing themselves through texting. Is their grammar correct? Do they use proper punctuation? Is capitalization used appropriately? Do the word choices reflect positively on the creator of the text?

*   Twister is a faux Twitter account hosted by Classtools.net. Learners can generate fake tweets based on historical figures that include factual information about their role in history and the time period. Challenge learners to consider an appropriate use of hashtags. What purpose do the hashtags serve? Are they to make the tweet more discoverable by topic and/or do they provide more information about the subject?

*   Fakebook is another favorite in that it allows learners to simulate the Facebook experience through interactive dialog. Fakebook users can set up an account that signifies a historical figure, a book character, a politician, a scientist, or any other individual that learners are studying. This activity encourages Fakebook creators to consider perspective, historical accuracy, and explore facts about literature or an important time period. Characters and their friends can interact on the Fakebook page to represent events as they happened. Fakebook creators can envision themselves stepping into the role of the subjects and create content according to how they believed the Fakebook friends would have engaged with one another.

The school librarian should be at the center of the efforts to promote the integration of social media into the learning community. In doing so, school librarians help ensure that the appropriate tools are being used in accordance with the law. Start a student social media club from within the library that is responsible for educating teachers about the age restrictions and safety measures relevant to each social media platform. Help teachers set up their class social media accounts so that they are using their professional email addresses and are cultivating a professional classroom profile within these platforms. Be the connected educator that brings new opportunities and relationships into the school to demonstrate the effectiveness of social media when channeled for good. Connecting with authors via social media before and after reading their books in student book clubs results in numerous Skype visits between authors and readers. Reach out to experts who can educate you, your faculty, and your students in innovative tools you are exploring as additions to the curricular experience. For example, through Twitter, we discovered a drone expert in Oregon who Skyped with our students about the pros and cons of drones in education. When a teacher or team of teachers is preparing to integrate a new technology tool into their learning that can expose students to external audiences, offer to host a pop-up seminar for their students so that they become familiar with the critical components of the digital tool. This might translate into walking students through the privacy settings, the location of the delete button, how to monitor comments, the sharing options, the points to consider before publishing, and more. Teachers will appreciate your support and your efforts to educate and assist the students. Become the role model that ignites a healthy, productive community of responsible, impactful social media users.

CHAPTER ELEVEN

Build Curiosity with QR Codes

"The QR code helps me show other people my work so that they can say it's cool."

—Phillip, age 7

A QR code, which stands for quick response code, has a mysterious allure to it. Perhaps it is their curious appearance, their ability to be placed in the strangest of places, and/or the knowledge that some earth-shattering message could be hidden behind the wall of the QR code only to be discovered by scanning the code with a QR reader. Once my eyes were open to the possibility of QR codes being in the most unlikely of places, I started to notice them more often. I saw them on stickers placed on bananas in the grocery store, in restaurant windows, and on movie posters, as just a few examples. In an educational setting, QR codes can add an element of creative fun to the learning process, the sharing of student work, and the discovery of media-rich content. This chapter will explore the benefits of using QR codes in a school environment, the innovative uses, and the technology that can be used in conjunction with QR codes.

Trick Plays

The enticing mystery behind QR codes makes it difficult to resist scanning them, especially when posted with a catchy phrase nearby to elicit curiosity. QR code technology now allows QR code creators to customize QR codes with colors and images embedded into the QR design making them even more appealing. Using QR codes to generate excitement, curiosity, and publicity makes it possible to elevate one's game without it even being realized. School librarians can demonstrate their ease of use starting in the library by using QR codes to share professional development resources, host scavenger hunts for the patrons, and as tools to showcase student work. However, before we get into all that, let us consider the history of the QR code.

The History of the QR Code

It is interesting to discover how QR codes became a part of the everyday consumer scene. They were invented in Japan as an iteration of the barcode allowing more than just numbers to be stored as data. In 1994, the company Denso Wave, which is a developer and manufacturer of data capture equipment, industrial robots, and other systems, developed the QR code as a way for Toyota Car Company to be able to track and control their inventory of car parts. Denso Wave decided not to patent the rights to the QR code, which has seemingly influenced QR code technology becoming one of the more common means to extract large amounts of data quickly (Anderson 2011). Once the reliability of QR codes had been established, other industries, such as food, pharmaceuticals, and contact lenses, started to use QR codes as a means to measure their inventory. It allowed the production process for various goods to become transparent. In 2002, cell phones began to be marketed as having the ability to read QR codes, which helped contribute to the spread of their popularity. Soon, people were using QR codes to access airplane boarding passes, coupons, and contact information. In 2014, QR code technology advanced. The codes became customizable so that QR code creators could personalize the appearance of the codes. This is known as FrameQR. According to Denso Wave's website, it was very important to the company that the QR code be universally accessible so that as many people could benefit from the technology as possible. QR codes act as shortcuts to access large (or small) amounts of data. Today, there are technology tools that embed additional shortcuts within the use of QR codes allowing content creators to produce QR codes directly within their websites. We will explore these tools later in this chapter. For now, read along to discover the benefits of creating with QR codes and myriad innovative approaches to entice curious learners. The games have just begun!

Benefits of Making QR Codes Part of Your Game Plan

QR codes make data sharing a mobile experience while being easily accessible. Rather than typing in a tricky URL, individuals can scan an image to receive large amounts of data. Another plus is that the data stored within the QR codes can be accessed from anywhere, as long as the QR code is readable. This creates opportunities for student engagement through interactive learning experiences. Learners also gain a sense of independence with QR codes. Students can self-check their work by scanning the answer keys found within QR codes and they can proceed at their own pace. This level of independence, even for learners as young as kindergarten, allows the educator to focus on small group or individual instruction when needed. As a result, QR codes can be a powerful tool to assist with classroom management, support differentiation, and allow for logistical flexibility. QR codes also save wall space while allowing educators to advertise special programs, tutorials, and strong resources to support learning. Content creators can use QR codes to brand their work creating signature logos behind QR codes to identify their work as their own. These simple square-shaped codes allow users to personalize their creations no matter the level of complexity behind the design. How can a librarian use QR codes to support innovative practices in a school? Read on for some imaginative examples of QR code usage at its best.

Going the Distance with QR Codes

You would not think that what originated as black and white squares could be used in so many inventive ways, but sometimes simple allows the most innovative outcomes. QR codes can be a prime example of such. I recommend starting by using QR codes in the school library so that all patrons interact with them in some form, then suggesting ways you can support teachers in integrating them into their classrooms, and finally encouraging students to generate their own QR codes for their own sharing.

Examples of Creative QR Code Uses

QR codes can be used to encourage content creators to produce their best work. When they discover how shareable their work becomes with QR codes, it is hard not to feel a sense of pride to do their best work. Accessibility for sharing resonates with content creators. They know that a larger audience can discover their efforts, giving richer meaning to its value.

QR codes as teasers are irresistible. Set up QR codes on the back of bathroom stalls to advertise library programming, such as book clubs, poetry readings, and author events. Entice potential readers by posting QR codes in the hallways with question marks next to them. When scanned, readers may discover a book trailer for a new book in the library, a link to a Google form to sign up for the next book club event, or an advertisement for a powerful database. Fun places to post QR codes include on the seat of chairs, on top of trash cans, inside stairwells, outside lockers, and inside cabinets. Encourage a scavenger hunt for students to scan the highest number of hidden QR codes advertising library-related information, with the student bringing back evidence of their findings for a prize. Cultivate a culture of learners who are trained to scan the codes when they stumble upon them, even in the most unlikely of places.

When planning QR code placement, consider access to devices. Are you advertising for younger students who primarily use mobile devices, such as tablets, in their classrooms? If so, consider planting QR codes in the unlikeliest of places within the classroom, such as on the door to the classroom as an entry ticket. If using a platform like Glogster, Blogger, Smore .com, or any other multimedia tool that can be updated, the QR code can remain the same while the creator of the content can simply update the information within the QR code from directly within the multimedia tool.

QR codes allow for an innovative approach to highlighting student authors. A great partnership between the school librarian and the language arts and/or homeroom teacher is to support not only the publication of student authors' works but also the ways in which their work is shared. Each May, our students in kindergarten prep through fifth grade debut books that they have written on what is known as Young Authors Night. Each grade level has a different theme for the books that

they write. For example, our kindergarten prep students create an All About Me book. On the cover is a QR code with an image of their face in the middle. When scanned, the QR code links to a self-portrait drawn by the student using the whiteboard app ShowMe, which includes an audio recording of the student announcing their book's title and to whom the book is dedicated, as shown in Figure 11.1.

Similarly, student authors can create an interactive

Figure 11.1   Scan the QR code to experience a multimedia book cover made with the whiteboard app, ShowMe, and a QR code.

All About the Author component to their books with the help of customized QR codes. Once the QR code in Figure 11.2 is scanned, you will see and hear one student sharing his biographical information through the whiteboard app known as Educreations. This is a fun way to learn more about the author while hearing their voice, as opposed to reading about them. It's a multisensory experience that helps the words jump right off the pages.

Students can create their own poetry anthologies. In our case, students were inspired by reading Sharon Creech's novel *Love That Dog*. When the QR code on their poetry anthology is scanned, it takes the reader to a public reading of one of the student's poems that they have filmed themselves reading in front of a green screen. Using the Green Screen app by DoInk and Creative Commons Search website, the poet drops in a background relevant to the poem that they are sharing.

Figure 11.2 Scan the QR code to hear one student author sharing his biographical information through the whiteboard app Educreations.

QR codes can be tools for active learning encouraging students to venture beyond their immediate space. One of my favorite collaborative projects involves creating littleBits challenges that relate to curriculum. Homeroom teachers or specialized teachers bring their classes to work together in smaller groups to achieve a goal with the help of littleBits that relates to what they are learning. For example, third graders were challenged with art-inspired activities in preparation for an upcoming field trip to the High Museum of Art in Atlanta. With the help of QR codes that link to informative videos, students can jointly view additional content. Using QR codes, as shown in Figure 11.3, to add depth to their understanding of the content influences the group's ability to work together and synthesize information. Upon grasping their task, they begin the design cycle

Yayoi Kusama's limitless *Infinity Mirrors* exhibit is all the rage at the High Museum of Atlanta right now. In fact, it was sold out in minutes! Watch this five minute video by scanning the QR code below. Can you create a work of art with littleBits inspired by the style of Yayoi Kusama's art?

Figure 11.3   Art-inspired littleBits challenge.

through a process of developing ideas, inquiring, evaluating and creating the end product.

QR codes allow a layer of multimedia enrichment to any student project. As school librarians take on the role of supporting the addition of media to traditional projects, a collaborative partnership is formed between the other educator and the school librarian. This is one strategy for developing strong relationships through innovative projects. For example, our fourth-grade students create a states project each year, in which they select and research one state. Naturally, the school librarian partners with the teachers and students for the research portion. In recent years, however, we have added an audio component with a little help from the friendly QR code. Using the AudioBoo app, students shared their research findings about their particular state alongside their poster board allowing viewers to hear the student's learning. While this project is done in fourth grade, the younger grade teachers make a point of allowing their classes to travel through the states project exhibit. With the inclusion of QR codes linked to audio, this creates a multisensory experience for the viewer while accommodating an auditory learner.

Sometimes QR codes can create an active experience in which it is not just the mind that travels to another time and place but also the body. Invite teachers that assign writing to partner with you on a project that will bring the writing to life with the aid of QR codes. One example of this includes our second-grade team assigning the following journal writing prompt: "If you could travel anywhere in the world, where would it be and why?" After students consider this, and possibly even do some research to support their position, invite the class to join you in the media center to recreate their destination in virtual reality using the CoSpacesEdu app. Educators can establish a free digital classroom allowing each student to have their own space under the framework of the teacher. You can push out an assignment so that once logged into their student account, students can create independently and have their work saved within the teacher's class account. This makes the sharing of the students work fairly simple. Once finished, we project each student's project onto a large drop down screen and allow the students to act as tour guides navigating their peers through their chosen place. This serves as an audio and visual representation of their journal writing. When parents come into the building for parent-teacher conferences, the teachers hang up their written journal entries creatively shared under the flap of a suitcase, alongside a personalized QR code that links to their virtual reality destination scene. This keeps parents busy as they await their turn to speak with their child's teacher.

Another collaborative win is using these same tools and resources to highlight to parents the innovative approaches to learning that their children are experiencing. Each year, we host a parent media center volunteer orientation in which we welcome our new parent volunteers, provide a Dewey Decimal System 101 training to make their shelving process more seamless, and mingle with the parents so that they have an opportunity to learn the library while getting to know the librarian. Arranging the orientation so that parents go through a QR code scavenger hunt in teams orienting themselves to the library's layout demonstrates interactive learning opportunities that you and the other educators regularly create for their children. This, in turn, helps the school librarian gain parental support toward volunteer hours, resources, and advocacy.

QR codes allow audiences to examine the work of student creators by providing a window into their process. Next time you want to highlight student work either as a presentation or as an exhibit, consider placing QR codes in the space so that audiences can get a closer look at the students' creation process. When presenting in front of parents about the programming opportunities for our students, I strategically place QR codes around tables so that parents can scan them and view sample projects. One of my favorite projects involved two fifth-grade boys that created a power table out of littleBits. The table consisted of a knife that cut vegetables and other items at a slow speed and another knife that cut food items at a faster speed, both of which were attached to cutting boards that were part of one table raised at two different levels. Rather than listen to me describe the project, by scanning the QR code that linked to a YouTube video, parents could view the students showcasing their project and sharing their creation process. Another example of this is our Math Museum created by kindergarten students. These students used the ShowMe whiteboard app to demonstrate how the number line worked to aid in addition and subtraction. Each student solved a math problem through ShowMe, explained and demonstrated their process using the number line, and each video was then saved as a QR code. Each QR code was framed as though it were part of a museum exhibit, and displayed on the walls outside their classroom. Students can also use the Educreations app for this activity as well as demonstrate how they solve a mathematical word problem. For example, if ten birds are sitting on a fence and two fly away, how many are left? The student can announce the problem and draw ten birds on a fence making two fly away to show that eight remain. Then, they can show how they would write this equation: $10 - 2 = 8$. This is one way for them to show what they know. Again, strategically putting the Math Museum on display at a time when parents are going to be in the building and noting the collaboration between the school librarian and the homeroom teacher demonstrates the value of the partnership.

Showcasing student work with QR codes can be done in a variety of ways with cross-curricular collaboration. Our art teacher, Rebecca Ganz, facilitates a project for our upper elementary students around the holiday of Purim, in which each student selects an artist and develops a mask around that artist's style. These students do biographical research on their artists with the school librarian, and create digital posters with Glogster .com that highlight the artist's work, their lives, and timelines of the author's life events. A QR code is placed next to each mask and, when scanned, audiences are directed to the digital poster board further educating the viewer about the artist who inspired the mask's design.

Students are the experts. Leverage the use of QR codes as a platform for students to share their expertise and their experiences. For example, work with the IT department to determine the most commonly asked questions that they wish they had the answer to on repeat. Do the same within the library department and/or among classroom teachers. Using a screencasting tool, such as the free Screencast-O-Matic.com, have students record themselves answering those commonly asked questions. For example, perhaps parents and students are constantly asking how students can remotely check their school email. Have a student demonstrate this process, host their screencast on YouTube, and turn the link into a QR code. When the question is asked about how to access email remotely, simply forward the QR code to the information seeker. It's a game changer in that it saves time, builds relationships across departments and empowers students to share their knowledge. Next time you put a book into the hands of a student, ask them to record an audio review of the book using the free website vocaroo.com. Vocaroo will generate a QR code within their website, which can be printed out and placed inside the book cover so that future browsers of the library can be persuaded (or not) to check out a book. The same can be done with student-made book trailers. Host their book trailers on YouTube, create a QR code that links to the YouTube video, and allow the student's movie making skills and book synopsis to come to life.

We have explored placing QR codes in some unlikely places but consider allowing QR codes to serve as human billboards showcasing student work. Students can create wearable QR codes, whether the QR codes are embedded into jewelry designs, placed as appliques ironed onto t-shirts, or even generated as removable tattoos. The latter is sure to be a hit among older students.

Favorite QR Code Tools to Amplify the Learning and the Sharing

When working with QR codes, I proactively encourage my community to download a QR code reader ahead of time. For example, if I launch a project with another educator that will be sent home via a QR code, I help draft language for the primary teacher to send home a letter or email to the families explaining what a QR code is and including the steps to download a QR code reader so that when the time comes, they are ready to scan. I have had great experiences with the i-nigma QR code reader and the Kaywa QR code reader. Both tend to be fast and adept at scanning the codes. In terms of generating the QR codes, qrcode-monkey.com is excellent in that it allows the creator to customize their QR code with an image and a variety of colors. Often, I use my Snipping Tool in Windows or the Grab tool in Apple to generate a jpeg file of the QR code. This step, however, is not necessary as the QR code can be downloaded as a Portable Network Graphics (PNG) file directly within qrcode-monkey.com. If you want to create a QR code scavenger hunt, a free resource can be found at https://www.classtools.net/QR that allows you to input a series of questions and answers, generate a QR code for each question, and place the QR codes around your space or building to send users on a digital quest. Once the QR code scavenger hunt questions and answers have been input into the classtools.net website, the website generates easy to follow instructions for the organizer, including how to explain the scavenger hunt to the participants. They can self-check their answers too. Classtools.net suggests dividing participants into small groups and giving each group one mobile device with which to scan the QR codes. If one person needs something additional to do within the group, they can be assigned the research role to help identify the answers before the group self-checks themselves. Another job within the group is to create an accountability officer that ensures that their group abides by the preestablished guidelines. School librarians can create QR code scavenger hunts as a professional development learning opportunity for faculty focused on specific growth areas, such as project-based learning while demonstrating a tool that requires active participation. School librarians can cofacilitate the creation of QR code scavenger hunts with other educators to accomplish a specific curricular goal and they can establish one for their parent community to demonstrate the innovative ways that their children are learning concepts. There are a variety of other platforms that make it simple to generate QR codes within their framework so that it is not necessary to input media into a third-party QR code generator. One example of this is the digital portfolio platform, Seesaw.

As QR code popularity continues to flourish and media sharing becomes more mobile, I suspect QR code generators will be integrated directly within digital tools. Regardless, QR codes make it easy for school librarians to partner with other educators, learners, and community members to share information and direct active learning opportunities. Luckily, we now have the ability to make them a little bit more attractive through improved technology. Embrace them!

CHAPTER TWELVE

Go Viral with Videoconferencing

"Mystery skyping with another school was entertaining and mysterious. I enjoyed guessing where they were located because I love a good mystery. The technology made it possible to reach students our age from another part of the country."

—Mia, age 15

New Plays with Old Equipment

According to Eventbrite, a global platform for connecting people to live events around the world, there are five reasons that motivate people to want to attend sporting events. The reasons are the following: networking and/or socializing, halftime shows, promotions and/or giveaways, team spirit, and impressing someone (Denton 2016). Each of these reasons is applicable to why a school librarian benefits from arranging videoconferencing events for their patrons with the ability to interact in real time with others outside their immediate community. Videoconferencing uses technology to make visual connections among people and places in real time. The concept of videoconferencing was first conceived in the late 1870s as a possibility for what the future might hold (Vasilyeva 2013). While the notion of videoconferencing has been around for quite some time, there are a variety of reliable and free videoconferencing tools to facilitate impactful curricular connections that can be shared among a larger learning community. In this section, we will explore some of these tools as well as address the benefits of videoconferencing in a variety of learning situations.

Extend the Playing Field

Powerful connections can be made in what is considered to be video-mediated communication. In fact, although unable to pick up on social cues in the same way that sharing a physical space allows, research reflects that people communicating via video are inclined to smile more often and raise the volume of their voice to compensate for not coexisting in the same space. Often times, videoconferencing results in seeing the other party from the chest up, diminishing the ability to pick up on body language (Croes et al. 2018). While this may sound like a disadvantage, it can actually serve as an advantage for learners who feel less confident in social settings and/or seek to understand content areas in which they feel like a novice. Let's go back to the five reasons mentioned previously for wanting to attend a sporting event. By relating each motivator to the potential effect that videoconferencing can have on the learning experience, it is hard to argue against school librarians establishing themselves as the catalyst for employing this technology first within the school library and ultimately into the classrooms through teacher partnerships. Naturally, a school's learning culture is on a continuum. At the 2019 Prizmah conference, author and educator George Couros asked the question, "How do we move from pockets of innovation to a culture of innovation?" This is exactly where the school librarian can be the game changer.

As mentioned above, one motivator for attending a sporting event is considered to be the entertainment provided. The halftime show appeals to the audience in its ability to dazzle the mind and ignite the senses. Video-conferencing can have the same impact on learners. Without the limitations of their usual surroundings, video communication allows audiences to enter into new and different territory, awakening a desire to soak up new knowledge and learn about and from others through a visual context. The biggest obstacle to employing videoconference capabilities within the classroom is not a lack of technology but rather a lack of confidence to set it up. However, if all educators knew how easy technology made it to connect on a global scale, they would give videoconferencing another look. Sometimes, I believe we feel paralyzed by the terminology, which can sound so intimidating. Take away the intimidation factor by taking the lead to educate the educators in your school community and model the possibilities.

Entertainment is always a draw to a sporting event. Whether it is the halftime show, the people watching, or the on and off the field stories of the player's lives, entertainment hooks audiences. In much the same way, school librarians can reel their audiences in to learning by exposing them to customs, cultures, places, and people different from their everyday norm. Ask yourself how you can leverage this approach to encourage literacy, innovative practices, and grow connections. We will explore specific examples further in this chapter. In the meantime, consider who and what would excite your learning community and who you need to videoconference with to entertain and educate your learners to access these subjects of interest.

Another reason people like to attend sporting events is to receive promotions and giveaways. In much the same way, videoconferencing opens up new opportunities for relationship building that has its own perks. Learners are exposed to people and places that otherwise may not be possible due to financial constraints, health issues, or logistical limitations. Despite these obstacles, videoconferencing makes meaningful connections possible. Demonstrate this by dazzling your school community with a memorable connection that leaves your learning community with a meaningful memory. Memorable experiences are the gifts that keep on giving. I will share some examples of memorable connections afforded via videoconferencing later on in this chapter.

Another favorite reason to attend a sporting event is the team spirit that comes from joining together to support the players. Have you ever been driving down the street and noticed another car with your alma mater's school logo and felt compelled to honk, wave, or give a symbol of being proud as a fellow supporter of that school? Sports allow different people, strangers included, to rally together to support a common interest. Believe it or not, videoconferencing can do the exact same thing! One of the greatest perks to being a librarian is to work within a profession that embraces a culture of sharing. There are countless school librarians connected on a variety of social media platforms sharing connection opportunities for students to come together and support a common cause. Whether it is to learn the ways we can save chimpanzees from extinction, sharing a Q&A session with other students around the country, connecting with Olympic athletes to learn about the hard work that goes into training for an Olympic medal, or for students to use their geography skills in a race against the clock to discover another class' location before they discover yours, be the bridge that connects your community to these opportunities. Build a spirited community in which your learners are linked to others beyond a physical space.

Finally, impressing someone is a reason why spectators attend a sporting event. What's most impressive, however, is not just spectating but being a part of the game. Interacting with the players, dining in the sky box, and swapping stories with fellow fans are what make an experience memorable and create lasting impressions. In much the same way, video-conferencing technology can allow learners to actively share and engage with incredible individuals in a comfortable setting. Be the powerhouse within the school that facilitates these valuable connections through videoconferencing.

Punt from the Library

Now that we have explored the reasons why videoconferencing makes for a memorable and positive learning experience, let's explore the what. What does videoconferencing from within the library look like for your learners? It is always a smart idea to associate extraordinary opportunities with the library space when possible (this is one reason I opt out of host-ing exciting author events in the gym when space permits). Often, the library is one of the larger spaces within the school that can accommodate a lot of bodies. The library often houses much of the school's technology, whether it is a large projector, interactive whiteboard, and/or webcam. Very importantly, perception can be everything. Public relations matter. Putting your community in front of those that they admire, will be impressed by, will learn from, and will delight in interacting with, all from within the comfort of the library, elevates the school library's public image as being a dynamic space where anything is possible. It is impor-tant not to underestimate the power of physically connecting rewarding opportunities to a specific place while allowing other educators to co-facilitate the experience. As learning through video-mediated communi-cation becomes more routine, other educators will feel more comfortable being the primary facilitator for specific groups with targeted content areas. This is when you will know that you have moved from pockets of innovation to a culture of innovation. The booster club will be in place. In the meantime, leverage the library as the place from which to punt this powerful play in learning.

Support from the Booster Club

Now that the stakeholders have witnessed and or heard about the amaz-ing connections made possible with videoconferencing, it is prime time to ramp up the integration. Take library programming to the next level with videoconferencing. Discover free technology tools so that these experiences do not cost a dime. With a little creativity, organization, and planning, the school library can be the portal to exploring the rest of the world.

The World Is Your Stadium with These Tools

There are a variety of videoconferencing tools available. Those that are free are often used in education while there are a variety of paid applications used in both education and business. The chosen tool is often dictated by the hardware that is available, the budget, and the size of the group. Let's explore the free tools:

- Google Hangouts: Often referred to as GHO, Google Hangouts are simple to use as long as you have a Gmail account. I recommend setting up a professional Gmail account not only for GHO usage but for any Google application that you may want to use for educational purposes in your school community. I have set mine up so that my professional school email account, which is not a Gmail account, is what I use to log into my Google apps. As I have done, it is possible to make your professional email account the primary email address to access Google applications. I prefer this so that I can compartmentalize the organization of my personal and professional Google creations. A personal Gmail address can be established as a recovery email address for the professional account. With GHO, you simply log into your Google account, go to Google apps, and click on the icon labeled hangouts. You can invite someone to join a hangout via their email address or by sharing the direct link to your Google Hangout. Settings can be restricted so that the connection includes video, audio, or video and audio. You can also text message your contacts with GHO. A nice feature is that video meetings can be recorded and shared later with those who could not be present or those who want to recap the details. Up to twenty-five participants can take part in a video call and invites for a hangout can be shared with a Google calendar or a Microsoft Outlook calendar. Additional features include sharing your screen or a portion of your screen, muting other participants, and accessing GHO from any computer or mobile device that has a camera or webcam.

- Zoom: Similar to GHO in that it is simple and quick to set up a videoconference call, Zoom.us is another strong free option. Zoom can host up to 100 participants for forty minutes but one-to-one videoconferencing has unlimited time. There is an unlimited number of meetings that can take place. Users can share their screens as well as have private and group chats. By clicking schedule a meeting and adding the details, the meeting can be shared on Google, Outlook, or Yahoo calendars or by sharing a link. Video calls can also be recorded with Zoom.

- Skype: Skype is a great tool to videoconference with up to ten people. However, what makes Skype special for educators is Skype in the Classroom, now a part of Microsoft. Skype in the Classroom offers amazing opportunities for connections geared specifically to schools. In fact, my students have Skyped with scientist and environmentalist Dr. Jane Goodall to learn about caring for animals, the planet, and the environment. We will explore more of these opportunities in the next section. Skype can be installed on a desktop computer (and automatically comes installed on Windows 10 devices), mobile devices, and can be used with Alexa and Xbox One. Skype was the first free videoconferencing tool to evolve into a verb. It is easy to use, has been around since 2003, and specifically supports a learning community with a variety of built-in connection opportunities making its integration seamless for educators. Users will need to set up a Skype account or a Microsoft account to use Skype.

- Facebook Live: This is another free option for videoconferencing. While Facebook users can select a specific audience for their live streaming video, the interaction is limited in that viewers can communicate via chat. Facebook Live events can be scheduled ahead of time to generate excitement. There is a four-hour time limit for Facebook Live broadcasts.

- YouTube Live: This is similar to Facebook Live in that it is live streaming but hosted on YouTube. The first time you use YouTube Live, you may have a delay so that YouTube can verify that your account is in good standing. This is an important detail if you are looking to establish an impromptu event for the first time.

- FaceTime: For a one-on-one videoconferencing app, FaceTime is a quick and easy option for iOS devices. With AirServer or Apple TV, it is possible to share FaceTime with larger audiences by projecting onto a large screen.

- Periscope: Similar to YouTube Live and Facebook Live, this is an iOS app that allows audiences to create or view live streams. Interaction is limited to comments and hearts. You cannot control what other viewers say in their comments so it is not uncommon for profanity or even edgy usernames to pop up on the screen. Keep this in mind when considering your age group, whether you host a public Periscope or pipe into someone else's.

Many other tools make up the playing field so if you have not found the one that you are most inclined to use listed above, don't lose hope. There are myriad other options. Now that we are equipped with some tools, let's explore what kind of beneficial plays we can make with them.

Plays to Improve the Scoreboard

As mentioned above, once videoconferencing happens a few times, it becomes routine for learners to interact with a global audience. Below, I will share some of my favorite options for videoconferencing. With an internet connection, these are learning opportunities without boundaries.

- Bon Voyage but Wait, We Are Coming Too: If you have any co-educators or parents that take interesting trips, ask them if you can tag along with your students for an outing. Using FaceTime, a homeroom teacher and I co-facilitated a videoconferencing experience for her students with two parents that were on a Mediterranean cruise. The parents served as our tour guides and answered questions from the class about their cultural experiences as their journey unfolded. Tap into your resources and discover upcoming voyages that members of your community may be willing to share with your students in real time. Visiting the Northern Lights, the Eiffel Tower, or the rainforests of Costa Rica? Let us join you. The more the merrier and anything is possible with technology.

- Dial an Expert: As school librarians, we pride ourselves on being resourceful. We may not know everything but we have a good idea about how to find out anything. Also common in our culture is stretching ourselves to bring unique experiences to our learners, even if it is beyond our knowledge base. We find ourselves facilitating opportunities in which we may not be the experts but we provide a forum for exploration of these topics. Videoconferencing is a remarkable strategy to expose your learners to experts when they are ready for the next level of content expertise. For example, when we started exploring drones in education with our student technology leaders, we found that we did not have all the up-to-date knowledge on privacy laws and flight paths. As a result, we Skyped with an expert at the University of Oregon who was well-versed on this topic and was able to educate us. On occasion, we have run into a conflict with time zones in these instances but often times we can share our questions ahead of time and the expert will record their answers as a video so that we can hear directly from the source. Coordinate with another teacher to bring a subject expert for their class via videoconferencing. Interested in Skyping with a scientist? Visit https://www.skypeascientist.com to arrange a science-related Skype visit. Looking to Skype with an artist, a mathematician, a game designer? Look no further. Skype in the Classroom has an entire section on their website devoted to connecting learners with a variety of experts. Visit the site at https://education.microsoft.com/skype-in-the-classroom/find-guest-speakers to discover what will work best in your classrooms and connect with your school's curriculum.

- The Amazing Race: One of my favorite uses of videoconferencing is to mystery Skype. If you have not yet mystery Skyped with a class within your school, you are missing out! A mystery Skype is when one class or group of students videoconferences with another class or group of students without knowing where the other is located. By taking turns and asking open-ended questions that are not too specific as to spoil the fun (and there is an art to this), it is a race against the clock to discover where the other group is located first. We follow the mystery Skype model that was crafted by Paul Solarz, a fifth-grade teacher in Illinois, who has mastered the process and supports other educators in their mystery Skype efforts. You can follow his model by reading about it here: https://psolarz.weebly.com/how-to-set-up-and-run-a -mystery-skype-session.html. Like Paul Solarz, every student elects to do a job and is placed in a specific spot in the room according to the demands of their job. Every time we do a mystery Skype, it reminds me of an air traffic control tower, in which organized chaos and deep concentration are the vibes. We go to great lengths to mask our location in that we turn our shirts inside out, if necessary, put labels over our school name on our shirts, turn-over our school's personalized mouse pads, and anything else that needs to be done to mask our location. With a mystery Skype, no one can refuse the pull of trying to figure out the other group's location first. We have had a variety of visitors just "drop in" to check out our mystery Skype in action only to be pulled into the fun not being able to tear away until the race is over. We have had the good fortune of connecting with students in parts of the country very different from our own. One school, located in Lubbock, Texas, surprised us at the end of a mystery Skype by bringing in their exotic animals that they house on their property. That was quite an experience for our students! Partner with your social studies teacher and schedule a Skype that will take your students to the other side of the country. Microsoft's Skype in the Classroom website has a variety of mystery Skype resources to help connect with other classrooms. My primary method of connection, however, is made through Twitter or the Future Ready Librarians Facebook group. Sometimes, other librarians will circulate a Google Doc around in which you can sign up for the date and time that works best for your students. Just be sure to check the time zones!

- Get Real With Your Favorite Authors: Videoconferencing is a phenomenal strategy for connecting your learners with their favorite authors and illustrators. More often than not, authors and illustrators will donate fifteen to thirty minutes of their time to videoconference with your students. You simply have to ask. The worst that can happen is that they say no. We ask almost every time we select a new book club pick. This certainly adds a level of excitement to our book club event and we have found that many authors really enjoy connecting with their readers in this way. It allows the author to be in the comfort of their home or office, get direct feedback from their readers, and bounce new ideas off of prospective fans. Videoconferencing with authors has also allowed us to grow our author podcast series. Our students can interview authors through videoconferencing and mix introductory and concluding music to create another addition to our growing list of author interviews. Now that we videoconference with authors from within our library, our teachers are also connecting with authors via videoconference technology within their own classrooms after reading a novel within the curriculum.

- Help Me, I'm Stuck: Videoconferencing for guidance on a larger project in which different areas of expertise are required to move forward is another benefit to connecting visually on a global level. The world is your classroom.

Whether it is feeling stymied on a programming project in which another programmer's expertise is needed, questioning the installation of a part on your student built 3D printer, or struggling to solve a complex math problem, videoconferencing can be the solution. After all, this is how Khan Academy came to be in existence. Troubleshooting by videoconferencing is an empowering way for learners to be resourceful in solving their own problems.

- The Special Occasion: It is a special occasion every day somewhere in the world. If you think about it, the programming opportunities are endless for videoconferencing around a special event. Microsoft's Skype in the Classroom also has an entire portion of their website devoted to upcoming special Skype events. It is worth checking out regularly and signing up to receive updates when these opportunities are announced. Not only is it amazing to connect your students with current Olympic athletes in real time or learn directly from Dr. Jane Goodall but it is extraordinary for them to interact with students from all over the globe who seek these same experiences. These connections create awareness of where we stand in the universe, both literally and figuratively, as one being and as one community within a vast and diverse world.

The reach of videoconferencing can be far and wide. Seize the opportunities that this technology can produce to expose your students to the amazing and incredible richness of our world. With a passionate school librarian leading the charge and co-educators who are ultimately inspired to get in the game, the possibilities are limitless. With these crowd pleasers, the fans will go wild.

CHAPTER THIRTEEN

Innovation Requires Leadership

"The entrepreneur leadership program was an amazing opportunity to see how future technology might be used to make the world a better place."

—Melanie, age 14

School librarians are in a unique position in that we work with everyone in the building. Let's use this power to influence student leadership opportunities by establishing a stage at every age from which learners can be empowered to go out into the world and serve others. In my experience, unless consciously asked to pause and think about it, students have not previously stopped to consider themselves in relationship to being a leader. Influencing a leadership mindset goes a long way.

In the same way that we may invest our time in considering the different tactical approaches to cultivate teacher leaders through professional development, we can approach student leadership under a similar model. For example, we may ask a specific teacher to consider leading a professional development strand on the ways in which they successfully integrate innovative practices into their classroom for other interested faculty. What if we empowered students to employ a similar approach to lead others grounded in sharing their experiences? What would that look like? For example, imagine if students (and not just faculty) went on a learning walk where they observed other students' learning in action? Student participants could meet again to engage in a reflective conversation. They would discuss what they noticed, what was surprising, and what was held in common with their own practices in the classroom. As a student tasked with influencing an environment to make positive changes to improve the learning, they are encouraged to think about others beyond themselves.

Strong leaders are compelled to serve others. While leading others can be natural for some, school librarians can create informal opportunities for all students to discover their potential to guide others.

Leadership shows itself in a myriad ways. As successful entrepreneur Derek Sivers and TED speaker states, "Being a first follower is an underappreciated form of leadership" (2010). First followers are the ones who follow someone else, igniting an entire movement of followers. Not to be devalued, this form of bravery is one of the most powerful forms of quiet leadership.

In this chapter, I share strategies to integrate leadership opportunities within those two models: one model being with a preestablished group of identified student leaders (scripted) and the other model being with the general student population (unscripted). In addition to supporting the pedagogy of leadership, it's just as important to emphasize the library as a place and a space for launching students who learn to guide others. You want the library to be the destination for leadership development and, in doing so, you demonstrate that you are invested in the students' ability to flourish.

Scripted Plays

The school calendar is our roadmap for creative programming and outreach opportunities. If your school has a master calendar, I recommend you submit your programming plans before the summer break to ensure your events are part of the master calendar. In this way, when another school event is tempted to conflict and potentially alter your plans, you can point back to the master calendar as evidence of the investment you have already put into making your program proceed as scheduled and be successful. In this same way, it is a good idea to consider your student population and anticipate your library's leadership needs prior to the summer break. This allows you to generate excitement for upcoming leadership opportunities and create buzz for what to look forward to in the next school year. Next, I will share some library leadership opportunities that a) help the school librarian do a job that often requires more hours than we can give, b) empower students as leaders, and c) inspire teachers to look to the library as the hub from which student leaders are launched and mimic a similar model in their individual classrooms.

The Network Sherpas

Strategy One: Consider your community's needs. What are some areas of growth within your school and how can your students positively

contribute to achieving these goals? We noticed that some of our teachers needed more technology support for areas that many of us take for
granted in knowing how to do. Examples of this included setting up a contact group in Microsoft Outlook, downloading one app to multiple devices,
or sharing a Google Doc so that others could edit the document. We also
noticed that while we had cornered the market on social media usage
within our school, we had an entire subset within our community that
didn't know how to use social media platforms: grandparents. We also
noticed that students love technology. From a school culture perspective,
we wanted to develop more opportunities for student leaders to emerge. As
a result, the Network Sherpa program was born. At its onset, the Network
Sherpa program was advertised to fifth graders at the beginning of the year
as a way for them to become student leaders as an extension of the IT
department. While the library team is in a different department than the
Network Administrator, our duties often overlap and educators come to
both of us for similar requests. The IT department in many schools, ours
included, feels stressed with device management, teacher inquiries, new
acquisitions, and more. The Network Sherpa program offered some relief
to these stressors. I advertised the program in classroom newsletters, during class library visits, in emails to teachers, and in one-on-one conversations with students popping into the library. An application deadline was
established and interested students had to complete an online application
via a Google form. The application required a teacher recommendation,
confirmation of parent approval (to accommodate early and later hours as
needed), and to ensure that students read through and understood the
responsibilities. The first year, I had several boys and one girl. Despite the
small group size, the program was beloved. These students were treated to
privileges that they considered to be quite special. They went on a behind
the scenes technology tour of The Davis Academy, wearing their winter
coats in the hot months for a visit to the server room. They ventured up
the ninety-degree angle ship ladder to learn about the intricate technology
in the state-of-the-art theater sound booth. They developed lesson plans
for the five year olds that focused on technology skills and digital citizenship and then implemented those lessons as student teachers. They conducted a lunch n' learn workshop on the topic of innovation and taught
our grandparents how to interact with The Davis Academy via social
media platforms, such as Twitter. They represented our school presenting
at national conferences on issues related to technology. They showcased
their technology fair projects at board meetings and parent-teacher organization (PTO) meetings. They went into the classrooms and downloaded
apps for teachers onto their class set of iPads. They made screencasts of

commonly asked questions and built up a library of "how to" videos to save our IT department time answering routine questions. They became the go to person during class time when a teacher or a student was having technical difficulties. They earned the right to be a member of the junior stage crew and to run the spotlights. They were deployed into the classrooms to provide additional support for students when teachers were using more technology than usual in their lessons. They piloted new technology prior to the larger roll out. They met with outside vendors to consider future acquisitions to spur innovation. It was a special group with rewarding privileges and they knew it.

The following year, the program tripled in size. In some ways, this program altered some of our school culture. It created a new pathway for students who loved technology, enjoyed being empowered, and were seeking something more as the eldest of our lower school campus. Ultimately, it became a subset of our Middle School Leadership Training Institute and is now offered to sixth, seventh, and eighth-grade students. The learning within this program extends well beyond our school walls. These students have visited cutting-edge workspaces to learn about the role that innovation and technology plays in society and a variety of creative job opportunities. Together, we have had exposure to unique experiences along the way. For example, one group of Network Sherpas ventured to a startup community and learned about the local businesses that are trying to make it big within their fields. They learned about the hierarchical structure that exists and how it is represented within the physical structure of the space. The higher the floor, the more successful the startup. The end goal is to reach the highest floor and ultimately outgrow the space, otherwise known as "the village." Throughout the tour, we saw nontraditional sights, such as the napping room. One sight included provocative artwork with overt nudity. I addressed it head on reminding the Network Sherpas that we were no longer in a controlled environment. Learning how to act in response to the unexpected is part of being a leader.

The responsibilities that the Network Sherpas are tasked with do not always conform to their class schedule. As a result, to participate in an event or activity that requires them to miss class, they are responsible for having a Sher-pass signed by the teacher of class they will be missing and with the understanding that the Sherpa is responsible for proactively making up any missed work. The Sher-pass becomes their entry ticket into the event. Being organized and responsible is an important component to leadership. The field trip opportunities are endless. Here are a few of the places that we have visited (for free with parent chaperones as drivers):

- Microsoft Store, to attend a coding workshop and later an entrepreneurship workshop (which resulted in one of our students earning two tickets to the Super Bowl and a new laptop computer)
- Coding bootcamp
- Technology startup hub
- 3D printing facility
- Savannah College of Art and Design's digital studios
- National technology conference

The Network Sherpas reapply each year should they wish to continue on in the program. Some Sherpas discover a passion for an interest that lay dormant, shaping their future in unpredictable ways. For example, Network Sherpas that work behind the scenes of the theater who were originally drawn to the technical side of the operations have, at times, realized that they too wish to experience being on stage in front of the audience. The Network Sherpa program offers a gateway to leadership opportunities, new school connections, and expanded content expertise. It's a win-win.

Figure 13.1 Barbara Braxton's S.T.A.R.S. Library Ambassador Program for elementary students.

Library Ambassadors

Does your school library have groupies? The kids that come in first thing in the morning just to chat and hang out? Nurture those library fans and turn them into library ambassadors. Students feel like they have superpowers when they are granted the privilege and trust of stepping into adult shoes and doing the tasks that they routinely observe adults doing. With this in mind, give students the chance to be modern day library leaders. New Zealand librarians Barbara Braxton and Sue Warren have developed excellent models for crafting library ambassador programs at the elementary and upper school level. They share their programs on their blogs and encourage other school librarians to use them and/or alter their versions to fit their own needs. Each program can be found by scanning the QR codes shown in Figure 13.1 and 13.2.

Figure 13.2 Sue Warren's Library Ninja Student Ambassador Training Program for middle school students and up.

Figure 13.3 Role-playing scenarios for library ambassador student training.

Launch the program with a training day activity that will help prepare student library leaders for the unexpected. I have prepared a series of role-playing scenarios that you can share with your students to practice their leadership skills viewable by scanning the QR code in Figure 13.3. They are color coded so that you can have students select a color, which will determine the scenario that they receive and they can partner with someone who either has the same color or a different color, depending on the time allotment. It will save time if you partner students together with the same colors so that they both focus on acting out and discussing how they would handle the same tricky scenario.

It's Not One Size Fits All

As I have shared in specific examples, the reality is that student leaders in the library should be influenced by the specific needs of your unique library culture. A robust library that operates as a well-oiled machine but would like to reach more patrons from a specific group of the student body may need Communication Outreach Specialists that gear their marketing efforts to a smaller subset. An active library that is a prime destination for the school community may need to cultivate a group of student mentors to serve as helpers for the younger population when it comes to selecting books. The library may be so busy that it is hard to keep the books organized neatly on the shelves and may necessitate an adopt-a-shelf student leadership program. The library may be hosting so many incredible programs that it is hard to find the time to toot the library's horn and, therefore, a student news team or an advocacy group is necessary to highlight the upcoming and past programs happening in the library. Perhaps a team of research specialists are needed to go into the classrooms and educate students and faculty about the variety of vetted resources available through the library and the ways in which they can be accessed. Maybe the collection feels stale and would benefit from a book selection committee to boost interest in resources. Consider the needs of your unique library and develop a scripted library leadership program that serves those needs. Keep in mind that as the environment changes, it may require routinely reinventing student leadership programs. This will ensure the current populations' needs are met and that the library remains relevant to the current school culture.

Unscripted Leadership Opportunities

While unscripted plays may take less effort in planning, they can have the biggest impact. These are those in the moment instances when you see a need for student leadership and, on the fly, select a student or groups of students to guide others through a situation. Sometimes, these are the students that are not typically recognized as leaders. As with a first-round draft pick, this is often the player that excels at one "big thing." They have a strong skill that sets them apart from the other players. Sometimes, these skills are a result of serious practice as well as being born with a knack for a specific component to a game. Not everyone is considered a star quarterback but they are out there. In this same way, we have students who are considered specialists or experts. They are intensely knowledgeable in an area so much so that it shapes their identity. For example, we have devoted gamers, voracious readers, and gifted coders. Each of these examples is pertinent to a future ready library as there is a responsibility to support the growth in these areas to set our students up for success upon graduation. Leverage your student experts in these areas to expose other learners to these skills.

The Gamer

There are countless ways in which gaming is being infused into school curriculums at a variety of entry points. With the influx of Esports, video game design courses, and MinecraftEdu as part of the learning environment, school librarians are expected to be the point person for supporting the infusion of these programs into the learning. Not to worry, however. That's where unscripted student leaders can be your game changers. No doubt you have students who are naturally drawn to these interests and spend as much of their free time as they can exploring them. Tap them as your student experts when integrating these tools into the curriculum. Empower them to be the leaders who drive the evolution of the curriculum forward. For example, when our third graders did their unit on Native Americans and worked in a multiplayer world to build a Native American village with the resources that would have been available, neither I nor the teacher taught the students who were new to Minecraft how to use the commands. Instead, we selected a student leader to teach the other students how to perform specific functions and what each command represents. These student experts are valued for their expertise, growing their connections to others.

The Voracious Reader

Most schools have students who would rather be reading while out on the playground than playing with the other kids. Additionally, most schools have teachers that will assign some form of a book report or reading project. Create a situation in which the voracious reader at your school becomes the guru for book recommendations for these projects. Ask other students to write down three to six adjectives that would describe their ideal book. Set up a booth for the voracious reader to receive these adjectives and make book recommendations accordingly. Now the voracious reader has a fan base that is eager to tap into their knowledge to help them discover a good read. Not only does this cultivate communication skills, forge student connections, and reward students for their interests, but it also assists the school librarian in serving their patrons.

The Programmer

While there are students who love to play games, there are also those that love to create them. Consider the web-based program, Scratch, developed by students at MIT. Scratch tends to have a following of students that find such joy in creating stories, games, and animated designs with this tool. Nurture those students to not only teach other students how to create in Scratch but to create something that you are striving to teach as well. For example, elect a student expert in Scratch to lead the class through a lesson in how to create an animated sprite that shares a digital citizenship tip. Allow the student leader to help set the parameters for the project. For example, the project must include more than one background, a movable sprite, use the voice command, and the program must include a conditional statement.

Student Leaders as Champions

Tapping student leaders based on their interests can result in a grassroots effort that positively alters the school culture. As the school librarian who is a connected educator, new digital tools come across your network regularly. Employ students to test out these digital tools and leave reviews of them for the purpose of sharing them with teachers. Figure 13.4

provides an example of a student leader evaluating the digital portfolio platform, Seesaw.

Student evaluations help teachers consider the tool from the perspective of the user to determine if it is a good fit for their classroom. Not only does this save time and a potential headache, it ensures that there will be someone besides the teacher who can support the adoption of a new digital tool when it is rolled out to a larger group.

Figure 13.4 Fifth-grade student leader evaluating Seesaw for teachers.

Some students are so enthusiastic about summer reading. Others, well, not so much. Empower the enthusiastic voices to help plan the summer reading program within your school. For example, we have a significant number of recreational baseball players in our student body. A few of them also really enjoy reading for pleasure. I have tapped them to spearhead a summer reading program designed around baseball to appeal to their peers. Those students that complete the optional summer reading program will return to school in the Fall to enjoy a concession stand summer reading celebration that includes cotton candy, Big League chew, and some fun souvenirs. Merge students' interests with leadership opportunities to grow the success of your programming.

Conclusion:
Reflect, Revise, Redo

"Taking the time to go back and reflect on my work is an opportunity to see what I need to work on and see what I am already good at doing."

—Nicole, age 11

As stated in Dr. Shiyali Ramamrita Ranganathan's book, *The Five Laws of Library Science*, "The library is a growing organism" (2006, 382). As our school communities change, so does the need to evolve within the library. Just as we teach students to reflect on their learning processes, school librarians must reflect on their efforts and calculate their library's ability to support and reach its patrons. Reflection is a critical component when considering the future. We may find that some programs have lasting power, whereas others may be a one-and-done situation. A program being done just one time does not necessarily mean that it was not a success. Changing the programming menu and the resources acquired can be the result of variables unique to that particular calendar year. Measuring the effectiveness of your school library can be gauged through a variety of factors. These include circulation reports, online surveys, face-to-face feedback, and program participation. In 2018, the American Association of School Librarians (AASL) recently launched the School Library Evaluation Checklist, shown in Figure C.1, as part of the national school library standards for learners, school librarians, and school libraries.

Consider the factors in the checklist as the backbone for creating a "State of the Library" report that can be used to gain continued support for resources, funding, and space; the support to execute programming initiatives; and/or changes in staffing.

Figure C.1. Scan this QR code to access AASL's School Library Evaluation Checklist.

With introspection comes change, and with change comes the opportunity for novelty. While the novel generates excitement, it also can bring about exhaustion as a side effect. It is critical to establish a pattern that feels comfortable so that as the library reinvents itself year after year, it is done in such a way that some programs are executed on autopilot, while others cycle in and out. Creating a balance in the approach to change is critical to avoid burnout and maintain a healthy mental state.

Similar to a training camp, the school library can be a discovery zone for piloting and implementing new ideas and resources. When librarians take the initiative to engage with their learning communities to drive the innovation and technology implementation within their schools, they become the ultimate game-changers.

Bibliography

Allocca, Kevin. *Videocracy: How YouTube Is Changing the World—with Double Rainbows, Singing Foxes, and Other Trends We Can't Stop Watching.* New York: Bloomsbury USA, an Imprint of Bloomsbury Publishing, 2018.

American Association of School Librarians. *AASL Standards Framework for Learners.* Chicago: ALA Editions, 2018. https://standards.aasl.org/wp-content/uploads/2017/11/AASL-Standards-Framework-for-Learners-pamphlet.pdf.

"American Football Field." Digital image. Wikimedia Commons. July 2004. Accessed December 8, 2018. https://en.wikipedia.org/wiki/Gridiron_football#/media/File:AmFBfield.svg.

Anderson, John. 2011. "Grasping, Employing QR Codes." *Bar Bulletin of the Maryland State Bar Association* 28 (10): 15–19. http://search.ebscohost.com/login.aspx?direct=true&db=lgs&AN=82364656&site=eds-live&scope=site.

Anderson, Laurie Halse. *Speak.* Harrisonburg, VA: Farrar Straus Giroux, 1999.

Any Given Sunday. Directed by Oliver Stone. Performed by Al Pacino, Cameron Diaz, and Jamie Foxx. United States: Warner Bros., 1999. Film.

Barack, Lauren. 2013. "A Minecraft Library Scores Big: Mattituck, NY, Branch Is a Hit with Kids." *The Digital Shift.* September 3. Accessed September 13, 2018. http://www.thedigitalshift.com/2013/09/k-12/a-minecraft-library-scores-big-a-virtual-version-of-the-mattituck-ny-branch-is-a-hit-with-young-patrons.

Bers, Marina Umaschi. *Coding as a Playground: Programming and Computational Thinking in the Early Childhood Classroom.* New York: Routledge, Taylor and Francis Group, 2018.

Borovay, Lindsay A., Bruce M. Shore, Christina Caccese, Ethan Yang, and Olivia (Liv) Hua. 2019. "Flow, Achievement Level, and Inquiry-Based Learning." *Journal of Advanced Academics* 30 (1): 74–106. doi:10.1177/1932202X18809659.

"Bring TED-Ed Student Talks to Your School." TED-Ed. Accessed June 21, 2019. https://ed.ted.com/student_talks.

Burgess, Dave. *Teach Like a PIRATE: Increase Student Engagement, Boost Your Creativity, and Transform Your Life as an Educator.* San Diego: Dave Burgess Consulting, 2018.

Burns, Marilyn. *The Greedy Triangle.* New York: Scholastic, 1994.

Center for Innovative Teaching and Learning. n.d. "Assessing Student Learning." Accessed January 5, 2019. https://citl.indiana.edu/teaching-resources/assessing-student-learning.

Cleaver, Samantha. "Hands-On Is Minds-On." Scholastic.com. Accessed January 12, 2019. http://www.scholastic.com/browse/article.jsp?id=3751901.

Code.org. n.d. "Hour of Code One Pager." Accessed October 31, 2019. https://hourofcode.com/files/hoc-one-pager.pdf.

Coding Outside the Computer Classroom. n.d. Accessed June 20, 2019. http://activity.pencilcode.net/home/worksheet/humanities.html.

Cole, Joanna, and Bruce Degen. *The Magic School Bus and the Climate Challenge.* New York: Scholastic, 2010.

Cooper, Charles. 2013. "Teaching with Aurasma." YouTube Video, 4:39. January 18. Accessed September 23, 2018. https://www.youtube.com/watch?time_continue=3&v=uHIxYpBW7sc.

Couros, George. 2019. "The Innovator's Mindset." Keynote Presentation, Prizmah Jewish Day School Conference, Marriott Marquis, Atlanta, March 10.

Couros, George. 2018. "We All Need a Champion." *The Principal of Change: Stories of Leading and Learning* (blog), May 18. Accessed October 5, 2018. https://georgecouros.ca/blog/archives/tag/rita-pierson.

Creech, Sharon. *Love That Dog.* London: Bloomsbury, 2001.

Croes, Emmelyn A. J., Marjolijn L. Antheunis, Alexander P. Schouten, and Emiel J. Krahmer. 2019. "Social Attraction in Video-Mediated Communication: The Role of Nonverbal Affiliative Behavior." *Journal of Social and Personal Relationships* 36 (4): 1210–1232. doi:10.1177/0265407518757382.

Curtis, Christopher Paul. *The Watsons Go to Birmingham—1963.* New York: Yearling, an Imprint of Random House Children's Books, 2013.

D'Auria, John. *Ten Lessons in Leadership and Learning: An Educators Journey.* Wellesley, MA: Teachers21, 2010.

"Decades of Scientific Research That Started a Growth Mindset Revolution." 2017. The Growth Mindset—What Is Growth Mindset—Mindset Works. Accessed January 26, 2019. https://www.mindsetworks.com/science.

Denton, Joe. 2016. "Update: 5 Reasons People Go to Sporting Events." *Eventbrite* (blog), October 31. Accessed March 17, 2019. https://www.eventbrite.com/blog/ds00-5-reasons-people-go-to-sporting-events-and-what-we-can-learn-from-them.

DePaola, Tomie. *Strega Nona's Harvest.* New York: Penguin Group, 2009.

Doorley, Scott, Sarah Holcomb, Perry Klebahn, Kathryn Segovia, and Jeremy Utley. 2018. "Design Thinking Bootcamp Bootleg." D.school at Stanford University. Accessed June 13, 2019. https://static1.squarespace.com/static

/57c6b79629687fde090a0fdd/t/5b19b2f2aa4a99e99b26b6bb/15284
10876119/dschool_bootleg_deck_2018_final_sm(2).pdf.

Draper, Sharon M. *Out of My Mind*. New York: Atheneum Books for Young Readers, 2010.

EGFI Dream Up the Future. n.d. Accessed June 21, 2019. http://teachers.egfi-k12
.org.

Engineering Is Elementary. n.d. Accessed June 21, 2019. https://www.eie.org.

Field of Dreams. Directed by Phil Alden Robinson. Performed by Kevin Costner,
James Earl Jones, Ray Liotta. United States: Universal Pictures International, 1989. Film.

Find Guest Speakers—Microsoft in Education. 2019. Accessed June 21, 2019.
https://education.microsoft.com/skype-in-the-classroom/find-guest
-speakers.

Foster, Stewart. *The Bubble Boy*. London: Simon & Schuster, 2016.

Future Ready Librarians. 2018. Accessed June 13, 2019. https://futureready.org
/wp-content/uploads/2017/01/Library_flyer_download.pdf.

Gadzikowski, Ann. *Robotics for Young Children: STEM Activities and Simple Coding*.
St. Paul, MN: Red Leaf Press, 2018.

Gee, James Paul. *What Video Games Have to Teach Us about Learning and Literacy*.
New York: Palgrave Macmillan, 2007.

Gibbs, Stuart. *The Complete Moon Base Alpha: Space Case; Spaced Out; Waste of Space*.
New York: Simon & Schuster, 2019.

Giffin, Emily. *All We Ever Wanted: A Novel*. New York: Ballantine Books, 2018.

Goodell, Jill Jeffers. 2015. "Welcome to Learning HTML for Kids." Learning HTML
for Kids." Accessed June 20, 2019. http://www.goodellgroup.com/tutorial
/index.html.

Graves, Colleen. 2016. "Invention Literacy Research-Part One." *Create Collaborate
Innovate* (blog), June 7. Accessed June 13, 2019. https://colleengraves.org
/2016/06/07/invention-literacy-research-part-one.

The Greatest Show. Written by Benj Pasek, Justin Paul, and Ryan Lewis. Performed
by Hugh Jackman, Keala Settle, Zac Effron, and Zendaya. Atlantic, 2017.

Gustafson, Brad. 2014. "Digital Leadership Challenge." *Adjusting Course: Responding to the Needs of The 21st Century Student* (blog), May 12. Accessed
June 13, 2019. https://adjustingcourse.wordpress.com/2014/05/12/digital
-leadership-challenge.

Hanover Research Brain Trust. 2014. *Impact of Student Choice and Personalized
Learning*. Report. November. Accessed December 21, 2018. http://www
.gssaweb.org/wp-content/uploads/2015/04/Impact-of-Student-Choice
-and-Personalized-Learning-1.pdf. (A report conducted by the Hanover
Research brain trust to examine the impact of personalized learning,
and educational strategies that emphasize student choice, on academic
achievement. The report focuses on promising practices that have the
potential to increase academic achievement, student persistence, and overall student engagement.)

Heath, Chip, and Dan Heath. *Made to Stick*. New York: Random House, 2008.

Herring, Cherie. 2013. "Aurasma in Music Class." YouTube Video, 2:06. October 15. Accessed September 5, 2018. https://www.youtube.com/watch?v=oxNDOMUbc18&feature=youtu.be.

Hill, Laban Carrick. *Dave the Potter: Artist, Poet, Slave*. Boston: Little, Brown and Company, 2010.

"Hour of Code: Join the Movement." n.d. Hour of Code. Accessed September 10, 2018. https://hourofcode.com/us.

Jeffers, Oliver. *This Moose Belongs to Me*. New York: Philomel Books, 2012.

Jensen, Eric. *Teaching with the Brain in Mind*. Alexandria, VA: Association for Supervision and Curriculum Development, 2008.

Kahoot! "Kahoot! Grows by 75% to Reach 70 Million Unique Users." 2018. January 18. Accessed June 13, 2019. https://kahoot.com/press/2018/01/18/kahoot-grows-reach-70-million-unique-users.

Kearney, Matthew, and Sandy Schuck. 2014. *Students in the Director's Seat: Teaching and Learning with Student-generated Video*. Working paper. Education, University of Technology Sydney. Sydney: University of Technology. Accessed January 19, 2019. https://www.researchgate.net/publication/2377 25746_Students_in_the_Director's_Seat_Teaching_and_Learning_with _Student-generated_Video.

Kelley, David M., and Tom Kelley. *Creative Confidence: Unleashing the Creative Potential within Us All*. New York: Random House, 2013.

King, Hope, and Wade King. *The Wild Card: 7 Steps to an Educator's Creative Breakthrough*. San Diego: Dave Burgess Consulting, 2018.

Kinney, Jeff. *Diary of a Wimpy Kid*. New York: Harry N Abrams, 2007.

Lange, Patricia G. *Kids on YouTube: Technical Identities and Digital Literacies*. New York: Routledge, 2016.

Lee, Harper. *To Kill a Mockingbird*. Reprint ed. New York: Harper, an Imprint of HarperCollins Publishers, 2015.

"LEGO® Education WeDo 2.0 Curriculum Pack." 2017. Accessed January 1, 2019. https://le-www-live-s.legocdn.com/sc/media/files/user-guides/wedo-2 /science-teacher-guides/scienceteachersguide-en-us-v1-971a0fa7ca998b2 284eb812936428571.pdf.

Lester, Helen. *Wodney Wats Wobot*. New York: Houghton Mifflin Harcourt, 2011.

Little Free Library. 2019. "Plans and Tips for Library Builders." May 20. Accessed June 21, 2019. https://littlefreelibrary.org/build.

Liukas, Linda. *Hello Ruby: Adventures in Coding*. New York: Feiwel & Friends, 2015.

Maiers, Angela. n.d. "You Matter Manifesto." *Angela Maiers Blog* (blog). Accessed December 18, 2018. https://www.angelamaiers.com/blog/you-matter -manifesto.html.

McNee, Darcy, and Elaine Radmer. 2017. "Librarians and Learning: The Impact of Collaboration." *English Leadership Quarterly* 40 (1). Accessed January 5, 2019. http://www.ncte.org/library/NCTEFiles/Resources/Journals/ELQ /0401-aug2017/ELQ0401Librarians.pdf.

Milgrom-Elcott, Talia. 2018. "STEM Starts Earlier Than You Think." *Forbes.* August 1. Accessed January 3, 2019. https://www.forbes.com/sites/taliamil gromelcott/2018/07/24/stem-starts-earlier-than-you-think/#5688345 6348b.

Moreillon, Judi. 2019. "Evaluation and Assessment for Learning." *Knowledge Quest* 47 (3): 6–7.

Moulden, Yolanda. 2019. "Latest News from AAEES." American Academy of Environmental Engineers and Scientists. Accessed June 20, 2019. http://www .aaees.org.

"MS-ESS1-1 Earth's Place in the Universe." 2013. Next Generation Science Standards for States, by States. April. Accessed December 8, 2018. https:// www.nextgenscience.org/pe/ms-ess1-1-earths-place-universe.

Nast, Phil. 2017. "Authentic Assessment Toolbox." NEA. Accessed January 6, 2019. http://www.nea.org/tools/lessons/57730.htm.

National Aeronautics and Space Administration (NASA). 2014, June 12. "Dynamics of Flight." Accessed January 1, 2019. https://www.grc.nasa.gov/www/k -12/UEET/StudentSite/dynamicsofflight.html#lawofmotion.

National School Library Standards for Learners, School Librarians, and School Libraries. Chicago: ALA, 2018.

Novel Engineering. 2018. Accessed June 21, 2019. http://www.novelengineering .org.

Park, Linda Sue. *A Long Walk to Water: A Novel.* New York: Houghton Mifflin Harcourt, 2010.

Paulsen, Gary. *Hatchet.* New York: Atheneum Books for Young Readers, 1987.

PBS Kids Design Squad Global. n.d. Accessed June 21, 2019. https://pbskids.org /designsquad.

Pera, Mariam. 2014. "Championing Introverts." *The Scoop Blog* (blog), July 2. Accessed June 13, 2019. https://americanlibrariesmagazine.org/blogs/the -scoop/championing-introverts.

Plaskoff, Melissa (President and co-founder, ON-AIR MEDIA, LLC), in discussion with the author. June 18, 2019.

Polacco, Patricia. *Thunder Cake.* New York: Putnam & Grosset Group, 1990.

QRCode.com. n.d. "History of QR Code: How Was the QR Code Created? How Has It Come to Be Used so Widely? And What Is Its Future?" Accessed March 4, 2019. https://www.qrcode.com/en/history.

Rabganathan, S. R. *The Five Laws of Library Science.* New Dehli: Ess Ess Publications, 2006.

Ramsay, Julie D. 2014. "Writing to the World." *Educational Leadership* 71 (7): 54–58. http://search.ebscohost.com/login.aspx?direct=true&db=eric&AN =EJ1043827&site=ehost-live.

Reid, Calvin. 2018. "Macmillan Podcasts Promote Authors, Create New Content, Boost Sales." *Publishers Weekly* 265 (16): 8–10. http://search.ebscohost.com /login.aspx?direct=true&db=tfh&AN=129089265&site=ehost-live.

Reynolds, Jason. *Ghost.* New York: Atheneum Books for Young Readers, 2016.

Reynolds, Peter. *The Dot*. Cambridge, MA: Candlewick Press, 2003.

Rideout, Vicky. 2015. *The Common Sense Census: Media Use by Teens and Tweens*. Report. Edited by Seeta Pai. Accessed January 13, 2019. https://www .commonsensemedia.org/sites/default/files/uploads/research/census _executivesummary.pdf.

Robbins, Dean. *Margaret and the Moon*. New York: Knopf, 2017.

Robertson, Joanne. *The Water Walker*. Toronto: Second Story Press, 2017.

Sarcone-Roach, Julia. *The Bear Ate Your Sandwich*. New York: Random House, 2015.

Shernoff, David J., and Suparna Sinha, Denise M. Bressler, and Lynda Ginsburg. 2017. "Assessing Teacher Education and Professional Development Needs for the Implementation of Integrated Approaches to STEM Education." *International Journal of STEM Education* (Springer Nature) 4 (13): 1–16. doi:10.1186/s40594-017-0068-1.

Sivers, Derek. 2010. "First Follower: Leadership Lessons from a Dancing Guy." *Derek Sivers* (blog), February 11. Accessed March 31, 2019. https://sivers .org/ff.

Skype a Scientist. n.d. Accessed June 21, 2019. https://www.skypeascientist.com.

SmithScience. 2013. "Using Aurasma in the Science Classroom." YouTube Video, 50. September 9. Accessed October 5, 2018. https://www.youtube.com /watch?v=xInuGQRBPTc&feature=youtu.be.

Solarz, Paul. n.d. "How to Set Up and Run a Mystery Skype Session." What's Going on in Mr. Solarz's Class? Accessed June 21, 2019. https://psolarz.weebly .com/how-to-set-up-and-run-a-mystery-skype-session.html.

Spencer, John. 2016. "Design the Ultimate Roller Coaster." YouTube Video, 2:02. February 22. Accessed January 1, 2019. https://www.youtube.com/watch ?v=PaKtnAsqlt4.

Stanford D.school. 2019. Accessed June 21, 2019. https://dschool.stanford.edu.

"Statistics." n.d. Code.org. Accessed October 26, 2019. https://code.org/statistics.

Stein, Michelle. 2014. "Together We Can Change." Class lecture, 6th Grade Language Arts, The Davis Academy, Atlanta, August 25.

Swanson, Kristen. 2015. Panel Presentation, Building Learning Communities, Park Plaza Hotel, Boston, July.

Try Engineering. 2019. Accessed June 21, 2019. https://tryengineering.org.

Vasilyeva, Zinaida. 2010. "Video-Mediated Communicative Interaction: An Analysis." *Antropologicheskii Forum (Forum for Anthropology)* 13: 177–210. https:// www.researchgate.net/publication/280560191.

Verde, Susan. *The Water Princess*. New York: G. P. Putnam's Sons, 2016.

Wagner, Tony. *Creating Innovators: The Making of Young People Who Will Change the World*. New York: Scribner, 2012.

Watson, Jude. *Loot*. New York: Scholastic Press, 2014.

"When It Comes To Tech, The Best Parental Control . . . Is You!" 2017. *Savvy Cyber Kids* (blog), October 11. Accessed February 16, 2019. https://

savvycyberkids.org/2017/10/11/when-it-comes-to-tech-the-best-parental
-control-is-you.

Yamada, Kobi. *What Do You Do with an Idea?* Seattle: Compendium, 2013.

Yolen, Jane. *The Devil's Arithmetic.* New York: Puffin Books, 2004.

"YouTube by the Numbers." n.d. YouTube for Press. Accessed January 13, 2019.
https://www.youtube.com/yt/about/press.